# LIFE, LIBERTY, AND THE PURSUIT OF UTILITY

WB —————— Welfare

——————— Cumbersome

——— Dignity —— Choice

—— Value

—— Prestige

# ST ANDREWS STUDIES IN
# PHILOSOPHY AND PUBLIC AFFAIRS

Founding and General Editor:
John Haldane
University of St Andrews

Volume 1:
*Values, Education and the Human World*
*edited by John Haldane*

Volume 2:
*Philosophy and its Public Role*
edited by William Aiken and John Haldane

Volume 3:
*Relativism and the Foundations of Liberalism*
by Graham Long

Volume 4:
*Human Life, Action and Ethics:*
*Essays by G.E.M. Anscombe*
edited by Mary Geach and Luke Gormally

Volume 5:
*The Institution of Intellectual Values:*
*Realism and Idealism in Higher Education*
by Gordon Graham

Volume 7:
*Life, Liberty, and the Pursuit of Utility:*
*Happiness in Philosophical and Economic Thought*
by Anthony Kenny and Charles Kenny

Volume 8:
*Distributing Healthcare:*
*Principles, Practices and Politics*
edited by Niall MacLean

# LIFE, LIBERTY, AND THE PURSUIT OF UTILITY

## HAPPINESS IN PHILOSOPHICAL AND ECONOMIC THOUGHT

Anthony Kenny and Charles Kenny

St Andrews
Studies in
Philosophy and
Public Affairs

imprint-academic.com

Published in the UK by Imprint Academic
PO Box 200, Exeter EX5 5YX, UK

Published in the USA by Imprint Academic
Philosophy Documentation Center
PO Box 7147, Charlottesville, VA 22906-7147, USA

ISBN 1 84540 052 6
ISBN-13 9781845400521

A CIP catalogue record for this book is available from the
British Library and US Library of Congress

Cover Photograph:
St Salvator's Quadrangle, St Andrews by Peter Adamson
from the University of St Andrews collection

# Contents

Preface . . . . . . . . . . . . . . . . . . . . . . . . . . . . 7

*PART ONE: HISTORICAL INTRODUCTION*

Chapter  1    The Philosophy of Happiness . . . . . . . . . . 13

Chapter  2    Happiness in History . . . . . . . . . . . . . . 45

*PART TWO: WELFARE*

Chapter  3    The Goods of the Body . . . . . . . . . . . . . 57

Chapter  4    The Determinants of Welfare . . . . . . . . . . 65

*PART THREE: DIGNITY*

Chapter  5    Choice, Worth and Prestige . . . . . . . . . . 103

Chapter  6    The Economics of Dignity . . . . . . . . . . . 111

*PART FOUR: CONTENTMENT*

Chapter  7    Mental States and their Measurement . . . . . 135

Chapter  8    Subjective Well-being and its Correlates . . . . 149

*PART FIVE: CONCLUSIONS*

Chapter  9    Happiness and Morality . . . . . . . . . . . . 179

Chapter 10    Policies for Happiness . . . . . . . . . . . . . 189

Bibliography . . . . . . . . . . . . . . . . . . . . . . . . . 209

Index . . . . . . . . . . . . . . . . . . . . . . . . . . . . . 223

# Preface

'From the dawn of philosophy' wrote John Stuart Mill 'the question concerning the *summum bonum*, or, what is the same thing, concerning the foundation of morality, has been accounted the main problem in speculative thought and has occupied the most gifted intellects.' Happiness, or the supreme good, was indeed a major concern of philosophical inquiry throughout many centuries. In the twentieth century, however, the most gifted intellects in philosophy rather lost interest in the topic. In the heyday of analytic philosophy the word 'happiness' did not even occur in the index of the most influential texts of ethical theory. Only in the field of Aristotelian scholarship was the study of the topic kept alive.

In the latter part of the century, the ball that had been dropped by philosophers was taken up by economists. From 1974 Richard Easterlin published a series of empirical studies which entitled him to be called the father of the field of the economics of subjective happiness, a field that has been blooming over the last few years, as later chapters of this book will attest. Easterlin was also one of the first to systematically question the link hitherto assumed by economists between income and welfare.

Amartya Sen combines the skills of an economist with the insight of a philosopher. He has fused a broadly Aristotelian approach with his immense knowledge of development to build a theory based on the concepts of capabilities and functionings as keys to what is valuable in or important about the development process. This thinking, and writing by those that Sen has influenced, informs much of the work which will be cited in later chapters. He and his colleagues early pointed out that the success of countries and regions such as Kerala, China and Sri Lanka in improving health outcomes was largely to do with measures of public support rather than economic growth. More broadly, Sen's general approach to development has been explicitly based on the idea that income is an insufficient measure and a poor proxy for levels of the quality of life.

In this book we attempt, like Sen, to combine philosophy and economics in the consideration of happiness. We adopt, however, a different approach to the analysis of well-being. Consideration of the debates over centuries on the nature of happiness leads us to believe that overall human well-being  has three main constituents, which we call welfare, contentment, and dignity.

We structure the book around this basic scheme. In the first section we offer a historical introduction to the topic of happiness. The next three sections treat in turn of welfare, dignity, and contentment. We take the elements in this order because it corresponds to the order in which they are implied in the commitment of the US Declaration of Independence to 'life, liberty, and the pursuit of happiness'. The final section draws some moral and political conclusions from our analysis of well-being.

Each section contains two chapters. The first, odd-numbered, chapters deal with conceptual issues and were written by Anthony Kenny. The second, even-numbered chapters treat of empirical matters and were written by Charles Kenny. While the concepts are very much distinct, it is worth noting that welfare, dignity and contentment frequently reinforce one another. We will see that there is evidence that income equality, gender equality and measures of civil rights may all be causally related to welfare outcomes including infant mortality and life expectancy. A basic level of welfare is itself clearly critical to the ability to function in society. Subjective well-being appears to be as much a cause as a result of good health and a greater level of civil rights appears to be related to higher levels of contentment.

While welfare, dignity and contentment are often closely linked, one of the major themes of this book is that income is a poor proxy for any of these. Beyond some minimal level, increasing income appears at best weakly correlated with improvements of welfare, dignity or contentment within or across countries over time. Institutions which foster and preserve life and liberty do appear central, but these institutions can exist in poorer and richer countries, and their development over time is largely (causally) independent of the speed of economic growth.

We should at the outset address a few issues of definition: 'subjective happiness' and 'subjective well-being' are both used to describe answers to polls answering questions akin to 'taking your life as a whole, would you consider yourself very, happy, somewhat happy or not happy at all.' We take answers to such polls to be a fairly accurate proxy for what we term contentment. Gross National Product (GNP) and Gross Domestic Product (GDP) are distinct but very highly correlated measures of national output. Both are commonly used as measures of national income — so that GNP per capita or GDP per capita are taken in the text to represent good proxy measure for average individual incomes in a country. Unless otherwise specified, dollar figures presented in the text are measured in terms of the year 2000 purchasing power of a US dollar. In other words, the figures have been adjusted for inflation over time and the differing costs of goods and services in different countries. Finally, 'average,' unless otherwise indicated, is the mean value of an indicator.

We are greatly indebted to John Haldane, who encouraged us to write this book, and to Nancy Kenny and Pamela Street Kenny, for comments and editorial advice. We are particularly grateful to the Rockefeller Foundation for supporting a three week residency at the Villa Serbelloni in Bellagio, Italy, where the bulk of the manuscript was written in surroundings conducive to every aspect of well-being.

*Anthony Kenny, Oxford*
*Charles Kenny, Washington DC*
*July 2006*

# PART ONE
# HISTORICAL INTRODUCTION

# Chapter 1

# *The Philosophy of Happiness*

## Aristotle on Happiness

Since the earliest days of Western thought philosophers have concerned themselves with the nature of happiness. One of the earliest to ask the question 'what is happiness?' was Aristotle, who, in a manner typical of philosophers, before providing an answer insisted on making a distinction between two different questions. His first question was what was meant by the word 'happiness' – or rather, its ancient Greek equivalent *eudaimonia*. His second question was where happiness was to be found, that is to say, what is it that makes us truly happy. Reasonably enough he thought that it was futile to try to answer the second question without having given thought to the first.

The definition that he offers is that happiness is the supreme good that supplies the purpose, and measures the value, of all human activity and striving. 'It is for the sake of happiness' he wrote 'that we all do everything else we do' (Aristotle, 2002, 1102a3). This seems a very sweeping statement: surely it is implausible to suggest that every human action is explicitly aimed at some single goal. Indeed, the suggestion is inconsistent with things that Aristotle says elsewhere. He does not seem to wish to rule out the possibility of impulsive actions done for fun without any reference to one's long-term happiness. What he means rather is that if you plan your life – and any sensible person, he thinks, ought to have a plan of life, at least in the form of a set of priorities — your top priority, your overarching goal, will show what you take to be a worthwhile life, and thus what you mean by 'happiness'. Indeed, in the light of what Aristotle says, we might offer 'worthwhile life' as the most appropriate translation of his word 'eudaimonia'. But we will continue to use the traditional translation 'happiness', where necessary qualifying it as 'Aristotelian happiness'.

Aristotle was well aware that human beings may have the most varied and bizarre notions of what makes them happy. But whatever they present as their ultimate ambition, it must, he thinks, as a matter of logic, pass certain tests if it is genuinely to count as happiness. For there are two features, he maintains, that are built into the very notion of happiness.

One is that it must be an end rather than a means. We may do other things for the sake of happiness, but we cannot be happy as a means to some other goal. You may find, perhaps, that being cheerful helps you to make money, and for that reason you resolutely adopt a cheerful frame of mind. But that just shows, Aristotle would say, that cheerfulness is something different from happiness, and if your ultimate aim is to make money for its own sake, what that indicates is that you believe (wrongly) that happiness is to be found in riches. Happiness, he insists, is always sought for its own sake and never for the sake of anything else.

The second built-in feature of happiness is that is must be self-sufficient: that is, it must be some good, or set of goods, that in itself makes life worth living. One's life cannot be truly happy if there is something missing that is an essential ingredient of a worthwhile existence. Moreover, a happy life should, so far as human nature allows, be invulnerable to bad luck; otherwise, the constant fear of losing one's happiness will diminish that happiness itself. So happiness, Aristotle concludes, must have the properties of independence and stability.

On the basis of these definitional features of the concept of happiness, Aristotle was in a position to move on to his second question: in what does happiness consist? What sort of life is actually the most worthwhile? Some things can be ruled out from the start. There are some occurrences in life, e.g. sickness and pain, which make people want to give up life: clearly these are not what makes life worth living. There are the joys and adventures of childhood: these cannot be the most choice-worthy things in life since no one in his right mind would choose to be a child once more. In adult life there are things that we do only as means to an end; we go to war, for instance, in order to bring peace. Clearly these cannot, in themselves, be what makes life worth living (Aristotle, 1992).

If life is to be worth living it must surely be for something that is an end in itself. One such end is pleasure. The pleasures of food and drink and sex Aristotle regards as, on their own, too brutish to be a fitting end for human life. If we combine them with aesthetic and intellectual pleasures then we find a goal that has been seriously pursued by people of significance. Others prefer a life of virtuous public action — the life of a real politician, not like the false politicians, who are only after money or power. Thirdly, there is the life of scientific contemplation, as exemplified by the Athenian philosopher Anaxagoras, who when asked why one should choose to be born rather than not replied 'In order to admire the heavens and the order of the universe'.

Having weeded out a number of other candidate lives, Aristotle settled for a short list of three: a life of pleasure, a life of politics, and a life of study. The pursuit of wealth was ruled out briskly at the start of the inquiry. Money is only as good as what it can buy. It is how someone spends his money that shows us where he really thinks happiness lies: does he spend it on luxury, for instance, or does he use it to gain political power, or give it to those less well off?

What was Aristotle's own choice between the three types of life on his short list? There is no single answer to this question: Aristotle wrote more than one treatise on happiness, and he gave different accounts in different treatises. But in all of them, we are offered a definition of happiness as activity in accordance with virtue, that is to say, doing well what is worth doing and what we are good at. Aristotle's definition derives from a consideration of the function or characteristic activity (*ergon*) of human beings. Man must have a function, the

Nicomachean Ethics argues, because particular types of men (e.g. sculptors) have a function, and parts and organs of human beings do likewise. What is this function? Not growth and nourishment, for this is shared by plants, nor the life of the senses, for this is shared by animals. It must be a life of reason concerned with action. So human good will be good human functioning, namely, activity of soul in the exercise of virtue (Aristotle, 2002, 1098a16).

So much is common to all of Aristotle's ethical treatises. Where they differ is in determining which are the particular virtues whose exercise constitutes happiness. For, as Aristotle explains, there are many different kinds of virtue or excellence: there are the moral virtues displayed in the active life, such as courage and temperance, and there are the intellectual excellences, such as wisdom and understanding, that are exercised in a life of scientific inquiry. In the best known of his moral treatises, the Nicomachean Ethics, Aristotle identified happiness with the enjoyment of philosophical study. The life of the philosopher provided the best fit, he argued, to the definitional features of happiness.

On the one hand, it was the most independent and the most stable. To philosophise you need only the bare necessities of life: you do not need a vast staff or expensive equipment. Riches may be stolen, political allies may desert you, and age and sickness may take away your appetite for pleasure. But as long as you live nothing and no one can take away the enlightenment you achieve by philosophising. On the other hand, philosophy is always an end, and not a means: it cannot be pursued for the sake of some superior goal, since it is totally useless for any other purpose.

Aristotle's identification of happiness with the pursuit of philosophy strikes some people as engaging, and others as irritating. Few, however, have found it totally credible. Perhaps Aristotle did not do so himself, because in his lesser known but more professional treatise, the Eudemian Ethics, he claims that the happy life must combine the features of all three of the traditional candidates on his short list. The happy person must not be a purely contemplative philosopher, but must possess and exercise the practical virtues that are necessary for the pursuit of worthwhile ambitions. Someone who is really virtuous will find virtuous actions in pursuit of noble goals a pleasure and not a burden. It is wrong to think that the only pleasures are those of the senses, but these too have a role in the happy life when enjoyed in accordance with the virtue of temperance – a virtue which is violated not only by an excess of sensual pleasure but also by a lack of sensual pleasure (Aristotle, 1992).

This kind of ideal of life, Aristotle believed, which assigns a role to philosophy, to the practical virtues, and to pleasure, could claim to combine the features of the traditional three lives, the life of the philosopher, the life of the politician, and the life of the pleasure-seeker. The happy man will value contemplation above all, but part of his happy life will be the exercise of political virtues and the enjoyment in moderation of natural human pleasures

## Epicureans and Stoics

In making an identification between the supreme good and the supreme pleasure, Aristotle entitles himself to be called a hedonist: but he is a hedonist of a very unusual kind, and stands at a great distance from the most famous hedonist in ancient Greece, namely Epicurus. Epicurus' treatment of pleasure is less sophisticated, but also more easily intelligible than Aristotle's. He is willing to place a value on pleasure that is independent of the value of the activity enjoyed: all pleasure is, as such, good.

For Epicurus, pleasure is the final end of life and the criterion of goodness in choice. He suggests that this is something that needs no argument: we all feel it in our bones.

> We maintain that pleasure is the beginning and end of a blessed life. We recognize it as our primary and natural good. Pleasure is our starting point whenever we choose or avoid anything and it is this we make our aim, using feeling as the criterion by which we judge of every good thing (Diogenes Laertius, 1972, 128–9).

This does not mean that Epicurus makes it his policy to pursue every pleasure that offers itself. If pleasure is the greatest good, pain is the greatest evil, and it is best to pass up a pleasure if it will lead to long-term suffering. Equally, it is worth putting up with pain if it will bring great pleasure in the long run.

These qualifications mean that Epicurus' hedonism is far from being an invitation to lead the life of a voluptuary. It is not drinking and carousing, he tells us, nor tables laden with delicacies, nor promiscuous intercourse with boys and women that produces the pleasant life, but sobriety, honour, justice and wisdom. A simple vegetarian diet and the company of a few friends in a modest garden suffice for Epicurean happiness.

What enables Epicurus to combine theoretical hedonism with practical asceticism is his understanding of pleasure as being essentially the satisfaction of desire. The strongest and most fundamental of our desires is the desire for the removal of pain. Hence, the mere absence of pain is itself a fundamental pleasure. Among our desires some are natural and some are futile, and it is the natural desires to which the most important pleasures correspond. We have natural desires for the removal of the painful states of hunger, thirst and cold, and the satisfaction of these desires is naturally pleasant. But there are two different kinds of pleasure involved, for which Epicurus framed technical terms: there is the kinetic pleasure of quenching one's thirst, and the static pleasure that supervenes when one's thirst has been quenched. Both kinds of pleasure are natural: but among the kinetic pleasures some are necessary (the pleasure in eating and drinking enough to satisfy hunger and thirst) and others are unnecessary (the pleasures of the gourmet).

Unnecessary natural pleasures are not greater than, but merely variations on, necessary natural pleasures: eating simple food when hungry is pleasanter than stuffing oneself with luxuries when satiated. Hunger, indeed, is the best sauce. But of all natural pleasures, it is the static pleasures that really count. 'The cry of the flesh is not to be hungry, not to be thirsty, not to be cold. Someone who is not in any of these states, and has good hope of remaining so, could rival even Zeus in happiness' (Long & Sedley, 1987, 21G).

Sexual desires are classed by Epicurus among unnecessary desires, on the grounds that their non-fulfilment is not accompanied by pain. This may be surprising, since unrequited love causes such anguish. But the intensity of such desire, Epicurus claimed, was due not to the nature of sex but to the romantic imagination of the lover. Epicurus was not opposed to the fulfilment of unnecessary natural desires, provided they did no harm – which of course was to be measured by their capacity for producing pain. Sexual pleasure, he said, could be taken in any way one wished, provided one respected law and convention, distressed no-one, and did no damage to one's body or one's essential resources. These qualifications added up to substantial constraint, and Epicurus thought that even when sex did no harm, it did no good either.

Epicurus is more critical of the fulfilment of desires that are futile: these are desires that are not natural and, like unnecessary natural desires, do not cause pain if not fulfilled. Examples are the desire for wealth and the desire for civic honours and acclaim But so too are desires for the pleasures of science and philosophy: 'Hoist sail' he told a favourite pupil 'and steer clear of all culture' (Diogenes Laertius, 1972, X,5). Aristotle had made it a point in favour of philosophy that its pleasures, unlike the pleasures of the senses, were unmixed with pain: now it is made a reason for downgrading the pleasures of philosophy that there is no pain in being a non-philosopher. For Epicurus the mind does play an important part in the happy life: but its function is only to anticipate and recollect the pleasures of the senses.

In the ancient world the great opponents of Epicureans were the Stoics, a school founded in the fourth century by Zeno of Citium. The Stoics found it disgusting to believe that the virtues were merely means of securing pleasure. Zeno's successor Cleanthes told his pupils to imagine pleasure as a queen on a throne surrounded by the virtues. On the Epicurean view of ethics, he said, these were handmaids totally dedicated to her service, merely whispering warnings, from time to time, against incautiously giving offence or causing pain. In reality, according to the Stoics, happiness consisted in nothing other than virtue itself.

Like the Stoics, Aristotle had placed happiness in virtue and its exercise, and had counted fame and riches no part of the happiness of a happy person. But he thought that it was a necessary condition for happiness that one should have a sufficient endowment of external goods. Moreover, he believed that even a virtuous man could cease to be happy if disaster overtook himself and his family, as happened to King Priam as his sons, his city and finally he himself fell in Trojan War (Aristotle, 2002, 1101a8-17). By contrast, the Stoics thought that happiness, once possessed, could never really be lost; at worst it could be terminated only by something like madness.

The weakness in the Stoic position is its refusal to come to terms with the fragility of happiness, the insistence that happiness cannot be constituted by any contingent good which is capable of being lost. Given the frail, vulnerable natures of human beings as we know ourselves to be, the denial that contingent goods can constitute happiness is tantamount to the claim that only superhuman beings can be happy.

The Stoics in effect accepted this conclusion, in their idealisation of the man of wisdom. Happiness lies in virtue, and there are no degrees of virtue, so that a person is either perfectly virtuous or not virtuous at all. The most perfect virtue is wisdom, and the wise man has all the virtues, since the virtues are inseparable from each other. One Stoic went so far as to say that to distinguish between courage and justice was like regarding the faculty for seeing white as different from the faculty of seeing black. The wise man is totally free from passion, and is in possession of all worthwhile knowledge: his virtue is the same as that of a god:

> The wise man whom we seek is the happy man who can think no human experience painful enough to cast him down nor joyful enough to raise his spirits. For what can seem important in human affairs to one who is familiar with all eternity and the vastness of the entire universe? (Long and Sedley, 1987, 61J, 63F).

The wise man is rich, and owns all things, since he alone knows how to use things well; he alone is truly handsome, since the mind's face is more beautiful than the body's; he alone is free, even if he is in prison, since he is a slave to no appetite. It was unsurprising, after all this, that the Stoics admitted that a wise man was harder to find than a phoenix. They thus purchased the invulnerability of happiness only at the cost of making it unattainable.

## Happiness as a Gift of God

It will be seen that what view a philosopher takes of the nature of happiness makes a great difference to whether he thinks it easy or difficult to achieve, Aristotle, having defined happiness to his own satisfaction had gone on to ask the question: how is it acquired? He had offered a number of candidate answers, derived from the reflections of previous philosophers. Does it come about, he asked, by nature, by training, by learning, by luck, or by divine favour? (Aristotle, 1992, 1214a15). In the course of his treatise he tried to show that each of these elements has a part in the acquisition of happiness. There is no need to follow how he spells this out, because the importance of his list is that each item on it has been seized upon by one or other later thinker as crucial. Some have claimed that happiness is in our genes, others have written how-to manuals setting out regimes to be followed for its acquisition. Some have believed that there is a secret science whose mastery will bring happiness to the initiate. Others have thought that happiness is owed above all to a fortunate environment. Finally, for many centuries the dominant account was that supreme happiness was a gift of God, obtainable only through divine grace.

The foremost exponent of this last view was St Augustine. Like everyone in the ancient world, Augustine starts from the premise that everyone wants to be happy, and accepts that it is the task of philosophy to define what this supreme good is and how it is to be achieved. If you ask two people whether they want to join the army, Augustine says in the *Confessions*, one may say yes and the other no. But if you ask them whether they want to be happy, they will both say yes without any hesitation. The only reason they differ about serving in the army is that one believes, while the other does not, that that will make him happy (Augustine, 1992, 10, 31).

In another work, Augustine tells the story of a stage player who promised to tell his audience, at his next appearance, what was in each of their minds. When they returned he told them 'Each of you wants to buy cheap and sell dear'. This was smart, Augustine says, but not really correct — and he gives a list of possible counterexamples. But if the actor had said 'Each of you wants to be happy, and none of you wants to be miserable' then he would have hit the mark perfectly (Augustine, 1963, 13,3,6).

Again like Aristotle, Augustine defines happiness as the supreme good. This is the good which provides the standard for all our actions: it is sought for its own sake, not as a means to an end, and once we attain it we lack nothing that is necessary for happiness (Augustine, 1972, VIII,8). Then Augustine goes on to take a step beyond Aristotle and all his pagan predecessors. He claims that happiness is truly possible only in an afterlife, in the vision of God.

First, he argues that anyone who wants to be happy must want to be immortal. How can we hold that a happy life is to come to an end at death? If a man is unwilling to lose his life, how can he be happy with this prospect before him? On the other hand, if his life is something he is willing to part with, how can it have been truly happy? But if immortality is necessary for happiness, it is not sufficient. Pagan philosophers who have claimed to prove that the soul is immortal have also held out the prospect of a miserable cycle of reincarnation. Only the Christian faith promises everlasting happiness for the entire human being, soul and body alike (Augustine, 1963, 13, 8, 11–9,12).

> The supreme good of the City of God is eternal and perfect peace, not our mortal transit from birth to death, but in our immortal freedom from all adversity. This is the happiest life — who can deny it? — and in comparison with it our life on earth, however blessed with external prosperity or goods of soul and body, is utterly miserable. None the less, whoever accepts it and makes use of it as a means to that other life that he longs for and hopes for, may not unreasonably be called

happy even now — happy in hope rather than in reality (Augustine, 1972, 19, 20).

Virtue in the present life, Augustine says, is not equivalent to happiness: it is merely a necessary means to an end that is ultimately other-worldly. Moreover, however hard we try, we are unable to avoid vice without grace, that is to say without special divine assistance that is given only to those selected for salvation through Christ. The virtues of the great heroes of Roman history were really only splendid vices. They received their reward in Rome's imperial glory, but did not qualify for the one true happiness of heaven.

The treatment of happiness by Thomas Aquinas, like his treatment of many topics, combines elements from Aristotle and Augustine. He agrees with both of them that everyone necessarily desires happiness, and he agrees with Augustine that happiness is truly to be found only in the beatific vision of God after death. But he raises a different question with a new urgency. How can the necessary desire for happiness, he asks, be reconciled with that freedom of the will that is an essential attribute of human beings? If I cannot help but desire happiness, and if happiness is only to be found in God, how can I ever turn away from God and commit sin? He gives his answer:

> There are some particular goods that have no connection with happiness because a human being can be happy without them; nothing necessitates the will to want these. There are other things which do have a necessary connection with happiness, the things that unite men to God in whom alone true happiness is to be found. But until the necessity of this link is established by a vision of God, the will is not necessitated either to want God or the things of God (Aquinas, 1993).

Aquinas' attempt to reconcile a belief in freedom with the postulate that humans cannot help but pursue happiness, though neat and clear, is not really satisfactory. On the one hand, the mere fact that a particular good is not necessarily connected with happiness is not sufficient to establish my freedom not to choose it. If I am a chain-smoker who gets through 200 cigarettes a day, am I free at any moment to stop smoking? To establish that I am, something more is needed than the observation that human beings can be happy without smoking. On the other hand, there seems to be something wrong with the fundamental premise that Aquinas shares with both Aristotle and Augustine, namely, that one cannot help but pursue whatever one regards as necessary for one's happiness. A wife may be convinced that she will never be happy unless she leaves her husband, and yet stay with him for the sake of the children.

This example brings out the fundamental weakness of the eudaimonism that is common to the ethical systems of all the thinkers we have considered: namely, that they place morality on a basis that is ultimately self-centred. Compared with this feature common to both the pagan and the Christian forms of eudaimonism, it is less important whether the ultimate satisfaction that is held out is envisaged as being realised in this world or in the next. To be sure, Aristotle admitted that a happy man would need friends, and that even a philosopher could philosophise better in company. Again, Augustine and Aquinas taught that we must love our neighbour, as we are commanded to do by the God whose vision we seek. But in each case the concern for the welfare of others is presented as a means to an ultimate goal of self-fulfilment.

### Fulfilment and Altruism

The first philosopher in the Christian tradition to break with this eudaimonism was the fourteenth century Oxford Franciscan, John Duns Scotus. While Augustine and Aquinas had followed Aristotle in placing happiness at the apex of their ethical systems, they accepted, as Aristotle did not, the idea that human beings must obey a natural law laid down by a creator God. Aquinas concurred that such things as murder, abortion, and usury were all violations of the natural law of God. But he structured his ethical system not around the concept of law, but around the idea that virtue was the route to self-fulfilment in happiness. It was Duns Scotus who gave the theory of divine law the central place that it was to occupy in the thought of Christian moralists henceforth. Simultaneously, Scotus removed happiness from its position of solitary dominance in ethical theory.

Scotus agreed with Aquinas that human beings have a natural tendency to pursue happiness; but in addition, he postulated a natural tendency to pursue justice. This natural appetite for justice is a tendency to obey the moral law no matter what the consequences may be for our own welfare. Human freedom, for Scotus, consists in the power to weigh in the balance the conflicting demands of morality and happiness.

In denying that humans seek happiness in all their choices, Scotus was turning his back not only on Aquinas but on a long tradition of eudaimonistic ethics. He was surely right to do so. Unless a philosopher seeks to makes it true by definition, it is surely wrong to maintain that one's own happiness is the only possible aim in life. A person may map out his life in the service of someone else's happiness, or for the furtherance of some political cause which may perhaps be unlikely to triumph during his lifetime. A daughter may forego the prospect of marriage and congenial company and a creative career in order to nurse a bedridden parent. No doubt such people are doing what they want to do, in the sense that their actions are voluntary and not coerced. But 'doing what you want to do' in that sense is not the same as seeking one's own happiness or doing what would give one most pleasure.

In the eudaimonistic tradition freedom was conceived as the ability to choose between different possible means to happiness; and wrongdoing was represented as the outcome of a failure to apprehend the appropriate means. For Scotus, freedom extended not just to the choice of means to a predetermined end, but to a choice between independent and possibly competing ultimate goals (A. Kenny, 2005, 272–4).

## The Greatest Happiness of the Greatest Number

The disagreement between Aquinas and Scotus was replayed, in a different key, at the end of the eighteenth century. It was re-enacted as a difference of opinion between the philosophers Bentham and Kant. Bentham, like Aquinas, made happiness the central concept of morality. Kant, like Scotus, thought that morality needed a different basis: he called it the sense of duty.

Where Scotus had placed the appetite for justice on equal terms with the pursuit of happiness, Kant regarded duty as the supreme motive which must triumph over every other.

Bentham's fundamental moral principle, on his own account, was owed to David Hume. When he read the *Treatise of Human Nature*, he tells us, scales fell from his eyes and he came to believe that utility was the test and measure of all virtue and the sole origin of justice. The principle of utility was interpreted by Bentham as meaning that the happiness of the majority of the citizens was the criterion by which the affairs of a state should be judged. More generally, the real standard of morality and the true goal of legislation was the greatest happiness of the greatest number.

Bentham, like Aristotle, is eudaimonistic in making happiness the key notion of morality. But there are two important differences. First, for Bentham what should guide choices is not the individual's own happiness, but the general happiness. Second, Bentham equated happiness with pleasure, while Aristotle made a sharp distinction between the two. Indeed, Aristotle denied that there was any such thing as pleasure, *tout court*: there were pleasurable experiences and pleasurable activities, and the moral evaluation of a pleasure depended simply on the evaluation of the activity or experience enjoyed. For Bentham on the other hand, pleasure was a single indefinable feeling — produced, no doubt, in many different ways — and this feeling was the one thing that was good in itself and was the point of doing anything whatever. 'In this matter we want no refinement, no metaphysics. It is not necessary to consult Plato, nor Aristotle. Pain and pleasure are what everybody feels to be such.'

It is pleasure that is the supreme spring of action. Bentham's *Introduction to the Principles of Morals and Legislation* famously begins:

> Nature has placed mankind under the governance of two sovereign masters, pain and pleasure. It is for them alone to point out what we ought to do, as well as to determine what we shall do. On the one hand, the standard of right and wrong, on the other the chain of causes and effects, are fastened to their throne. They govern us in all we do, in all we say, in all we

> think: every effort we can make to throw off our subjection,
> will serve but to demonstrate and confirm it (Bentham, 1982).

To maximise happiness, therefore, is the same thing as to maximise pleasure, and pleasure itself is simply a straightforward sensation.

It was, Bentham was careful to point out, a sensation that could be caused not only by eating and drinking and sex, but also by a multitude of other things, as varied as the acquisition of wealth, kindness to animals, or belief in the favour of a Supreme Being. So critics who regarded Bentham's hedonism as a simple call to sensuality were quite mistaken. However, whereas for a thinker like Aristotle pleasure was to be identified with the activity enjoyed, for Bentham the relation between an activity and its pleasure was one of cause and effect. Moreover, whereas for Aristotle the value of a pleasure was the same as the value of the activity enjoyed, for Bentham the value of each and every pleasure was the same, no matter how it was caused. 'Quantity of pleasure being equal' he wrote 'push-pin is as good as poetry'. What went for pleasure went for pain, too: the quantity of pain, and not its cause, is the measure of its disvalue.

What is of prime importance for a utilitarian, therefore, is the quantification of pleasure and pain. In deciding on an action or a policy we need to estimate the amount of pleasure and the amount of pain likely to ensue. Bentham was aware that such quantification was no trivial task, and he offered recipes for the measurement of pleasures and pains. Pleasure A counts more than pleasure B if it is more intense, or if it lasts longer, or if it is more certain, or if it is more immediate. In the 'felicific calculus' these different factors must be taken into account and weighed against each other. In judging pleasure-producing actions we must also consider fecundity and purity: a pleasurable action is fecund if it is likely to produce a subsequent series of pleasures, and it is pure if it is unlikely to produce a subsequent series of pains. All these factors are to be taken into account when we are considering our own affairs, If we are operating the calculus for purposes of public policy, we must further consider another factor, which Bentham calls 'extension' — that is, how widely the pains and pleasures will be spread across the population.

Bentham offered a mnemonic rhyme to aid in operating the calculus:

> Intense, long, certain, speedy, fruitful, pure —
> Such marks in pleasures and in pains endure.
> Such pleasures seek if private be thy end;
> If it be public, wide let them extend.
> Such pains avoid, whichever be thy view
> If pains must come, let them extend to few.
>                                   (Bentham, 1982,4,2)

In using the felicific calculus for purposes of determining public policy, extension is the crucial factor.

'The greatest happiness of the greatest number' is an impressive slogan: but when probed it turns out to be riddled with ambiguity. The first question to be raised is 'greatest number of *what?*' Should we add 'voters' or 'citizens' or 'males' or 'human beings' or 'sentient beings'? It makes a huge difference which answer we give. Throughout the two centuries of utilitarianism's history most of its devotees would probably give the answer 'human beings', and this is most likely the answer that Bentham would have given. In principle he thought that in the pursuit of the greatest happiness 'the claim of [the female] sex is, if not still better, at least altogether as good as that of the other'. Only tactical considerations prevented him from advocating female suffrage.

In recent years many utilitarians have extended the happiness principle beyond humankind to other sentient beings, claiming that animals have equal claims with human beings. Though a great lover of animals (especially cats) Bentham himself did not go as far as this, and he would have rejected the idea that animals have rights, because he did not believe in natural rights of any kind. But by making the supreme moral criterion a matter of sensation he made it appropriate to consider animals as belonging to the same moral community as ourselves. Animals do not share Aristotelian rationality with humans, but it is beyond doubt that many animals as well as humans feel pleasure and pain. The classical and Christian moral tradition had placed supreme moral value in activities not of the sense but of the reason, and regarded non-rational animals as standing outside the moral community. Bentham's moral theory represented a break with this tradition, and that has turned out, in the long term, to be one of its most significant legacies.

A second question about the principle of utility is this: should individuals, or politicians, in following the greatest happiness principle attempt to exercise control over the number of candidates for happiness (however these are defined)? Does the extension of happiness to a greater number mean that we should try to bring more people (or animals) into existence? What answer we give to this is linked to a third, even more difficult question: when we are measuring the happiness of a population, do we consider only total happiness, or should we also consider average happiness — should we take account of the distribution of happiness as well as of its quantity? If so, then we have to strike a difficult balance between quantity of happiness and quantity of people.

In introducing his Greatest Happiness principle, Bentham was less concerned to provide a criterion for individual moral choices than to offer guidance to rulers and legislators on the management of communities. But it is precisely in this area, when we have to consider not just the total quantity of happiness in a community but also its distribution, that the greatest happiness principle, on its own, fails to provide a credible decision procedure.

Suppose that, by whatever means, we have succeeded in establishing a scale for the measurement of happiness: a scale from 0 to 10 on which 0 represents maximum misery, 10 represents maximum happiness, and 5 a state of indifference. Imagine that we are devising political and legal institutions for a society of 100 people, and that we have a choice between implementing two models. The result of adopting model A will be that 60 people will score 6, and 40 will score 4. The result of adopting model B will be that 60 people will score 10 and 40 will score 0. Faced with such a choice, anyone with a care either for equality or humanity will surely wish to implement model A rather than model B. Yet if we operate Bentham's felicific calculus in the obvious manner, model A scores only 520 points (60x6 + 40x4), while model B achieves a total of 600 (60x10).

The principle that we should seek the greatest happiness of the greatest number clearly leads to different results depending on whether we opt to maximise happiness or to maximise the number of happy people. The principle needs, at the very least, to be supplemented by some limits on the amount of inequality between the best off and the worst off, and limits on the degree of misery of the worst off, if it is not to permit outcomes which are gross violations of distributive justice.

But even if we restrict our consideration to matters of individual morality, there remains a problem raised by the initial passage of the *Introduction* quoted above. The hedonism there proclaimed is twofold: there is a psychological hedonism (pleasure determines all our actions) and an ethical hedonism (pleasure is the standard of right and wrong). But the pleasure cited in psychological hedonism is the pleasure of the individual person; the pleasure invoked in ethical hedonism is the pleasure (however quantified) of the total moral community. If I am, in fact, predetermined in every action to aim at maximising my own pleasure, what point is there in telling me that I am obliged to maximise the common good? This was a problem which was to exercise some of Bentham's successors in the Utilitarian tradition.

The best known, and the most talented of these successors was John Stuart Mill. Mill was, like Bentham, a consequentialist, that is to say he thought that the morality of an action depended on its foreseen consequences. But in other ways he toned down aspects of Bentham's teaching that had been found most offensive. In his treatise *Utilitarianism,* written in his late fifties, he acknowledges that many people have thought that the idea that life has no higher end than pleasure was a doctrine worthy only of swine. He replies that it is foolish to deny that humans have faculties that are higher than the ones they share with animals. This allows us to make distinctions between different pleasures not only in quantity but also in quality. 'It is quite compatible with the principle of utility to recognise the fact that some *kinds* of pleasure are more desirable and more valuable than others' (Mill, 1962, 258).

How then do we grade the different kinds of pleasure? 'Of two pleasures' Mill tells us 'if there be one to which all or almost all who have experience of both give a decided preference, irrespective of any feeling of moral obligation to prefer it, that is the more desirable pleasure'. Armed with this distinction a utilitarian can put a distance between himself and the swine. Few humans would wish to be changed into a lower animal even if promised a cornucopia of bestial pleasures. 'It is better to be a human being dissatisfied than a pig satisfied.' Again, no intelligent, educated person would wish, at any price, to become a foolish ignoramus. It is 'better to be Socrates dissatisfied than a fool satisfied' (Mill, 1962, 260).

Happiness, according to Mill, involves not just contentment, but also a sense of dignity; any amount of the lower pleasures, without this, would not amount to happiness. Accordingly, the greatest happiness principle needs to be restated.

> The ultimate end, with reference to and for the sake of which all other things are desirable (whether we are considering our own good or that of other people), is an existence exempt as far as possible from pain, and as rich as possible in enjoyments, both in point of quantity and quality; the test of quality, and the rule for measuring it against quantity, being the preference felt by those who in their opportunities of experience, to which must be added their habits of self-consciousness and self-observation, are best furnished with the means of comparison (Mill, 1962, 262).

Let us suppose, then, that a critic grants to Mill that utilitarianism need not be swinish. Still, he may insist, it does not appeal to the best in human nature. Virtue is more important than happiness, and acts of renunciation and self-sacrifice are the most splendid of human deeds. Mill agrees that it is noble to be capable of resigning one's own happiness for the sake of others — but would the hero or martyr's sacrifice be made if he did not believe that it would increase the amount of happiness in the world? A person who denies himself the enjoyment of life for any other purpose 'is no more deserving of admiration than the ascetic mounted on his pillar.'

Mill strives to explain how various notions connected with justice — desert, impartiality, equality — are to be reconciled with the utilitarian principle of expediency. With regard to equality, he cites a maxim of Bentham's 'everybody to count for one, nobody for more than one' — each person's happiness is counted for exactly as much as another's. But he does not really address the problem inherent in the Greatest Happiness Principle, that it leaves room for the misery of an individual to be discounted in order to increase the he overall total of happiness in the community.

## Happiness vs Duty

At the opposite extreme from utilitarianism, in modern times, stands the moral theory of Kant. Kant's starting point is that the only thing that is good without qualification is a good will. Talents, character, and fortune can be used to bad ends and even happiness can be corrupting. It is not what a good will achieves that matters; good will, even if frustrated in its efforts, is good in itself alone. What makes a will good is that it is motivated by duty: to act from duty is to exhibit good will in the face of difficulty. Some people may enjoy doing good, or profit from doing good, but worth of character is shown only when someone does good not from inclination, but for duty's sake.

Happiness, Kant argues in his *Groundwork of the Metaphysic of Morals*, cannot be the ultimate purpose of morality.

> Suppose now that for a being possessed of reason and will the real purpose of nature were his preservation, his welfare, or in a word his happiness. In that case nature would have hit on a very bad arrangement by choosing reason in the creature to carry out this purpose. For all the actions he has to perform with this end in view, and the whole rule of his behaviour, would have been mapped out for him far more accurately by instinct; and the end in question could have been maintained far more surely by instinct than it ever can be by reason (Kant, 1991, 395).

The overarching concept in Kantian morality is not happiness, but duty. The function of reason in ethics is not to inform the will how best to choose means to some further end: it is to produce a will that is good in itself; and a will is good only if it is motivated by duty. Good will, as has been said, is for Kant the only thing that is good without qualification. It is not what it achieves that constitutes the goodness of a good will; good will is good in itself alone.

> Even if, by some special disfavour of destiny, or by the niggardly endowment of stepmotherly nature, this will is entirely lacking in power to carry out its intentions, if by its utmost effort it still accomplishes nothing, and only good will is left… even then it would still shine like a jewel for its own sake as something which has its full value in itself (Kant, 1991, 394).

Good will is the highest good and the condition of all other goods, and good will is within our power, while happiness is not. Happiness is an impossible goal to pursue, because no finite being, however powerful and insightful, can say definitely and consistently what he really wants. Riches may bring with them anxiety, long life may turn out to be nothing but long misery. Only an omniscient being could determine with certainty what would make him truly happy.

## No Consensus among Philosophers

Our survey of philosophers from Aristotle to Kant shows a great variety of understandings of the concept of happiness and of the relationship between happiness and morality. Hardly any two thinkers give the same set of answers to the following questions. Is happiness something subjective or objective? Is it a sensation detectable at a single moment, or is it a quality of an entire life? Is it a motive for endeavour, or is it a state of satisfaction? Does everyone pursue happiness? *Should* everyone pursue happiness? Is it something achievable at will, or something that depends on factors outside oneself? However it is brought about, is it something to be hoped for in this life or only in some afterlife? Is happiness the key concept that determines the structure of morality? If so, is it the happiness of the individual or is it the general happiness that stands at the apex of the moral system?

For Bentham happiness is clearly a subjective phenomenon: a warm sensation that each of us can recognise when we feel it. Pleasure and pain are opposites, and it is as natural to take someone's word for it that she feels pleasure as it is to take her word for it that she is in pain. According to Aristotle and his followers, however, most people are ignorant of the true nature of happiness and therefore do not really know whether they are happy or not. If the Nicomachean Ethics is right that ultimate satisfaction is to be found only in the intellectual delights of the philosopher, then the nature of happiness is a secret known only to very few. Without going so far as this in the glorification of their own discipline, other philosophers have taken the Aristotelian view that happiness is an objective, not a subjective condition, and that it takes inquiry, not just introspection, to ascertain what it is and whether one possesses it.

Feelings of pleasure are fleeting and variable, and if happiness is to be equated with pleasure then it is possible to be happy at one moment and unhappy the next — though of course in operating Bentham's felicific calculus one will attach more weight to the more durable pleasures. For Aristotle on the other hand stability is a conceptual requirement for happiness, and whether someone is happy or not can be judged only over a long period. Indeed there was an ancient tradition that only a whole lifetime would permit such a judgement: 'call no man happy' the sage Solon had famously said 'until he is dead'. Aristotle did not go so far as that. Though happiness must be an enduring condition, none the less, given the contingencies of human life, it is something that can be lost. King Priam of Troy came to an unhappy end, as every reader of Homer knew; but that did not mean that he was not genuinely happy at a time when he was a wise and popular monarch with a large and gifted family. Happiness, Aristotle had to agree, might turn into tragedy; but he insisted that anyone who was truly happy must have within himself the ability to cope in a dignified manner with whatever adversity might present itself.

All the thinkers we have considered regard happiness both as a motive in advance of action, and as a benefit resulting from action. But different philosophers link the two features of happiness in different directions. Bentham and his followers start from utility as a satisfactory goal, and seek the means to achieve it. Aristotelians start from our desire to have a good life, and ask what kind of end state will possess the features that are built into our desire. Again, while everyone agrees that happiness can motivate action, there are some who think that happiness is a necessary goal (every action is consciously or unconsciously aimed at happiness) others think of it only as a possible motive, and not necessarily an ultimate goal.

How far is happiness achievable? Among the philosophers discussed in this chapter there are very variable degrees of optimism. Everyone agrees that some factors necessary for happiness — the essentials for life and health — may be lacking through no fault of our own. Aristotle and his Christian followers see virtue (whether moral or intellectual) as the road to happiness, and they regard the virtues as excellences that, given basic luck, we can and should acquire. For Augustine and Aquinas, happiness demanded, in addition to moral virtues like courage and temperance and intellectual excellences such as knowledge and understanding, the theological virtues of faith, hope, and love, and these were gifts of God that might be freely given or denied. The happiness that was the reward of these virtues could be fully enjoyed only in the next life; on the other hand the imperfect happiness that attached to a life of virtue in this world was compatible with an almost complete lack of worldly goods. By comparison with the Aristotelians, the utilitarians were much more optimistic about the possibility of achieving true happiness in the present life (which, for most of them, was the only life). This contrast is unsurprising, given the differences between the underlying conceptions of happiness. The more exalted one's notion of happiness is, the less one is likely to think it achievable, and the best that the optimist can hope for, the human condition being what it is, will be something rather down-to-earth.

Aristotle and Bentham agree that happiness is the single overarching concept of ethics, in contrast to Scotus, who thinks that the concept of happiness rests on an equal level with the concept of justice, and Kant, who thinks that it ranks below the concept of duty. But in addition to their differences about the nature of happiness, Aristotle and Bentham disagree about the extension of the happiness that is to be the goal of action. For Aristotle the virtuous individual's ultimate aim is his or her own well-being; for Bentham it is the greatest happiness of the greatest number. Though Scotus and Kant do not give such a dominant position to happiness of any kind, on the issue of general vs individual good they in effect take sides on this issue with Bentham against Aristotle. For Scotus the interests of others than oneself are what determine the independent principles of justice; for Kant, the nature of duty is to be determined by a procedure of universalisation that treats other rational beings as on an equal footing with oneself.

Because of the overwhelming influence of Kant, many moral philosophers in the nineteenth and twentieth centuries lost interest in the study of happiness. The utilitarians, of course, continued to pay homage to the concept, but their interests began to diverge in two different directions. The philosophers among them were mainly interested in the relationship between utilitarianism and other moral intuitions, while the economists sought to explore what methods were available to measure utility.

The most influential utilitarian philosopher of the nineteenth century, Mill's disciple Henry Sidgwick, came to hold that there was an inconsistency between two great principles of Mill's system. One could not simultaneously maintain psychological hedonism (the doctrine that everyone seeks their own happiness) and ethical hedonism (the doctrine that everyone should seek the general happiness). One of the main tasks Sidgwick set himself was to resolve this problem, which he called 'the dualism of practical reason'.

In the course of his thinking Sidgwick abandoned the principle of psychological hedonism and replaced it with an ethical principle of rational egoism, that each person has an obligation to seek his own good. This principle, he believed, was intuitively obvious. Ethical hedonism, too, he decided, could only be based on fundamental moral intuitions. Thus, his system combined utilitarianism with intuitionism, which he regarded as the common-sense approach to morality. However, the typical intuitions of common sense were, he believed, too narrow and specific: the intuitions that were the foundation of utilitarian morality were more abstract. One such was that future good is as important as present good, and another is that, from the point of view of the Universe, any single person's good is of no more importance than any other person's.

The remaining difficulty was to reconcile the intuitions of utilitarianism with those of rational egoism. Sidgwick came to the conclusion that no complete solution of the conflict between my happiness and the general happiness was possible on the basis of calculations related to the present life alone (Sidgwick, 1907). For most people, he accepted, the connection between the individual's interest and his duty is made through belief in God and personal immortality. As he himself was unwilling to invoke God in this context, he concluded sadly that 'the prolonged effort of the human intellect to frame a perfect ideal of rational conduct is seen to have been foredoomed to inevitable failure.' He consoled himself by seeking, through the work of the Society for Psychical Research founded in 1882, empirical evidence for the survival of the individual after death.

## From Philosophy to Economics

The first utilitarians thought of happiness as something that it was possible to quantify and measure: otherwise the notion of the 'felicific calculus' would have no content. Moreover, since utility was the goal of economics, the success of an economic venture or policy must depend upon the amount of utility produced. Throughout the nineteenth century many economists believed that the most efficient method of producing utility is the free operation of the market. Whether or not this belief is correct — and the disastrous history of command economies in the latter part of the twentieth century gave it formidable support — it clearly supposes that the operation of the market and the production of utility are two separate entities that can be described and measured independently. Otherwise talk of 'efficiency' would have no meaning.

Economists such as Pigou and Marshall clearly thought of utility in this way as an independent variable. They regarded it as a quantity comparable to temperature, to which one could assign a cardinal value. (Layard, 2005, 133) But since, in line with the empiricist tradition, they conceived of mental states and events as private entities accessible only to introspection, there was a problem in seeing how utilities could be subject to any comparative measurement. In the first part of the twentieth century many philosophers and psychologists became sceptical about not just the measurement but the independent existence of mental states such as contentment.

Behaviourists such as Watson and Skinner accepted the prevailing notion that feelings were incommunicable mental events; rightly rejecting the notion of irreducibly private events, they wrongly concluded that there were no such things as feelings. Accepting an over-simplified view of the relation between a name and what it names, they thought that since words like 'anxiety' and 'contentment' were not names of private sensations, they must be names of publicly observable reactions.

Watson, the founder of behaviourism, concluded, as a result of his investigations on children, that there were three main types of unconditioned stimuli producing emotional reactions in infancy. Loud sounds and sudden loss of support produced checking of the breath, crying, a start of the whole body, and marked visceral responses. Holding or restraint produced crying with open mouth, prolonged holding of breath, and reddening of the face. Stroking the skin, and especially the genitals, produced smiling, cessation of crying, changes in respiration, cooing, gurgling and erection. These three behaviour patterns, he maintained, are the starting points from which are built up the complicated conditioned habit patterns that we call the emotions of fear, rage, and love. The complication of adult emotional life is achieved by an increase in the number of stimuli, due to conditioning and transfers, and additions and modifications to the responses (A. Kenny, 1963 ,29).

The behaviourist account of emotions and feelings was a crude oversimplification that did not long remain popular with philosophers and psychologists. It lasted long enough, however, to infect the thought of economists who wished to offer an operational definition of utility. They sought for measurable behaviour that would constitute happiness in the way that, for Watson, crying, cooing, and gurgling constituted more basic emotions. Surely, in economic terms, the behaviour most indicative of satisfaction is the set of actual choices that a person makes in his market transactions. So economists such as Robbins and Samuelson developed the theory that utility was nothing other than the revealed preferences of the those who purchased goods or services. Only an ordinal, not a cardinal, magnitude could be assigned to utility, so conceived. Moreover, critics suspected that there lurked in the system a certain circularity that made it impossible to undertake a genuinely empirical evaluation of the efficiency of an economic practice or institution.

Towards the end of the twentieth century economic fashion once again followed a change in fashion in psychology. Psychiatrists studying depression found it unsatisfactory to treat it merely as a behavioural pattern, and social psychologists began to explore ways to investigate happiness by means of population surveys. Some of these were open-ended inquiries about what people wanted out of life, which required detailed volunteered answers. Others, vaguer but more easily comparable across countries and across cultures, asked questions such as 'How satisfied are you with your life as a whole: very, somewhat, so-so, not very or not at all?' Such self-ascribed happiness was once again a quantity measurable on a cardinal scale, even if only a scale that ranged from one to five. It therefore offered economists a measure of utility independent of market activity.

Despite some obvious methodological problems, which will be discussed in a later chapter, such surveys have developed into a respectable branch of social science, the discipline of 'happiness studies' that straddles psychology and economics. Later in this book a number of the results of such studies will be presented and evaluated for their possible implications for public policy. In this introductory chapter two examples will be mentioned by way of illustration.

Aristotle, it will be remembered, inquired whether happiness came by nature, by luck, or by training. Twentieth century psychologists, likewise, have sought to discover how much of a person's subjective happiness is determined by heredity, how much by environment, and how much is a result of individual endeavour. A number of studies have suggested that good or bad luck, that is to say external events outside one's control, has much less effect on self-ascribed happiness than might be expected. Some psychologists claim that each individual has a determined 'set-point' of subjective well-being — a level of contentment with life that is set by one's genes and one's personality. Key events in one's life, such as marriage or divorce, acquiring or losing a job, even serious injury, appear to make a dramatic increase or decrease in one's level of satisfaction only for a comparatively brief period. Their longer term effects are muted. In time — so this theory suggests — everyone adjusts to the new condition and returns to the set-point. Whatever the merits of this theory, the evidence collected in its favour suggests that human adaptability — even among paraplegics — is much greater than might have been anticipated.

Another well-confirmed result that is surprising — at least to economists — is that above a certain minimum level the amount of money a person has bears very little relation to how subjectively happy she is. In the period since happiness studies began the average incomes in the most developed countries have more than doubled. Yet people's answers to pollsters during the same period suggests that they are very little, if at all, happier.

Later parts of this book will refine and analyse this brief statement of an economic paradox, and discuss its relationship to philosophical discussions of happiness across the centuries.

## The Elements of Well-being

If we reflect upon the different accounts of happiness given in philosophical, psychological, and economic tradition, we may conclude that there are three distinct elements to be identified in human well-being. We may call them contentment, welfare, and dignity. Contentment is what is expressed by self-ascriptions of happiness. It is not so much a feeling or a sensation as an attitude or state of mind; but of the elements of well-being it is the one that is closest to the utilitarian idea of happiness. If it is to amount to a constituent of well-being, however, it must be an enduring and stable state, and not mere temporary euphoria or passing glow of satisfaction.

Welfare, in the most obvious sense of material welfare, consists in the satisfaction of one's animal needs, for food, drink, shelter and the other things that conduce to bodily flourishing. Self-ascription does not have the same central role in the measurement of welfare as it does in the case of contentment; we may be mistaken about the state of our bodily health and other people are often better placed to make a judgement in this area. But welfare is the least controversial element in well-being. As we shall see in a later chapter, almost all philosophers who have considered the topic have considered it either a constituent or a necessary condition of happiness.

In addition to material welfare there is psychological welfare, which is less easy to quantify. Clearly there are negative conditions necessary for well-being: freedom from mental illness or defect, and freedom from tragedies occurring within one's family or immediate social circle. But there are also positive abilities of a mental as well as a physical kind, which may well be regarded as basic constituents of a good life. Literacy is a good whose possessors prize in themselves and wish to confer on others. But perhaps it is not so much an element in welfare as in the third element of well-being, which in this book we label 'dignity'.

Dignity is a much more complicated notion to define. We may say initially that it involves the control of one's own destiny and the ability to live a life of one's choice. But in addition, it seems to be necessary for total well-being that one's chosen way of life should have worth in itself, and should enjoy the respect of others. Because dignity concerns, among other things, one's position in relationship to others, measurements of dignity cannot be as absolute and objective as those of welfare. Dignity is the element of well-being most emphasized in the Aristotelian concept of happiness.

These three elements of well-being are independent of each other and may vary independently. Though they are, as a matter of empirical fact, correlated with each other in various ways, each may exist without the others, and more importantly, pairs of the triad may occur without the third.

It is possible for someone to have welfare and contentment without dignity. A well-housed and well-fed slave who looks for nothing better than his servile lot and has no complaints about the way he is treated may be thought of as being in a certain sense quite happy: but he lacks the dignity that only liberty could confer.

Contentment and dignity may be present without welfare. A devout and ascetic hermit, revered by all who come in contact with him, may regard himself as blessed even though he may be undernourished and unhealthy. Such is the 'man on the pillar' despised by John Stuart Mill. If we look for a secular example, we may think of hunger strikers, admired by a throng of supporters, suffering resolutely to further a cause they believe to be paramount. Both religious and secular martyrs have died proclaiming their own happiness.

Finally, it is all too easy for welfare and elements of dignity to be present without contentment, as in the case of a pampered member of a rich and dominant elite, active perhaps in charitable causes and feted as a celebrity in popular newspapers, but bored and irritable and finding little satisfaction in her life. Lack of contentment in the presence of welfare and dignity need not betray a defect of character: it may even be the result of something admirable, for instance the decision to stay loyal to a spouse who has become intolerable, in order to ensure a stable home for the children of the marriage.

Many of the problems and paradoxes that have perplexed those who have sought to understand the nature of happiness are removed if we resolve it into these separate elements and consider them in turn.

Our purpose in breaking down the notion of well-being is not to show that no one can be happy who does not score highly in each of these dimensions. Throughout history, few have been fortunate enough to be in possession of all the desirable characteristics we have identified. The purpose of the analysis is to show that when we pursue happiness for our-selves or for others, the goal is not a simple but a complex one, and if we are trying to measure well-being, a single metric will not suffice. Policies for the maximisation of happiness may involve trade-offs between dignity and contentment, between welfare and dignity, and between contentment and welfare.

The three items that we have identified correspond to the unalienable human rights whose existence the American Dec-laration of Independence regarded as a self-evident truth: life, liberty, and the pursuit of happiness. 'Life', broadly inter-preted, includes the necessities that we have entitled 'welfare'. 'Liberty' is the foundation of a career of dignity. And the 'hap-piness' that was to be pursed was conceived of by the founding fathers as a state of contentment, such as was soon to be given the name of 'utility'.

In the remainder of this book we shall consider the constitu-ent elements of well being in the order suggested by the words of the Declaration. Section Two will consider welfare, Section Three dignity, and Section Four contentment. In a final section we will discuss what conclusions with regard to moral behav-iour as well as national and international policy should be drawn from the study we have undertaken.

Chapter 2

# Happiness in History

In the seventeenth century, the Dutch Republic built up immense wealth on the basis of a trading empire. It became the richest country in the World — richer than any country at any point in prior history. Famines became almost unknown and even poorhouse food included milk, bread, cheese, vegetable and meat stews as well as fowl. The real social divide, according to Simon Schama (1997), was between those who could only afford butter to spread on their bread and those that could also buy it as a substitute for lard in cooking. Paintings from the time depict overweight peasants feasting and drinking merrily[1] and other scenes of widespread excess.[2]

Moralists cried out for restraint. As well as painting scenes of debauch, artists composed pictures both depicting and adorning simple houses which would symbolize the transience of earthly pleasures — the guttering candle, the peacock feather, the skull. Calvin's *Commentary on Isaiah* warned his Dutch adherents: 'it too often happens that riches bring self-indulgence, and superfluity of pleasures produces flabbiness as we can see in wealthy regions and cities.' Popular authors predicted that excess would bring on plague, poxes, rheums and insomnia. Schama notes that 'preachers and mor-

---

[1]    For example, Vinckboons' *Peasant Kermis*, The Royal Cabinet of Paintings, The Hague.
[2]    Van Scheyndel, *Bacchus Wonder-wercken*, Koninklijke Bibliotheek The Hague.

alizing writers made no social distinctions in their attacks on corrupt manners. Their assumption was that abundance was a common, if unevenly distributed patrimony, and that middling and common people quite as much as the elite needed warning of the dangers of drink and gluttony.' There were even attempts to place legal limits on excess — in 1655, a law was passed limiting wedding feasts to two days.

The widespread concern in the seventeenth century Dutch Republic that the country had too much wealth, and was having too jolly a time, for its own good might not be considered surprising given that it was the richest country in the world at the time. But it might seem strange to modern readers given that the average income in the Republic was around $2,100 (this expressed in year 2000 US dollars).[3] This is approximately the same income as was reached in the UK in 1820, by Lesotho in 2000, or somewhere around one thirteenth the average income per capita of the US today. Wealth and poverty are not what they used to be.

The apparent general level of contentment in the Dutch Republic at the time might also come as a surprise given the comparatively atrocious status of health indicators. Despite adequate nutrition, perhaps one third of children died before their first birthday and average life expectancies were no higher than in other (poorer) parts of Europe at the time — in the low thirties. (This was due in considerable part to the poor state of knowledge about health, to be discussed in a later chapter).

More broadly, in Western Europe as a whole, GDP per capita at the beginning of the Christian era has been estimated as approximately $450 (Maddison, 2001). One thousand years later, it was approximately the same. By 1820 it had climbed to $1,232. In the period after 1820 the region saw dramatic growth with income climbing to $18,742 over the next 180 years. This suggests that, for most of history, the average Western European has lived on an income which is less than one tenth the average income of the *poorest ten percent* of US citizens in 2000 ($5,760, from World Bank, 2005). We will see

---

[3]    Even poorer for a time in terms of tulip-adjusted incomes.

that health in Western Europe was also broadly stagnant over the period before 1850, declining slightly as globalization and urbanization created better environments for new diseases. Life expectancies were between one third and one half of late twentieth century US levels. Again, given that polls suggest ten percent of Americans remain unhappy today despite all of their comparative health and wealth, if there were a close link between income and contentment, weeping, wailing and gnashing of teeth must surely have been the major preoccupation of people everywhere before the late twentieth century.

And yet, the Dutch Republic was hardly the exception in managing to produce considerable amounts of cheer, as well as considerable concern with non-absolute-income (and non-health) elements of the good life despite this overwhelming poverty compared to the modern world. While we lack survey data based on a representative sample of Anglo-Saxons in 800 AD regarding states of self-reported happiness measured on a scale of one to ten, considerable circumstantial evidence suggests that happiness (including elements of welfare, dignity and contentment) was considered a widely achievable goal well before the period of modern economic growth or the explosive improvements in health of the last two hundred years.

## Views of Income and the Good Life in History

It appears that welfare — adequate food, shelter and health followed by a peaceful death — has long been an element of the good life. Hesiod, writing in the eighth century BC describes a Golden Age that provides an early example of the perfect life:

> Nothing for toil or pitiful age they cared
> But in strength of hand and foot still unimpaired
> They feasted gaily, undarkened by sufferings
> They died as if falling asleep; and all good things
> Were theirs, for the fruitful earth unstintingly bore
>     unforced her plenty ...

> (*Works and Days*, 110ff; quoted in Claeys and Sargent, 1999)

Whatever human powers of adaptation to circumstances, then, it appears implausible that widespread lack of basic necessities of life or early death or disability would be discounted as problems. Nonetheless, from early in Western writing it appears that such problems were considered significant for only a minority of people, and more income was not seen as the answer to those problems.

Those who were absolutely poor in the sense of being hungry, thirsty and cold were a small enough group in Western Europe, even in the Middle Ages, that theologians such as Aquinas suggested such people had the right to steal what they needed (A. Kenny, 2005, Geremek, 1997). Fogel (1995) presents evidence that, while diets were inadequate, famine deaths had already, by the Tudor period, become only a minor cause of mortality.

In part as a result, well before the Industrial Revolution, the idea of poverty in the United Kingdom had changed. No longer a conception of an absolute lack of the basic necessities of life (adequate food and shelter), it has become a social status. For example, in the Fifteenth Century, Sir John Fortescue returned from a visit to France noting the superior life of the British peasant. French countryfolk drank water rather than beer, ate brown rather than white bread, ate little meat, and only the men had shoes. In short, he argued, French peasants 'live in the most extreme poverty and miserie' compared to their English counterparts (Landes, 1998). It was not that the French peasant lacked the basic needs of life, but that they lacked the comforts of white bread.

This is why long before the Industrial Revolution 'combating poverty' moved from a concern with welfare (supplying basic needs) to a concern with dignity (supplying needs generated by social conditions). By the eighteenth century, when annual UK income per capita was somewhere around $2,000, Adam Smith argued that the rich, by employing the poor 'for their own vain and insatiable desires ... make nearly the same distribution of the necessities of life ... had the earth been divided into equal portions among all its inhabitants' (Smith, 1982). Necessities for Smith meant 'not only those things which nature, but those things which the established rules of decency have rendered necessary.' Indeed, he argued for the creation of a minimum wage set at a level considerably above brute subsistence to ensure that the poor could afford social necessities required to avoid social stigma. For example, in England, one could not go out in public barefoot without embarrassment, so the minimum wage should be set high enough to allow for the purchase of shoes. (In Scotland, where wandering around barefoot was common, the minimum wage could be set lower, argued Smith.)

At comparatively low levels of income, 'social poverty' rather than 'absolute poverty' became the dominant concern of political thinkers, then. Similarly, at quite low levels of income, concerns with the deleterious effects of too *much* money on morals and the search for the good life became a concern. Calls for limits to luxuries hark back as far as the mythical lawgiver of Sparta, Lycurgus, who (according to Plutarch) 'banished the unnecessary and superfluous arts', banned foreign wares and denied entry to rhetoric teachers, soothsayers and harlot keepers (translated by Claeys and Sargent, 1999). Plato was an early (non-mythical) exponent of limiting wealth—'the community which has neither poverty nor riches will always have the noblest principles' he argued (quoted in Bronk, 1998).

It is an idea that has frequently reappeared throughout the history of thought and in politics. Tacitus praised the Lapps for having 'achieved the most difficult thing of all: they have ceased to feel the harrying of men's desires' (quoted in Fernandez-Armesto, 2001). Sumptuary laws were introduced in the Roman Empire and again in many parts of Medieval and early modern Europe (as well as China, Japan, and amongst the Aztecs) in order to limit consumption in the cause of vanity (Mason, 1998). In medieval France, a lord could purchase only four costumes a year, only one of which could be for summer wear (Bernstein, 2004). The Dominican friar Savonarola put a torch to the original 'bonfire of the vanities' (a 60 foot high pile of luxury goods) in Florence in 1497. Parliamentarians during the English Civil War called for a maximum income of 2,000 pounds a year (Hill, 1991).[4]

---

[4]    About 150,000 pounds in today's money (C. Kenny, 2006).

The idea of the 'hedonic treadmill' — that more goods do not slake the appetite for ever more goods — also predates the Industrial Revolution. In 1753, Rousseau argued heatedly that too much concern with the fripperies of civilization was the chief cause of the corruption of man. In all people, he argued, there is a 'consuming ambition, the burning passion to increase one's relative fortune, less out of real need than to make oneself superior to others.' The result that was all people grew attached to ever more luxury, without gaining satisfaction from it: 'in time ... commodities lost all their pleasantness through habit, and as they had at the same time degenerated into true needs, being deprived of them became more cruel than possessing them was sweet; and people were unhappy to lose them without being happy to possess them' (Rousseau, 1984).

Conceptions of the potential widespread extent of happiness suggest once more that low income was not seen as the major barrier to its achievement, although it took some time for such conceptions to become commonplace. Philosophers in the ancient and medieval period held out little hope of universal happiness. Plato, Aristotle, and the Stoics defined happiness in such a way as to place it out of the reach of many people — both amongst the rich and amongst the poor. Only Epicurus gave an account of happiness that made it a realistic aspiration for the multitude. But even an Epicurean like Lucretius regarded the world as being a place of woe, clearly not designed by any gods for human benefit. No wonder that newborn children wail:

> Thus, like a sailor by the tempest hurled
> Ashore, the babe is shipwrecked on the world
> Naked he lies, and ready to expire
> Helpless of all that human wants require;
> Exposed upon inhospitable earth,
> From the first moment of his hapless birth.
> Straight with foreboding cries he fills the room
> (Too true presages of his future doom).
>
> (quoted A. Kenny, 2004, 303)

Many medieval thinkers too thought of the world as a vale of tears from which only the few elect would escape to eternal happiness in heaven. In this world, rich and poor alike were doomed to misery, and it was the poor, rather than the rich, that had the best chance of finding themselves in bliss hereafter.

But with the Enlightenment, we see for the first time an egalitarian notion of happiness in this life. McMahon (2006) notes an explosion of works on the subject of achieving earthly happiness in the final two decades of the seventeenth century which suggested a wide range of different approaches (including, on the side of the rock, temperance and, on the side of the hard place, the consumption of 'wine of English grapes'). By the eighteenth century, Diderot's Encyclopedia was suggesting all people had a right to happiness, and Helvétius argued that this was 'the century of happiness'. Neither poverty nor ill-health was seen as an insurmountable barrier to ubiquitous happiness.

Whilst this was perhaps the first time that the potential for general happiness in this life became a commonplace amongst philosophers, it is worth noting that it became commonplace as early as the 1700s, well before the Industrial Revolution. Even Adam Smith, while clearly interested in national output, already felt that in wealthy nations 'all are often abundantly supplied.' As a result, he argued, it was a deception that the rich man owned more means to happiness than the poor (Gilbert, 1997). The poor man in pursuit of wealth 'sacrifices a real tranquility that is at times in his power' and 'in the last dregs of life… he begins at last to find that wealth and greatness are mere trinkets of frivolous utility' Smith suggested in the *Theory of Moral Sentiments* (1982).[5]

Furthermore, as the Industrial Revolution got under way, this was the very moment that the 'maladie du siecle' spread. Rousseau's idea that civilization brought with it discontent 'enjoyed widespread currency among analysts of the modern malaise' in the early nineteenth century according to McMahon. As industrialization spread, the apocalyptic — and sadly accurate — descriptions of proletarian life provided by

[5]    Nonetheless, Smith argues in the Wealth of Nations that greed is good because such motives keep 'in continual motion the industry of mankind.'(quite to what end is never made clear).

(not least) Engels and Marx were seen to be the forerunner to political revolution. The increasing misery of industrial conditions was highlighted in the writing of Dickens (*Hard Times*) and Upton Sinclair (*The Jungle*) amongst many others. Indeed, it was in the century of industrialization that the cottage industry of complaint against economic progress turned into a significant manufacturing enterprise, Dickens alone producing output in the millions of words.

This brief history suggests a high absolute level of income is neither necessary nor sufficient for the good life. On the one hand, many political thinkers through history have thought that welfare and contentment were achievable at levels of income which have become common even in the poorest countries at the close of the twentieth century. On the other hand, high income is no guarantee of happiness, and indeed many thinkers went so far as to argue that economic advance, if not ameliorated by significant government intervention, was a source for reduced welfare and contentment. What is true of welfare and contentment is undoubtedly true for dignity. Rousseau's analysis led him to conclude that man, born free, was everywhere in chains thanks to the advance of civilization. Conversely, elements of dignity have been achieved far enough back in history to suggest that their provision does not presuppose a high level of average income in a society. For example, slavery was abolished in the UK in 1833, and suffrage regardless of race or gender was introduced in New Jersey in 1776.[6]

## The Role of Technology and Institutions in the Good Life

Thomas More's *Utopia* is a book that needs careful interpretation. It is as much a satire as a signpost. Nonetheless, it is worth noting how he described the perfect country. Utopia was free from the ills of poverty, war and crime. This was not because of considerable advances in economic or technological knowledge, which are limited to certain elements of animal husbandry. It was instead because of a considerably improved social and political model (Adams, 1949). The introduction of women priests, for

---

[6]   There were (disputed) property requirements.

example, is one of the significant social advances that separate
Utopia from sixteenth-century England.

As later chapters make clear, More's *Utopia* is typical in the
history of political philosophy in that improvements in the
social and political model of countries are seen as key to an
improved life for all. Technology and income are largely extra-
neous. It might be argued that, for thinkers living before the
Industrial Revolution, this is because they could not imagine
significant change in general levels of income. The same cannot be argued for Mill or Marx, however, and even they saw
economic advance as at best a tool or an input to social and
political change.

Since the Eighteenth Century, it has become clear that technology can be a force for improved welfare. Not least, the
invention of a range of vaccinations has been a powerful
weapon in the fight against diseases of civilization. It is technological progress that means countries with considerably
lower average incomes per capita than the Dutch Republic in
its golden age still have considerably lower infant mortalities
and longer life expectancies, as we will see. But it is worth noting again here that it is technological progress as opposed to
greater incomes that has driven this change, with slow growing and fast growing economies benefiting alike. It is also
worth noting that the impact of technology has been on welfare, not necessarily contentment. In other words, while philosophers in the past were perhaps too little concerned with
the potential role of technology to improve welfare, they were
right to see income alone as a poor catalyst for the better life.

As to the twentieth century, a fascination with income has
certainly grown. George Painter, writing in 1922, noted that
'the present century seems to glory in material progress as
nothing else.' At least amongst economists, GDP per capita
remains widely taken as a good measure of welfare and contentment. At the same time, it is also the case that the role of
income in increasing welfare and contentment remains a subject of continual debate. That this is the case even after a worldwide 'natural experiment' of massively increasing incomes
occurring within single lifetimes should perhaps give pause to
those convinced of the utility of income.

## Conclusion

William Petty, writing in seventeenth century Britain, felt compelled to publish a book aimed at the many who were sure 'the whole Kingdom grows everyday poorer and poorer...' by using the 'not very usual' approach of utilizing empirical evidence. Similarly, in 1995, Julian Simon published *The State of Humanity*, a book dedicated to demonstrating the many ways that we were doing better than we ever have before. The chapters that follow will provide numerous examples of this being the case. Today, more people have more of the constituents of welfare than ever before in history. It is at least arguable that dignity is more widely enjoyed than ever before. It is more difficult to suggest the same about contentment. The following chapters might help illustrate potential causes for growing levels of dignity and welfare, and perhaps some of the reasons behind stagnant levels of contentment, and thereby provide evidence for policy recommendations to speed the spread of welfare, dignity and contentment worldwide.

# PART TWO

# **WELFARE**

Chapter 3

# The Goods of
# the Body

## Aristotle on External Goods

In his discussions of happiness, Aristotle often makes a distinction between different kinds of goods. There are, he tells us, three classes of goods: goods of the soul, goods of the body, and external goods. On his own account it was the goods of the soul that were crucial to happiness; but he also considered the relationship between happiness and external goods.

> Happiness seems to be in need also of external goods; for it is impossible, or not easy, to perform noble deeds without the appropriate endowment. Many deeds are done using friends and wealth and political power as instruments; and there are some things whose lack takes off the gloss from blessedness, like good birth, good children, and bodily beauty; for a man who is hideous, or ill-born, or solitary and childless is not the kind of person to be happy, and even less so, perhaps, if he had worthless children or friends, or had lost good ones by death. Happiness seems to need this sort of prosperity (Aristotle, 2005, 1099a31).

In the passage we have just quoted Aristotle uses 'external' to mean 'external to the soul'. He counts the goods of the body as external goods, for bodily beauty is treated as an externality. Elsewhere by 'external goods' he means goods that are external to body as well as to soul: friends and family, wealth, position and the like. In a later section of the book we will consider these elements of well-being that are completely external to an individual. In the present section we will focus on the 'external' goods that are goods of the body.

In another place Aristotle makes a distinction between different kinds of goods that are chosen for their own sake. There are some that are objects of praise: such are actions expressing virtues like justice and temperance. These are not just valuable but noble . Health and strength on the other hand (like wealth and honour) though they are genuine goods are not objects of praise and therefore they are not noble. Indeed, though they are naturally good, they may in an individual case be harmful, materially or morally. Their goodness depends on the goodness of their possessor: it derives from their being used by a good person. They are no longer goods if used by a bad man for bad purposes (A. Kenny, 1992, 10).

It was Aristotle's view that the possession of health and strength and other external goods, was not itself a constituent part of happiness, but that it was a necessary condition of the happy life. A happy person, he wrote 'is one who is active in accordance with complete virtue, and is sufficiently endowed with external goods, not for some chance period, but through a complete life' (Aristotle, 2002, 1101a15).

The endowment with external goods is not, for Aristotle, part of happiness itself: the sentence just quoted is not a definition of happiness but a thesis about the happy person. At any given time the happy person will be doing many other things beside the virtuous activities which, for Aristotle, constitute his happiness. He will, for instance, be digesting, breathing, seeing and hearing. If he is to be happy many other things will have to be true of him besides the fact that he performs the activities in which happiness consists. As Aristotle himself insists, there is a great difference between the things in which happiness is to be found and the things without which happiness is not possible. Aristotle makes a comparison with the difference between the constituents of bodily health and its necessary conditions. A good climate is essential for health, but living in a certain place is not what being healthy consists in (A. Kenny, 1992, 41).

It is surprising that in his list of bodily goods Aristotle, a physician's son, does not mention the most important of all bodily goods, namely health. He does, however, mention 'good birth'. He is often taken to be insisting here that noble birth as a necessary condition of happiness. There is, however, no need to take his remark in that sense. If one does, it means that he was ruling out the possibility of happiness for himself, since he was himself no nobleman. The Greek word he uses is the one from which our word 'eugenics' is derived, and he may simply be meaning that a requirement for a happy life is to have the kind of genetic constitution that provides one with a healthy body. The actual enjoyment of health throughout life, he seems to have believed, depended greatly on one's exercise of virtue and avoidance of vice—in other words, on the goods of the soul.

Here as elsewhere Aristotle is trying to reduce the role of luck in happiness: he is anxious to exhibit happiness as something robust. But he realises that the happy person cannot be more invulnerable than the human condition allows. Some of his contemporaries claimed that a good life is simply a lucky gift from the gods, and nothing to do with human striving. Others, by contrast, said that luck has no role at all in happiness, and that all the constituents of a good life are within the happy person's own control. Aristotle wants to take a middle stance between these positions. Against the one group he insists that life would not be worth living if there was no more to life than the things we do and experience through luck. Against the other group he says that it is absurd to claim that those who are unlucky enough to encounter catastrophe are happy as long as they retain their virtue. Only a doctrinaire philosopher, Aristotle maintains, will say that the virtuous man is happy under torture (A. Kenny, 1992, 32).

However, a person may be racked with pain through disease no less than through the malevolence of a tyrant, so that in consistency Aristotle should agree that a modicum of good health is a necessary condition for the good life. It is true that people suffering from painful disease and physical disablement may remain cheerful and achieve remarkable things. Remarkable men have also shown resilience and creativity in prison. Remember Thomas More, who answered his wife's laments about his captivity with the words 'is not this house as nigh heaven as mine own?'. Or, to take a secular example, Bertrand Russell wrote his best philosophical monograph while imprisoned as a conscientious objector. Stoical characters in chains, however admirable, are not, according to Aristotle, truly happy. But if he is not prepared to allow the political prisoner to be living the good life, he should equally exclude the bedridden invalid.

## The State of Nature and the Simple Life

In the history of philosophy, Aristotle was not alone in underplaying the importance of physical health as a constituent of happiness. It was only in comparatively recent times that welfare began to figure explicitly as a criterion and measure of well-being. In earlier centuries, philosophers were more concerned with the possibility of human life being threatened by other human beings than by disease.

The classic statement of the view that security from attack is the foundation of well-being was made in Thomas Hobbes' *Leviathan*. For Hobbes the natural state of free human beings was one of perpetual warfare, and a prime task of the philosopher was to justify the consent of individuals to live in peaceful subjection to a government.

Hobbes drew a sombre picture of the natural condition of mankind. Men, he said, were roughly equal in their natural powers of body and mind. 'From this equality of ability, ariseth equality of hope in the attaining of our ends. And therefore if any two men desire the same thing, which nevertheless they cannot both enjoy, they become enemies.' Not only when they are seeking pleasure, but when they are aiming simply at self-preservation, men find themselves in competition with each other. Unless and until there is a common power to keep men in awe, there will be constant quarrelsome and unregulated competition for goods, power, and glory – a war, in short, of every man against every man. Happiness of any kind is impossible in such conditions: there will be

> No knowledge of the face of the earth, no account of time, no arts; no letters; no society; and, which is worst of all, continual fear and danger of violent death; and the life of man, solitary, poor, nasty, brutish and short (Hobbes, 1996, 84).

People may be sceptical whether there ever was such a time of universal war, but we can see traces of it, Hobbes says, in the America of his day. Even in civilized countries men are always taking precautions against their fellows. Let the reader consider that 'when taking a journey, he arms himself, and seeks to go well accompanied; when going to sleep, he locks his doors; when even in his house, he locks his chests; and this when he knows there be laws and public officers.'

Each man, Hobbes maintains, has a natural right to preserve his own life and limbs with all the power he has. Since he has a right to this end he has a right to all necessary means to it, including a right to the bodies of others. As long as men retain this right, no man has security of living out his natural life. Rational self- interest therefore leads men to give up some of their unfettered natural liberty, and to be content with so much liberty against other men as he would allow other men against himself. Thus men transfer all their rights, save that of self-defence, to a central power that is able to enforce the laws of nature by punitive sanctions. Thus is sovereignty brought into existence. 'This is the generation of that great Leviathan, or to speak more reverently, of that mortal god, to which we owe under the immortal God our peace and defence'.

Hobbes took a gloomy view of the human condition, and even under a benevolent sovereign he held out little hope of happiness on earth. Our desires succeed each other incessantly, and what men call happiness is nothing but continual success in satisfying each desire that comes. Tranquillity is unattainable; we can never be without desire or fear while we retain consciousness. Men are ruled by 'a perpetual and restless desire of power after power, that ceaseth only in death' (McMahon, 2006, 185).

The Whig philosopher John Locke had a much more optimistic view than Hobbes of man's natural state. The state of nature, for him, is not a state of war, because everyone is aware of a natural law that teaches that all men are equal and independent, and that no one ought to harm another in his life, liberty, and possession. This law is binding prior to any earthly sovereign or civil society. It confers natural rights, notably the rights to life, self-defence and freedom.

Despite his comparative optimism about man's natural state, and despite the generally undogmatic nature of his own Christianity, Locke was as certain as any medieval theologian that true happiness was only to be found in an afterlife. If death ended all human concerns, then there would be no reason to prefer study and knowledge to hawking and hunting, or sobriety and riches to luxury and debauchery. It would be futile to seek whether the supreme good consisted in virtue, or pleasure, or contemplation. One might as well ask 'whether the best relish were to be found apples, plumbs, or nuts'. Only in heaven would there be found a taste to suit all palates (McMahon, 2005, 183–4).

In his account of the workings of pleasure and pain on human actions, however, Locke came close to Epicurus. Every choice to perform an action, he maintains, is determined by a preceding mental state: one of uneasiness at the present state of things. Uneasiness alone acts on the will and determines its choices. We are constantly beset with sundry uneasinesses, and the most pressing one of those that are removable 'determines the will successively in that train of voluntary actions which make up our lives.' The only degree of freedom that we have is that we can suspend the execution of a particular desire while we decide whether to act on it would make us happy in the long run (Locke, 1975, 250–63).

Some of those influenced by Locke drew the Epicurean conclusion that the road to happiness was to keep one's desires as simple as possible, and to limit them to a concern with basic welfare. This often found expression in a profession (sincere or not) of preference for a rural over an urban life. Thus the young Alexander Pope:

> Happy the man whose wish and care
> A few paternal acres bound
> Content to breathe his native air
> On his own ground.

Such an attitude reached its summit in the thought of Jean Jacques Rousseau. Rousseau agreed with Hobbes against Locke that there were no property rights in the state of nature: no paternal acres there. But he was, like Locke, an optimist about the natural condition of human beings. Indeed, in his early writings he went much further than Locke and maintained that humanity was naturally good and had been corrupted rather than improved by social institutions. The ideal human being was the 'noble savage' whose simple goodness put civilised man to shame. Later, Rousseau came to accept that social institutions could liberate as well as enslave. But he continued to idealise the state of nature.

In such a state, he maintained, men are not necessarily hostile to each other. They are motivated by self-love, indeed, but self-love is not necessarily egoism. It can be combined, in both humans and animals, with sympathy and compassion for one's fellows. In a state of nature a man has only simple, animal, desires: 'the only goods he acknowledged in the world are food, a female, and sleep; the only ills he fears are pain and hunger.' The crucial point, for Rousseau, is that these desires are not as inherently competitive as the quest for power in more sophisticated societies (A. Kenny, 2006, 296).

The French Revolution and its consequences brought about first the canonization and then the anathematisation of Rousseau's ideas. It was, however, the Industrial Revolution that caused a fundamental re-examination of the welfare requirements for human well-being.

Thomas Carlyle maintained that the pursuit of utility by capitalists, instead of bringing great happiness to great numbers, had enriched the few by reducing the masses to a state resembling Hobbes's original chaos. 'Our life is not a mutual helpfulness' he wrote 'but rather, cloaked under due laws-of-war, named 'fair competition' and so forth, it is mutual hostility' (McMahon, 2005, 364).

Both John Stuart Mill and Karl Marx agreed with Carlyle that the industrial revolution had brought the working classes into a state of unparalleled misery. But for Mill the cure for this malady was a further dose of the same medicine. The application of utilitarian principles tempered by liberal concerns would improve the condition of everyone and lift the poor out of their misery. The great majority of human ills were removable by human effort. It was vain to look for happiness in some future life: immortality would turn out to be much more

depressing than death. It was true that in the appalling conditions of early industrial England the only hope of happiness
that many had was to imagine it in another life. But Mill went
on

> It is not only possible but probable that in a higher, and above
> all, a happier condition of human life, not annihilation but
> immortality may be the burdensome idea; and that human
> nature, though pleased with the present, and by no means
> impatient to quit it, would find comfort and not sadness in the
> thought that it is not chained through eternity to a conscious
> existence which it cannot be assured that it will always wish to
> preserve (Mill, 1889, 122).

Karl Marx, in a similar manner, believed that the prospect of
future happiness held out by religion was no more than an
opium to dull the pain of the life of the manufacturing classes.
He did, also, share the optimism of Mill that a life of general
happiness could be looked forward to on this earth. But it
could brought about only by the abolition of the private property that Locke had thought one of the foundations of
well-being. And to achieve the final consummation of communist felicity, society would have to pass through a series of
painful birth-pangs.

Acutely aware of how ill their poorer contemporaries were
faring in the newly industrialised societies, both Mill and
Marx gave a prominent place to welfare in the centre of their
notion of happiness. In subsequent chapters we will see to
what extent their different prophecies of eventually increased
welfare were achieved, and what effect this has had on the
other components of well-being, namely dignity and
contentment.

# Chapter 4

# The Determinants of Welfare

## Introduction

The view of poverty that has become most widespread in development economics and international politics is one based around income. The UN's Millennium Development Goals, for example, would 'halve poverty' through reducing the number of people living on one dollar a day or less by fifty percent.

At the same time, it is widely agreed that there are dimensions of welfare that cannot be easily aggregated with consumption of market goods. The Millennium Goals themselves contain a list of other targets regarding attributes that people would be poorer, in a broader sense, without.

Our definition of welfare from the previous chapter is the satisfaction of animal needs—food, drink, shelter and other things that contribute to 'bodily flourishing.' The presence or absence of such satisfaction is surely better measured by levels of health in the population than income.

What is a matter of some debate is the extent to which there is congruence between income and non-income measures of welfare. On the one hand, some have suggested that 'wealthier is healthier' (Pritchett and Summers, 1993).[1] As a result, economists frequently conflate income and welfare. For example, Robert Lucas (1988) asked: 'Is there some action a government could take that would lead the Indian economy to grow like Indonesia's or Egypt's? If so, what exactly? If not, what is it about 'the nature of India' that makes it so? The consequences for human welfare involved in questions like this are simply staggering ...' On the other hand, there is a growing consensus that the relationship between income and broader measures of welfare is not as strong as it might appear at first examination.

It is true that richer people have been healthier people through most of history in most places. Fathers able to provide the largest dowries for their daughters in fifteenth-century Florence had less than half of the mortality rates of poorer fathers (Coniff, 2002). In the first half of the Nineteenth Century in the UK, child mortality rates amongst the British peerage were 109 per 1,000 live births compared to a national average closer to 156 per 1,000 live births for the country as a whole (Hill, 1995). Today, high income countries see average life expectancies 20 years longer than low income countries and child mortality rates of 0.7 percent compared to 12.3 percent (World Bank, 2005). Given this, it is unsurprising that a range of regression analyses have found income a significant correlate with health and education outcomes across countries at a given time.[2]

Nonetheless, there is plentiful evidence that income is a poor proxy for health. Table One compares the United Kingdom in the early nineteenth century to Vietnam in 2000. They had approximately the same income per head, a level approximately one tenth of current UK GDP per capita. In the early nineteenth century, the UK was considerably more unequal than modern-day Britain or modern-day Vietnam, with the richest ten percent of the country accounting for nearly half of

---

[1]  Although it is worth noting that even Pritchett and Summers conclude that 'income changes explain less about mortality changes than economists might have supposed.'

[2]  Including World Bank, 2004b, Hanmer and White, 1999, Thorbecke and Charumilind, 2002, Filmer and Pritchett, 1997, Wang, 2002, Leipziger et al., 2003.

national income. As befits the first industrial nation, it was also highly urbanized, with nearly two fifths of the population living in towns and cities — this is almost twice the level of modern Vietnam. One could argue either way on the relative state of democracy between Vietnam today and Britain in the early 1800s — in one country only ten percent of the people had a vote, in the other everyone can vote, but only for approved candidates. There are two sets of striking differences, however. One is the extent of technology — Vietnam has access to telephony, electricity production and aircraft, the UK in the early nineteenth century did not. The second set of differences involves welfare outcomes. Life expectancy at birth in Vietnam today is 69 years as opposed to 41 years in the UK in the 1800s.

| Indicator | UK, Early 19th Century | Vietnam, 2000 |
|---|---|---|
| Income per Capita ($) | 1,700 | 1,860 |
| Share of Income to top 10 Percent of Population (%) | 49 | 29.9 |
| Life Expectancy (years) | 41 | 69 |
| Infant Mortality (per 1,000) | 160 | 37 |
| Literacy (% population) | 69 | 95 |
| Electricity Production (billion kwh) | 0 | 22 |
| Urbanization (% population) | 39 | 20 |
| Army (% population) | 1.2 | 0.6 |
| International Telephone Traffic, (minutes/subscriber) | 0 | 22 |
| Voters (% Eligible, Choice) | 10 (Multi-party) | 100 (Party Approved) |
| International Aircraft Passengers (million passengers/year) | 0 | 3.0 |
| Source: C. Kenny (2005a) | | |

*Table One.* Comparing The UK and Vietnam at Similar Income Levels

Infant mortality is less than one quarter of the level of the UK two hundred years ago. The child mortality level for the very richest in the UK in the early nineteenth century is three times the average level for modern day Vietnam.[3]

The amount of welfare a given income can 'buy' has apparently risen considerably since the 1800s, no doubt in large part to the massive technological change we have seen in the last two hundred years. Along with no access to electricity, British subjects in 1815 knew nothing of the germ theory of disease and little of refrigeration. The most advanced sewer systems they were likely to have known were those found in Roman ruins from 1,500 years earlier. It may also reflect differences in access to education — Vietnam's literacy rate today is considerably above the rate for the UK at the start of the 1900s.

This chapter discusses the relationship between income and welfare in detail, and looks at the role of other causes of the global improvement in welfare that we have witnessed over the past 100 years. It opens with a discussion of the historical path of changes in welfare and potential determinants before looking at more recent evidence as well as a theory of determinants. The chapter also briefly discusses the changing nature of mortality from violence. It concludes that the strength of institutional structures is key to harness the state for positive health outcomes as well as to control the risk of state-sponsored violence.

## Welfare, Civilization and Globalization

For most of world history, global average life expectancies have hovered a little over 20 years. Health indicators began to make dramatic progress in the West in the second half of the Nineteenth Century and globally during the twentieth century. Global average life expectancy was 24 years in 1000 AD, 31 years in 1900 and reached 66 years in 1999. At the same time, the human population of the planet has increased from four

---

[3]   More broadly, within countries at a given time, child mortalities amongst the richest quintile are considerably higher than would be expected given their income and the cross-country relationship between average national incomes and average infant mortalities (C. Kenny, 2005b).

million 10,000 years ago (Simon, 1995), passing one billion in the nineteenth century and reaching over six billion today.

While populations and levels of health have recently expanded, so have incomes. In 1820, perhaps 84 percent of the world's population of one billion people lived on an income of below one dollar a day. By 1910, this had declined to two thirds of a population of 1.7 billion. In 1992, less than one quarter of a population of 5.5 billion lived in what by then was defined as 'absolute poverty' (Bourguignon and Morrisson, 2002). Despite this apparent correlation between health and income indicators, however, the historical link between economic advance and advances in welfare has not always been straightforward.

Life expectancy at birth for our stone-age ancestors was around 25 years (Cutler et al., 2006). It appears that early hunter-gatherer societies had reliable, and frequently abundant, food supplies. Indeed, crop domestication may actually have started not as a way to improve diets for the majority but to generate delicacies for the privileged. The first domesticated crops were chili peppers (a Mayan status symbol to this day), wheat (first used for beer) and the bottle gourd (used as a serving vessel for feasts) (Conniff, 2002). The move from hunter-gathering to farming may have favoured the elite who oversaw the earth moving required to create large fields and the construction of storage facilities, but the diets and health of those working the fields appear to have declined, while hours of work increased.

Looking at nine foraging and shifting-cultivation societies extant today, we find that they produce an average of nearly twice the kilocalories per hour than did an English farmworker in 1800. Partially as a result they work only 60 percent of the hours (Clark, 2005). Furthermore, the comparatively restricted sources of nutrition provided by early agriculture not only increased the risk of famine when the staple failed (such as in Ireland in the nineteenth century) but also fostered the spread of deficiency diseases such as pellagra, marasmus, kwashiorkor and scurvy. The widespread introduction of monoculture cash-cropping in colonial systems

similarly led to a decline in the nutritional status of the colo-
nized (Porter, 1999).

The rapid increase in disease prevalence was another result
of civilization. Of prehistoric society, Porter (1999) writes that
'infections like smallpox, measles and flu must have been virtually unknown, since the micro-organisms that cause contagious diseases require high population densities to provide
reservoirs of susceptibles. And because of the need to search
for food, these small bands did not stay put long enough to
pollute water sources or accumulate the filth that attracts dis-
ease-spreading insects. Above all, isolated hunter-foragers
did not tend cattle and other tamed animals which ... proved
perennial and often catastrophic sources of illness, for infectious disease riddled beasts long before spreading to humans.'
Infections that humankind received from animals included
poxes, tuberculosis, colds, the flu, measles, salmonella, polio,
cholera, typhoid, hepatitis and whooping cough. Diseases
such as malaria, elephantiasis, river-blindness, schistosomiasis and bilharzia spread only thanks to settlement required by
agriculture.[4] In parts of North America that adopted farming
in the twelfth century AD, Jared Diamond (1987) reports a
fourfold increase in iron-deficiency anemia, a threefold rise in
bone-lesions from infectious diseases, a 50 percent rise in
enamel defects indicative of malnutrition and a seven year
drop in life expectancy.

Average heights are a good measure of the material living
conditions of humans because disease and poor diet in childhood both lead to reduced adult stature. Average heights were
on the decline for much of the last two thousand years. They
were greater prior to 1 AD than they were for eighteenth-century Britain. When the people of Tahiti (who lived a stone-age
existence) were 'discovered' in 1767, they were taller than the
British sailors who discovered them. Their average heights
were indeed greater than those of British citizens 100 years
later, at a time most of the way through the Industrial Revolution (Clark, 2005). Modern Greeks and Turks are still shorter

[4]    Until the nineteenth century, towns remained so unsanitary that their
       populations never replaced themselves by reproduction, multiplying
       only thanks to the influx of rural surpluses (Porter, 1999).

than the hunter- gatherers who lived in the same area at the end of the last ice-age.

The health risks of civilization were exacerbated by globalization and the growing interaction between previously isolated communities. The danger faced by Europeans in Africa before modern medicine is well-illustrated by a letter from Mungo Park, a Scottish explorer, who led an expedition up the Niger River in 1805. In a letter from 'on board of H.M. Schooner Joliba at anchor off Sansanding' on the Niger on November 17th to Earl Camden, he wrote

> Your Lordship will recollect that I always spoke of the rainy season with horror, as being extremely fatal to Europeans; and our journey from the Gambia to the Niger will furnish a melancholy proof of it … We had no contest whatever with the natives, nor was any one of us killed by wild animals or any other accidents; and yet I am sorry to say that of forty-four Europeans who left the Gambia in perfect health, five only are at present alive … but I assure you I am far from desponding … I have changed a large canoe into a tolerably good schooner, on board of which I this day hoisted the British flag, and shall set sail to the East with the fixed resolution to discover the termination of the Niger or perish in the attempt.

Perish he did, along with the others left with him.[5]

As much as African diseases were of immense risk to Europeans, the diseases which European explorers, conquerors, missionaries, colonists and slavers brought with them killed many more. Ninety percent of the Mexican Indian population was wiped out by 'the white man and his fellow-traveling pathogens' as Landes (1998) puts it. The native population of Hawaii also fell 90 percent after its discovery by James Cook, Tahiti by over 75 percent and New Zealand by over 60 percent.[6] In North America, as European diseases (including smallpox, chickenpox, measles, mumps and scarlet fever) killed off Amerindian populations, the burgeoning slave trade

---

[5] Source: the last letter written in Park's hand from *The Journal of a Mission to The Interior of Africa*.

[6] In Africa, colonization spread sleeping sickness, especially in the Belgian Congo, where over half a million people died of the disease 1896–1906 (Porter, 1999).

brought an additional set of maladies from Africa— the first outbreaks of yellow fever occurred in Boston in 1693. This is to say nothing of the toll to the slaves themselves. There was a 50 percent mortality rate amongst the 20 million slaves who were forced to take the Middle Passage. For those who survived the journey, life expectancy at landing was less than seven years in 1682 (Fernandez-Armesto, 2001).

Back in Northern Europe, average heights fell from 173 cm in the 800–1000 AD period to 166 cm in the seventeenth and eighteenth centuries, not recovering until as late as the mid-twentieth century—in part due to urbanization and the importation of new diseases. It may be that syphilis was a gift of the new world to the old. Typhus spread to Europe from the East at about the same time. Continued urbanization and globalization had a particularly significant impact on the age of disease victims. 'Infections which at one time ravaged isolated susceptible populations in catastrophic waves now became endemic within densely crowded urban environments with high levels of demographic immunity' writes Porter (1999). 'Diseases which at one time were responsible for high levels of mortality among adults in secluded communities were reduced to attacking new susceptibles: that is, infants and children.'

Even as the spread of technology has improved health outcomes, economic integration continues to be a force for the globalization of disease. The influenza pandemic circled the world in 1918, killing over 25 million people in six months. Tuberculosis is in resurgence, cases increased by 12 percent in the US from 1985–91, 30 percent in Europe and 300 percent in parts of Africa, piggybacking on the new global pandemic of AIDS. Diphtheria has returned to the former Soviet Union, and cholera to the Americas, from where it had been absent since 1895.

## Welfare and the Industrial Revolution

The welfare costs of urbanization in a globalizing world absent sanitation and public health are well illustrated by the British Industrial Revolution. In the century after 1750, Britain's population increased threefold (Porter, 1999). The agricultural revolution combined with rapid improvements in transport (including canal and rail systems) allowed for particularly rapid growth in city sizes. Between 1800 and 1850, the population of London grew from one to 2.7 million (Friedman, 2005). But this symptom of rapid economic advance was a cause of declining health.

In 1798, Malthus wrote in his *Essay on Population* that:

> The increasing wealth of the nation has little or no tendency to better the conditions of the working poor. They have not, I believe, a greater command of the necessaries and conveniences of life, and a much greater proportion of them than at the period of the revolution [1688] is employed in manufactures and crowded together in close and unwholesome rooms.

This situation only deteriorated as the Industrial Revolution advanced. Life expectancies in the urban areas of England and Wales dropped from 35 to 30 years between the 1820s and 1840s. It is not hard to figure out why. Urbanization put unsustainable pressure on traditional modes of waste disposal while grouping people so close together that disease outbreaks would inevitably spread: 'Cesspools turned into manure swamps and seeped into local water supplies and wells. Dry middens and their consequent dungheaps turned into mountains infested with flies and vermin ... disease victims died and their corpses remained rotting among families in single-roomed accommodations for days, as the family scraped together pennies to bury them ...' (Porter, 1999). Easterlin (2004) quotes contemporaries describing 'town dairies ... dens and cellars in which cows were kept for the greater part of the year, standing knee-deep in filth ... tailors making soldiers' clothing having their children, from whom scabs were falling, wrapped in the garments' and a dunghill that 'contains a hundred cubic yards of inpure filth' on which flies would settle and then pass into houses: 'Every article of food and drink must be covered, otherwise, if left exposed for a minute, the flies immediately attack it, and it is rendered unfit for use, from the strong taste of the dunghill left by the flies.'[7]

---

[7]  Not all were so horrified by the situation. Thomas Macaulay wrote confidently in his *History of England* that 'It is now the fashion to place the

The spread of child labour in new industries had a particularly dramatic impact on health. The average age of boys starting work at the coal mine in the 1840s was a little over eight and a half. Long hours underground meant that they had almost no exposure to sunlight. As a result, rickets was widespread, and the average stature of twelve year old children in the coal mines was nearly three and a half inches shorter than boys working on farms (Kirby, 1995).

Rickets, along with smallpox and tuberculosis were three 'old' diseases that spread most dramatically in expanding industrial towns. The new disease of cholera joined them when it hit London for the first time in 1832, killing 7,000. These diseases attacked an increasing number of malnourished, brought on by growing pauperism (Fogel, 1995). Poor relief records from the village of Compton and the town of Shefford in Bedfordshire, for example, show a doubling of paupers in Compton and a full quadrupling in Shefford between 1794 and 1830 (Williams, 2005). Partially as a result of this growing underclass, Fogel (2004) argues that from the beginning of the Industrial Revolution to the end of the Nineteenth Century, the gap in life expectancies between rich and poor expanded from around seven to seventeen years (declining again to four years today). Overall, between 1800 and 1900 statures remained unchanged, and between 1820 and 1870, life expectancies rose only by a couple of years – all while average incomes approximately doubled (Table Two).[8]

---

Golden Age of England in times when... men died faster in the purest country air than they now die in the most pestilential lanes of our towns, and when men died faster in the lanes of our towns than they now die on the coast of Guinea' (quoted in Friedman, 2005). Macaulay's optimism was based on erroneous comparisons of death rates.

[8]    Famines had long been a very minor source of mortality in the UK. In the period 1540–1750 in the UK, famines accounted for less than 0.6 percent of total mortality (Fogel, 1995).

| Date | Income (1990 US$) | Stature (cm) | Life Expectancy | Calorie Intake | Literacy (%) |
|---|---|---|---|---|---|
| 1700 | 1250 | | | 2095 | |
| 1725 | | | | | |
| 1738 | | | 34.6 | | |
| 1750 | | 165 | | 2168 | |
| 1756 | | | 37.3 | | 47.5 |
| 1776 | | | 38.2 | | 49.5 |
| 1800 | | 167 | 35.9 | 2237 | 56.5 |
| 1811 | | | 37.6 | | 51.5 |
| 1820 | 1707 | | 39.2 | | 54.0 |
| 1830 | | | 40.8 | | 58.0 |
| 1840 | | | 40.3 | | 59.2 |
| 1850 | | 166 | 39.6 | 2362 | 61.9 |
| 1866 | | | 40.3 | | 74.2 |
| 1870 | 3191 | | 41.3 | | 76.9 |
| 1900 | | 167 | 48.3 | | |
| 1913 | 4921 | | | | |
| 1931 | | | 60.1 | | 100 |
| 1934 | | | | 3042 | |
| 1950 | 6907 | 175 | 69.0 | | |
| 1970 | | | 72.1 | 3316 | |
| 1973 | 12022 | | | | |
| 1990 | | | | 3282 | |
| 1998 | 18714 | | | | |
| 1999 | | | 77 | | 100 |
| Source: C. Kenny (2006) | | | | | |

*Table Two.* UK Historical Indicators of Welfare

It was only with the development of significant government interventions covering working hours, water, sanitation and hygiene that UK health indicators including stature and life expectancy began to improve — life expectancies climbing seven years from 1870 to 1900 and then a further twelve years from 1900 to 1931. As a result, broadly similar increases in income were accompanied by remarkably different rates of improvement in health in the early and later periods of the process of industrialization. Annual income growth was approximately 1.3 percent over 1820–70, while annual life expectancy growth was 0.1 percent. Between 1870 and 1950, annual income growth slowed to 0.9 percent while life expectancy growth reached 0.6 percent per year — a sixfold increase in the rate of improvement from the earlier period. The central role that technological advance and public action has for health improvements is one that remains to the present day.

## Technology, Public Action and Health in History

As we have seen, the Dutch Republic in the seventeenth century was the richest country in the history of the World, and a country in which even the poor appear to have been well-fed. Indeed, the Republic may have been the first 'Supersize Me' nation. Visitors to the Republic frequently commented on the peoples' girth and height — 'big-boned and gross-bodied' according to one commentator disgusted by their continual cramming. By 1590, there were 180 breweries operating in Amsterdam alone. Fifty years later, there were also more than fifty sugar refineries. Smoking was widespread enough that the town of Gouda employed 15–16,000 people, or half the workforce, making pipes (Schama, 1997). But despite the highest incomes in history, life expectancies remained around the European average, in the low 30s (Maddison, 2001) and perhaps a third of children died in infancy.

The main reason for such poor health was that the medical community didn't know what it was doing. Take views of the efficacy of tobacco as a medicine extant at the time: it was though to cure toothaches, worms, ague, scurvy, gout, stones and chronic insomnia. It was also supposed to reduce labour pains and protected against the plague. The Dutch Republic in the seventeenth century did see advances in anatomy, the discovery of the circulation of nutrients in the blood and microorganisms in water and the first blood transfusion. But the limits of efficacious application of these discoveries is suggested by the fact that the blood transfusion used sheep's blood in an attempt to cure a man of insanity. Miraculously, it didn't immediately kill him (Gribbin, 2002, Jardine, 1999).

The history of medical knowledge and public health interventions up until the mid nineteenth century is a history of a few effective practices in a sea of misinformed, frequently harmful, quackery. Amongst the more effective measures introduced was quarantine. In fourteenth century plague outbreaks, Poland closed its borders with relative success, while Milan walled up houses containing plague victims and their families. During fifteenth-century plague epidemics, Venice and Majorca isolated travelers and goods for forty days (thus the word 'quarantine'). Other cities used household isolation of infected individuals, some banned festivals and public gatherings.[9] Medieval towns including Dublin, Basel and Bruges attempted to limit pollution of the water by preventing citizens from throwing dead animals, refuse or tanning dyes into streams. Milan even had ordinances regarding the building of cesspools and drains (Porter, 1999).

At the same time, Tuchman (1978) recounts a number of methods to overcome plague in the fourteenth century which ranged from the wicked — pogroms against Jews — to the merely pointless — dancing to drums and trumpets to keep jolly. Cures included burning aromatic substances, bleeding and purging, lancing and cauterization, and pills and potions of stag's horn, myrrh, saffron, gold, pearls and emeralds. Until the late nineteenth century, Europeans fought off disease with practices including leaving water in the sun to draw up 'noysome vapors,' eating chili to 'disolve windes,' drinking plentiful alcohol and eating sugar and chocolate (Kupperman, 1984).

[9] Thomas More was the first to issue orders regarding isolation of plague victims in Oxford in 1518 which, according to Porter (1999) means that he can be credited as the father of English public health policy amongst his other achievements.

Mathew Baille, author of *Morbid Anatomy of Some of the Most Important Parts of the Human Body* (1793) noted that 'I know better perhaps than another man, from my knowledge of anatomy, how to discover disease, but when I have done so, I don't know better how to cure it.' Porter (1999) notes that 'the one early striking instance of the conquest of disease — the introduction of the first smallpox inoculation (in the early eighteenth century) and then of vaccination (at the end of the century) — came not through "science" but through embracing popular medical folklore.'

An example of the ineffectiveness of the medical community was the considerable efficacy of hospitals in terms of killing their patients. In the United States, Canada, and Britain today there are about four hospital beds for every 1,000 people. In Africa there is one bed for every 1,000 people. In 1591, Rome had a ratio of more than 30 beds for each 1,000 people. In France in 1700, there were about five beds per thousand people (estimated from Porter, 1999 and Maddison, 2001). The problem was not a lack of beds, then, but what happened to those in them. When it came to surgery, well into the nineteenth century hospital mortality was as much as three to five times higher than in private houses (Porter, 1999).

In the first half of the nineteenth century, some useful cures and drugs were invented and adopted, including morphine, codeine, quinine and ephedrine. Compulsory vaccination for smallpox was introduced in Britain in 1853. Antiseptic techniques in surgery spread in the second half of the century. At the same time, research by a number of colonial medical surgeons at the end of the Nineteenth Century began to uncover the role of vectors (such as mosquitoes and ticks) in spreading diseases including elephantiasis and malaria, opening up the possibility of disease control through vector eradication. In the period 1880–1900, causal agents for typhoid, leprosy, malaria, tuberculosis, glanders, cholera, streptococcus, diphtheria, tetanus, pneumococcus, malta fever, gas gangrene, plague and dysentery were all discovered and in the period 1890–1930 vaccines for diphtheria, cholera, pertussis, tuberculosis, tetanus, yellow fever and typhoid fever were developed (Easterlin, 2004).

Of even greater significance than the discovery of new vaccinations was the spread of sanitation. Edwin Chadwick was a key figure in the design of the new British Poor Laws (passed in 1834) as Secretary to the Poor Law Commission. He believed that the old system of poverty relief had been too generous, encouraging waste and idleness, and leading to rising demands for relief. However, he reconsidered his theory in the light of ever-increasing pauperism even after the passage of his punitive poor law amendments (discussed in a later chapter). He concluded that much poverty was due to disease rather than fecklessness. Chadwick's *Report on the Sanitary Condition of the Labouring Population of Great Britain* (1842) detailed the link between poverty, disease and sanitary infrastructure. He suggested that 'The primary and most important measures, and at the same time the most practicable...are drainage, the removal of all refuse from habitations, streets and roads, and the improvement of the supplies of water.' As a result of the report, the first British Public Health Act was passed in 1848. This forced local authorities with high mortality rates to adopt a set of institutions designed to improve sanitary conditions by dealing with issues including water supply and sanitation.

A second mid-century health reformer in the UK was Dr. John Snow, whose investigations into the London cholera epidemics of 1849 and 1854 led him to conclude that contaminated water was the cause of the disease's spread. In an 1855 report to the Commons Select Committee he advocated massive improvements in sewage and drainage to counter the threat. This call provided the catalyst for a number of significant improvements in sanitary infrastructure in cities across Britain, including London's new water and sewage system, completed in 1875, which drew water from the Lea Valley and the upper reaches of the Thames (Porter, 1999).

Only with the sanitation and health reforms of the later nineteenth century did the UK rural-urban health gap decline. Deaths from infectious diseases, concentrated in the dense breeding grounds of urban areas, fell from accounting for 60 percent of all deaths in 1848 to six percent in 1951 (Easterlin, 2004 and Cutler et al., 2006).[10]

## Modern-Day Convergence in Welfare and the Role of Income

Until the dawn of the twentieth century, it appears that technological and institutional advance rather than income growth were behind changing patterns of health in the face of globalization and urbanization. A similar story holds true for more recent history, reflected in patterns of divergence and convergence in income and welfare measures. For measures of income, debate rages over the extent of convergence across countries. Answers depend in part on one's data, one's chosen measure of convergence and the weighting one applies. It remains fair to say that the consensus finding is for long-term divergence and weak convergence or stagnation in more recent periods since the Second World War (Pritchett, 1997, Quah, 1993). For almost any other measure of welfare that we possess, the image is of strong divergence in the nineteenth and early twentieth centuries followed by strong convergence since then.

Table Three displays data on India's performance on various measures of development as expressed as a percentage of UK scores on these measures. The picture for income is of falling behind followed by stagnation. In 1500, Indian incomes were 72 percent of UK incomes. Over the next 450 years they fell to nine percent, and they were still at nine percent in 1999. Compare that to calorie intake, which fell from 79 percent to 59 percent of UK values from 1700 to 1934 before recovering to 68 percent by 1990. Life expectancy, at approximate parity with the UK in the fourteenth century, fell to 44 percent in 1931 but recovered to 82 percent by 1999. In short, other welfare mea-

---

[10] Similarly, in 1900 in the US, waterborne diseases accounted for nearly one quarter of infectious disease deaths in major cities. The health cost of city living was such that, in 1880, infant mortality was 140 percent higher in cities than in rural areas. The introduction of water filtration and chlorination systems over the next 35 years accounted for three quarters of the decline in infant mortality and nearly half of the overall reduction in mortality (Culter and Miller, 2004).

sures have never been as divergent as income is today, and have been converging for at least the last fifty years or so.

At the global level, for life expectancy convergence began at some point between 1913 and 1950. The 1950-99 period saw average global life expectancy increasing by nineteen years while measures of variation in performance dramatically declined (the standard deviation has nearly halved, for example). Data for infant survival suggest a similar pattern of convergence beginning at some point prior to the Second World War (C. Kenny, 2005). Related to this, adequate nutrition has been spreading worldwide, with the percentage of the World's population where per capita food supplies are below 2,200 calories per day falling from 56 percent in the mid 1960s to below 10 percent by the 1990s (Johnson, 2000).

| Year | Income | Calorie Intake | Life Expectancy | Literacy |
|------|--------|----------------|-----------------|----------|
| 1363 |        |                | 99              |          |
| 1500 | 72     |                |                 |          |
| 1543 |        |                | 71              |          |
| 1700 | 39     | 79             |                 |          |
| 1738 |        |                | 69              |          |
| 1800 |        | 74             |                 |          |
| 1813 |        |                | 59              |          |
| 1820 | 25     |                |                 |          |
| 1913 | 13     |                | 46              | 9        |
| 1931 |        |                | 44              |          |
| 1934 |        | 59             |                 |          |
| 1950 | 9      |                | 56              | 19       |
| 1970 |        | 61             |                 |          |
| 1990 |        | 68             |                 |          |
| 1999 | 9      |                | 82              | 57       |
| Source: C. Kenny (2005b) | | | | |

*Table Three.* Historical Welfare Indicators: India as a Percentage of the UK

As these figures suggest, cross-country relationships between income and health are significant but subject to considerable variation. In 1992, Mozambique's GNP per capita (unadjusted for purchasing power parity) was $80. China's was $470 and the United States' was $24,740. Infant mortalities per one thousand live births were 146, 31 and nine, respectively. Moving 1.6 percent of the distance between Mozambique and the US in terms of income got you 84 percent of the distance in terms of infant mortality (C. Kenny, 1999). More broadly, Diener and Diener's (1995) index of basic needs, which includes factors such as access to clean water and infant mortality, is significantly related to income only up to a GNP per capita of about $4,000.[11]

This evidence of considerable recent convergence in welfare measures absent income convergence reflects a weak and complex underlying relationship between income and health, one that is not simply a result of declining health returns to income. Sen (1992) has noted that men in Harlem, New York have a lower chance of reaching the age of 40 than do Bangladeshi men. The United States as a whole spends twice the OECD average on healthcare — 13 percent. It is four times richer than Malaysia on a per capita basis, and yet its infant mortality rate is the same. Cities in the state of Kerala, India (average income per capita of $300, life expectancy of 72) are another well-known case — they have a lower infant mortality rate than do African-Americans living in Washington, DC (UNDP, 2005).[12]

Across time, income-health relationships can be even weaker. Deaton and Paxson (2003) looked at age-specific mortality in the UK and US since 1950 and conclude that neither average income nor changes in income distribution can explain the observed trends, which must have been driven by technology instead. Developing countries also see a weak rela-

[11] Within countries, in Bolivia in 1998, the average under five survival rate was 96.43 percent, but the poorest ten percent of households had a better survival rate than the top thirty percent of households (Klasen, 2005).

[12] In part these statistics reflect that more that three percent of US households were 'food insecure' in 2002, to the extent that every day people in more than 500,000 US households were hungry because they cannot afford more food (Nord et al., 2003).

tionship between economic advance and health improvements. Life expectancy in Japan increased from 40 years in 1900 to a little below 80 years in 1990. In India, life expectancy over that period increased from 23 years to about 60 years. In absolute terms, the increase has been about the same, then –and in percentage terms India is significantly ahead. The same is not true of income. India's income per capita approximately doubled over that period while Japan's average GNP per capita increased 1,500 percent (Maddison, 1995).

Post-War Sub-Saharan Africa tells a similar story. Over the last four decades of the twentieth century, GDP per capita in Sub-Saharan Africa climbed by less than $100 – from $477 to $561. It fell from about five to about two percent of the average GDP per capita of a high-income country over that period. Under-five mortality fell from 254 to 161 per 1,000 live births, suggesting considerable convergence in child survival rates with wealthy countries. Similar results pertain to infant mortality, overall life expectancy and primary enrollment (C. Kenny, 2005). Again, almost all of China's post-war reduction in infant mortality happened prior to the acceleration in economic growth after 1980 – and the period since then has seen relatively little progress (Cutler et al., 2006).[13]

If we look at a group of 27 countries for which we have life expectancy and income data over the period 1913–99, it is clear that even over the long term there is little link between changes in the two variables. In both 1913 and 1999, those countries with higher incomes saw longer life expectancies. Indeed, looking at income in 1999, one could predict 1999 life expectancy with an 89 percent accuracy. But, at the same time, the speed of income *growth* between 1913 and 1999 is completely unconnected with increases in life expectancy over that period. On average, amongst those 27 countries, income increased from $3,000 to $15,000, while average life expectancy increased from 47 to 76 years. But faster growing countries saw slightly (statistically insignificant) *smaller* increases in health.

---

[13] Once the passage of time has been accounted for, rates of economic growth are insignificant in explaining reduced mortality rates across China in the 1980s and 1990s (Banister and Zhang, 2005).

Similar results also hold for a larger sample of countries over the shorter period 1975–2000, as well as for a sample of poorer countries (those with a GDP per capita below $3,000 in 1975) over that period and for measures of female and male adult mortality in developing countries in the recent past.[14] Indeed, even countries that saw considerably negative income growth saw positive health outcomes. For example, Angola saw income per capita fall by 34 percent from 1950–90, while life expectancy increased by 50 percent over the same period (See Table Four).

| Country | Percentage Change in Income | Percentage Change in Life Expectancy |
|---------|:---:|:---:|
| Angola | –34 | 50 |
| Cuba | –18 | 28 |
| Nicaragua | –15 | 51 |
| Mozambique | –14 | 28 |
| Bolivia | – 7 | 44 |
| Source: Kenny (2005b) | | |

*Table Four.* Economic Performance and Health Performance 1950–90, Selected Countries

Why is there a weak link between income and health? In part it is because too much income might be bad for health outcomes. Until the 1820s, it was commonly assumed that increased riches would lower levels of health through 'diseases of civilization' such as obesity, gout and venereal disease (Szreter, 1997). Indeed, it may be the case today that, above a certain minimum level of income, 'diseases of the rich' are as significant problem as 'diseases of the poor.' In the United

---

[14]   As an example, and ignoring issues of causality and weak statistical significance, for Brazil between 1965-96, three percentage points of change in female adult mortality was due to income growth compared to a nine percent change due to the passage of time (capturing global technological change). C. Kenny (2005a) discusses data weaknesses. In sum, the data are indeed weak, but there appears little reason to believe that these weaknesses account for the limited correlational strength of the relationship between income and health. See in addition Hill et al., 1998. Korenromp et al., 2004.

States, heart attacks increase when unemployment falls, with a one percentage fall in unemployment countrywide estimated to raise heart attack mortality by 2,500 deaths (Ruhm, 2006).[15] Recessions in wealthy countries appear to improve health because people with less money and more time are more likely to exercise and less likely to drink and smoke (Cutler et. al., 2006). Even in developing countries, more people die each year from high blood pressure, high cholesterol, obesity, physical inactivity, tobacco, alcohol and illicit drug consumption than die of malnutrition, indoor smoke from solid fuels, unsafe water, or poor sanitation and hygiene (WHO, 2002).

Furthermore, even very poor people do not appear to use their consumption resources to maximize health or education outcomes. Within two years of electrification, rural households in surveyed areas of Indonesia where incomes per capita were around $2/day saw television ownership reach 30 percent. Within seven years of electrification, ownership rates reached 60 percent, despite the fact that a television cost four or five times the monthly income of poorer households in the survey sample. (Compare this to refrigerators, which were owned by fewer than five percent of surveyed electrified households). Households with a television were watching it on average four to five hours per day. When asked to rank their priorities in life, electrified households put food, shelter, clothing, health and education all above recreation (Madon, 2003). Given that 70 percent of them were watching television four to five hours a day, we might have to assume they had done all they felt they could to meet these other priorities.

This is not to cast aspersions on the poor in developing countries. It is only to emphasize that rich and poor people in both developed and developing countries use income in ways that do little good or positively harm their health all of the time. Not least, they purchase large quantities of alcohol and cigarettes. Worldwide, income is rarely spent in a way that maximizes welfare.

---

[15] This stands in marked contrast to the relationship between employment and contentment presented in a later chapter.

Potential conflicts between economic and health interests also have a long history. We have seen that the concentration of people required for both farming and industrialization had a significantly negative impact on health. Attempts to quarantine the city of Pistoia in Italy to control the plague in 1630 were defeated by wine traders keen to continue their business (Deaton, 2004). Schistosomiasis was worsened in Egypt by the construction of the Aswan Dam. More recently, small-scale irrigation dams in Ethiopia have been found to improve agricultural yield and farm profits at the same time as they have considerably increase the burden of disease (Ersado, 2005). Economic and public health interests can directly conflict.

Factors that provide potential negative links between income and welfare cannot help to explain considerable global improvement in health outcomes, however. For this, we have to look first to technological advance. Samuel Preston (1975) studied data regarding life expectancy and income across countries and argued that global technological change was three to nine times more important than changes in income in explaining growth in life expectancy. Since then, a number of different researchers using different techniques have come to similar conclusions.[16]

Between 1870 and 1999, the income per capita associated with a given life expectancy has fallen tenfold. Countries with a GDP per capita of $300 today are achieving similar welfare outcomes to those achieved by countries with an income per capita of $3,000 in 1870 (See Table Five).[17]

---

[16]  Not least Easterly, 1999, McGuire, 2001, Szretzer, 1997, Deaton, 2004, Easterlin 1995, 1998.

[17]  Given that, it appears likely that more than half the World's countries today containing over four billion people (or about 69 percent of the global population) have seen more advance in life expectancy from non-income factors than from economic growth over the 1870–1998 period (C. Kenny, 2005a).

| GDP per Capita (US Dollars) | Predicted Life Expectancy in Given Year | | |
|---|---|---|---|
| | 1870 | 1950 | 1999 |
| 300 | 23 | 33 | 46 |
| 3,000 | 44 | 59 | 64 |
| 30,000 | 65 | 85 | 83 |
| Source: Kenny (2005b). GDP per capita is in constant dollars using purchasing power parity. | | | |

Table Five. Income and Life Expectancy Over Time

## The Role of Technology and Governments in Welfare

Overall, our general measures of income growth appear to be missing considerable changes in the basket of goods available to, and consumed by, the poor thanks to technological change. The average American industrial worker in 1889 had nearly twice the purchasing power of a rural Indian in 1983. And yet a day's worth of calories (2,300) cost around ten percent of the American's wage, compared to less than five percent in rural India in 1983. While the average Indian in 1983 consumed nearly 2,100 calories, the average American in 1888 consumed 1,646 calories (Logan, 2005). The income required to sustain an adequate diet has declined to the point that weight problems have become epidemic even in fairly poor countries. Egypt has a GDP per capita approximately 15 percent of the US level, but more than three quarters of women over 30 are overweight – a similar percentage to the US (Bhattacharya, 2005).

More broadly, GDP measures our ability to produce and consume goods in general. It is a poor measure of the choice of goods available, and this choice appears to be a key factor in determining welfare outcomes. However rich a citizen of the UK was in the early 1800s, they could not buy a vaccine against measles. Today, Vietnam, at a similar level of average incomes to the UK in the early 1800s, sees vaccination rates of around 97 percent. Thanks to the invention and rollout of cheap vaccination technologies, even very poor countries can use scarce health expenditures far more effectively than could countries 200 years ago to reduce death rates from a number of diseases. As a result, over the recent past, there has been considerable global convergence in the percentage of children immunized for diphtheria polio, tetanus and measles, for example (Comin et al., 2006). Similarly, knowledge about the transmission of disease and engineering advances have given the incentive and the means for even very poor cities to roll out access to clean water and sanitation.

What non-income factors related to technology and institutions play a role in determining health outcomes? Numerous studies have thrown variables into cross-country and within-country regression analyses, some looking across a single time and some looking at changes across time. Few results are 'robust' to all different samples and all different techniques, but some of the stronger correlates include not only expected ones such as immunization levels, but also more interesting factors such as female education, gender and income inequalities, access to potable water and sanitation, institutional quality and geographic factors.[18] Time — a proxy for the general influence of global technological change — appears to be a particularly strong determinant.[19]

It is worth noting that, beyond measures of immunization, direct measures of health inputs such as the number of doctors, nurses or hospital beds per capita or public health expenditures per capita do not appear to be robustly related to health outcomes in developing countries.[20] This is not to say that public health measures are unimportant — they are far more

[18]  Such results have been found in World Bank, 2003, Hamner and White, 1999, Younger, 2001, Wang, 2002, Hanmer et al., 2003, Ranis and Stewart, 2001, Filmer and Pritchett, 1997, Waldmann, 1992, Leipziger et al. 2003, Shi, 2000, Hertz et al. 1994, Moore et. al., 1999 and Lena and London, 1993.

[19]  See, for example, C. Kenny, 2005a, 2005b, Easterly, 1999, Clemens et al., 2004.

[20]  See Ranis and Stewart, 2001, Filmer, Hamner and Pritchett, 2000, Younger, 2001, Leipziger et al., 2003, Hertz et al., 1994. Although see Wagstaff, 2001 and Baldacci et al., 2004. The role of health care in explaining health outcomes appears to be limited even in advanced economies. The introduction of Medicare had no effect on the mortality of US elderly, while

important in the developing than the developed world.[21] Instead, it is that the most effective measures require minimal amounts of money and numbers of doctors to implement.

Laxminarayan et al. (2006) rate the three most cost effective interventions in Sub-Saharan Africa as a whole to reduce mortality and morbidity as first, childhood immunization, second, interventions to reduce traffic accidents and third the extension of access to bednets, spraying and preventive anti-malarial treatment during pregnancy. At the low end, such interventions would cost as little as $1–2 per (disability-adjusted) life year saved. Not only do these numbers suggest how inexpensive effective interventions can be, but also that interventions do not need to involve hospitals or doctors.

Looking at child and maternal health, nearly three quarters of under-five deaths in the developing world are caused by diseases for which practical, low-cost interventions exist such as immunization, oral rehydration therapy use (for overcoming diarrhea) and antibiotics (Hill et al., 1998). That 63 percent of children are immunized is a likely factor behind rapidly declining under-five mortality in Mozambique, for example (IMF and World Bank, 2005).[22] Using cross-country analysis, McGuire (2005) repeats the finding that health care expenditure (as well as geographic access to health services and per capita availability of doctors, nurses and hospital beds) is not associated with lower under-five mortality. But he finds that reduced mortality is correlated with the quality of maternal and infant health programs and the share of births attended by trained personnel. McGuire concludes that 'the main challenge in many developing countries may be less to raise overall public health spending, or even the share of public health spending devoted to basic services, than to assure that a very small absolute amount of revenue is spent effectively...' Oral

the introduction of the National Health Service had no impact on class differences in health in the UK (Cutler et al. 2006).

[21] For example, in Sub-Saharan Africa, 42 percent of total health burdens are due to infectious and parasitic diseases, compared to 2.8 percent in Western Europe (Bloom and Sachs, 1998).

[22] Indeed, Lewis (2006) finds that once one accounts for the quality of governance and education, GDP per capita is an insignificant determinant of measles immunization coverage.

rehydration, promotion of breastfeeding,immunization —these very cheap interventions are very effective.

Malaysia and Sri Lanka have both made competent, professional midwives available in rural areas as well as ensuring access to drugs and equipment. Maternal deaths per 100,000 live births have dropped from 2,136 in 1930 to 24 in 1996 in Sri Lanka and from 1,085 in 1933 to 19 in 1997 in Malaysia (the 2000 estimate for the US is 17 per 100,000). Once again, these improvements were achieved with extremely limited resources. Expenditure on maternal and child health services in the two countries remains below 0.4 percent of GDP (World Bank, 2006).

Overall, a recent survey found that the cost of a basic package of primary health services in rural areas ranged from US$2.82 per head per year in Cambodia to US$6.25 per head per year in Guatemala. In all cases studied, the amounts represent less than one percent of gross national income (Loevinsohn and Harding, 2005). Similarly, Easterlin (2004) argues that, since the 1950s, 'the cost requirements of major improvement in life expectancy have probably been no more than 2 percent of GDP, even in the poorest countries.' Some very effective interventions are even revenue-creating for health systems. Controlling tobacco use through taxation is rated by Jamison and his colleagues (2006) as perhaps the most important intervention for reducing noncommunicable disease in developing countries.

## The Role of Institutions

Concerted public action has been central to improved prospects for global health in countries rich and poor. For example, the global community has eradicated endemic smallpox from 140 countries since 1920, a complex coordination effort which overcame multiple market failures. The results of this public action are clear worldwide. In particular, they can be seen in the pattern of urban-rural health differences. In nineteenth century Europe, prior to public health interventions, urban life expectancy was considerably below rural life expectancy. In early Twentieth Century developing countries with similar incomes per capita, that picture has been reversed – with urban populations living longer (C. Kenny, 2005). This central importance of public health and sanitation measures in improving welfare outcomes suggests a vital role for government institutions in determining levels of health (a later chapter will discuss the nature of institutions).

The state has become a far more powerful agent over time for both good and ill. The British government's revenues as a share of GDP rose from perhaps two percent of national income under Elizabeth I in the late sixteenth Century to four percent 100 years later. By 1788, they had reached 12 percent, and closed the Twentieth Century at around 45 percent of GDP (Ferguson, 2001). Today, the size of government bears little relationship to incomes per capita. Indeed, if anything, poorer countries have governments that consume a larger percentage of GDP on average than richer countries (Alesina and Wacziarg, 1998, Annett, 2001). This suggests that governments in poorer countries at the start of the twenty-first century are far larger than were European governments at a time when European countries had similar incomes per capita.

How effective the state is at using this growing power has become an ever more vital determinant of health outcomes. Amartya Sen (1999) has noted that:

> ... even the poorest democratic countries that have faced terrible droughts or floods or other natural disasters (such as India in 1973, or Zimbabwe and Botswana in the early 1980s) have been able to feed their people without experiencing a famine.... Famines are easy to prevent if there is a serious effort to do so, and a democratic government, facing elections and criticisms from opposition parties and independent newspapers, cannot help but make such an effort. Not surprisingly, while India continued to have famines under British rule right up to independence... they disappeared suddenly with the establishment of a multiparty democracy and a free press.

As a result, welfare appears closely related to measures of dignity. A second case highlighted by Dreze and Sen (1999) in a discussion of Kerala in India is that of gender equality. The state of Kerala is considerably more equal in terms of female to male literacy ratios than the rest of India, and has higher levels of literacy overall. Dreze and Sen suggest this has played an important role in achieving very high welfare measures in the state. At the cross-country level, similar findings regarding the importance of gender equality to welfare have been found in numerous other studies.[23] Furthermore, the extent of sanitation, clean water and immunization is significantly higher in countries that have been stable democracies and, reflecting this, life expectancy is considerably longer in such countries (Besley and Kadamatsu, 2006).

There is some evidence that general health expenditures do improve health outcomes at the cross-country level in the presence of strong institutions measured by good governance and low corruption.[24] Improving the quality of expenditure through improved institutions and reduced corruption is surely as important as improving the quantity of expenditure when absentee rates for health providers in developing countries appear to average around 35–40 percent (with levels significantly higher in rural clinics), when the average leakage rate for drugs supposedly destined to public health care facilities in Uganda was estimated at 73 percent in the late 1990s, or when the ratio of highest to lowest price paid for saline solution and cotton across public hospitals in Bolivia was 15 to one and 36 to one respectively (Lewis, 2006).[25]

In both the case of education and health, it is clear that progress is a long-term project with an upper bound in terms of the speed of improvement (Clemens, 2004, Clemens et al., 2005). In part this will reflect the fact that institutional development takes a long time. A later start in commencing progress towards improved health and education will have acted as a considerable cause of current differences in performance in these areas.

---

[23]   See Hanmer and White, 1999, Ranis and Stewart, 2001, Filmer and Pritchett, 1997, Leipziger et al., 2003.

[24]   See Baldacci et al., 2004 and Lewis, 2006.

[25]   A further example: surveys of public sector doctors in Delhi found rampant over-prescribing and mis-prescribing perhaps in part related to the fact that they did less than a third of what they knew to be important in terms of diagnosis and took about fifteen percent of the required time to fully diagnose complaints (Das and Hammer, 2005).

The skewed institutional models generated as a result of differing colonial histories are blamed by many development economists as a driving force behind income differences between countries, as we will see in a later chapter.[26] It is clear that they can also help to explain long term differences in health and education outcomes. Disease-rich environments will have a direct impact on health, but they may also have determined the strength or weakness of initial government institutional structures that could improve health outcomes over the long term.

Support for the thesis that long term factors perhaps connected with colonial history and institutions play a role in determining today's health outcomes is that we can predict 70 percent of today's variation in male life expectancy across countries using data on the mortality rates of early colonists, and data from the 1960s on the extent of ethnic fragmentation within a country (based on the number and extent of different languages within national borders) (C. Kenny, 2005a).

To conclude the discussion of non-violent morbidity, welfare is largely a matter of public health in developing countries, and public health takes strong institutions to overcome related market failures. The strength of such institutions may in part reflect different histories stretching back as far as the colonial period. It is worth emphasizing, however, that evidence of global welfare convergence suggests that developing countries are performing far better in the delivery of public goods related to welfare than did now-developed countries when they had similar levels of income. This is in part due to improved technology and in, part, perhaps, to the growing strength of government institutions. Some minimum level of income is surely required to promote welfare, but that level is minimal, and the scope for improved welfare outcomes even in the poorest countries is immense.

---

[26] See Easterly and Levine, 2003, Acemoglu et al., 2001, Engerman and Sokoloff, 2005.

## Violence

Hobbes may have had a point regarding the state of nature. For a number of stone-age communities in the twentieth century, figures suggest that male deaths were caused by warfare varied between just under 10 percent (for the Gebusi of Papua New Guinea) to nearly sixty percent (amongst the Jivaro of the Peruvian rain forest) (Pinker, 2002). Having said that, the extent of harm caused by warfare worldwide appears to be on the resurgence over the long term, thanks in large part to technological advance. Once again, the best defense against a growing level of death from warfare may be institutional change rather than income growth.

Whilst technological and institutional changes have been powerful forces behind improved health, they have also driven immense increases in the power of the state for violence. In the 1470s, during the British Wars of the Roses, UK-based armies made up about 0.6 percent of the population. By 1810, during the Napoleonic Wars, this had risen to five percent (Ferguson, 2001). By World War One, Britain had nine percent of its population under arms (calculated from Maddison, 2001 and Ferguson, 2003).

Not only were more people directly involved in the effort to kill one another, but the means to kill became considerably more effective. Overall, Ferguson (2001) looks at the modern history of war and concludes on the basis of annual casualty figures that between the seventeenth and the twentieth Century, the capacity of war to kill (in terms of deaths per year) rose by a factor of roughly 800. The annual death rate in the Thirty Years War was a mere 69,000 compared to 9.5 million in the Second World War. The percentage of people dying in wars grew from a little under one percent of the global population in the nineteenth century to over four percent in the Twentieth (Kenny, 2006). In the decades since the Second World War, global battlefield deaths rose from 0.5 to 1.2 per 1,000 of the world's population between the 1950s to the 1970s, falling back to 0.4 per 1,000 during 1990-7. It should also be noted that battlefield deaths account for a fairly small percentage of overall war deaths in many twentieth-century conflicts.[27]

There have also been more occasions to utilize increasingly effective killing machines. Brecke (2001) estimates that the number of conflicts including civil wars averaged somewhere around 50 per decade in the period 1400–1700, dropping closer to 30 conflicts per decade in the 1700s before rising to around 80 per decade in the post-1800 period. A measure of the number of wars ongoing annually for the post-World War Two period suggests that the period after 1961 saw a dramatic rise in conflicts around the globe, from around 20 that year to over 50 by 1994, dropping back to below 30 by 2002 (Human Security Centre, 2005).

This drop in the number of wars after 1994 coincides with the end of the Cold War rather than a period of dramatic global economic growth, one piece of evidence against a strong link between income growth and peace. Over the period 1975-91, wealthy countries were less often the target of invasion, as were democracies (Hermann and Kegley, 1996). But data on the extent of involvement in warfare suggests that neither income nor democracy are guarantors against war. The three countries that have been involved in the most armed conflicts since 1946 are the UK (21), France (19) and the US (16). The most conflict-prone countries (measured by the number of conflicts multiplied by their length) were Burma, India, Ethiopia, the Philippines and Israel (Human Security Centre, 2005).

It is true that poorer countries have hosted more that their fair share of the world's recent civil wars, and that wealthier countries have fought fewer wars with each other (Hegre and Sambanis, 2005). Civil wars do break out more often in poor countries (Collier and Hoeffler, 2004). But income growth does not appear to reduce the appetite for such acts over the long term.[28]

---

[27]  Battlefield deaths accounted for less than two percent up to 29 percent of total deaths in a range of post-war African conflicts. Data from Lacina and Gleditsch, 2005.

[28]  Even in the short term, the finding that civil wars occur more in countries which seen recent periods of low growth appears not to be robust (see also Easterly, 1999).

Again, the role of institutions including the presence of stable democracies (both at home and in the neighborhood) appears to be more significant in determining long term trends in the frequency of conflict (Hegre and Sambanis, 2005). In particular, democracy appears to be far more robustly linked with reduced severity of civil wars in terms of battle deaths than is economic development (Lacina, 2006). Similarly, terrorists appear to be richer and better educated than the average population from which they are drawn, and they come from countries that lack civil liberties rather than those which are comparatively poor (Krueger and Maleckova, 2003, Abadie, 2006).

The state as an engine for domestic oppression has also significantly grown in efficiency. In Sixteenth Century Britain, Queen Mary killed 300 people over a reign of five years to earn the title 'bloody'. Three hundred deaths were the matter of a few hours work for Mao during the Cultural Revolution or Stalin during the Purges. Once again, the direct role of income as compared to institutions in explaining such outbreaks appears limited.

Leviathans which use their power to control rather than extend violence have been responsible for considerable reductions in non state-sponsored violence. Homicide rates began to decline in the UK as early as the Fifteenth Century, dropping from 23 per 100,000 people per year in the 1200–1400 period to seven in the Sixteenth Century. They continued this decline until the second half of the Eighteenth Century, when levels reached as low as one per 100,000 people (lower than rates today). The Industrial Revolution was accompanied by a rise in violent crime, no doubt connected with social dislocation, so that rates doubled from the late Eighteenth Century to the first half of the Nineteenth. After that point they started declining again, until the 1970s.

Regarding the rest of Europe, dramatic declines commenced in the Low Countries by the end of the sixteenth century, in Scandinavia and Germany by the first half of the seventeenth century and in Italy by the end of that century. In other words, declines considerably predated modern economic growth, and periods of stronger growth since then have frequently been associated with rising homicide rates (Eisner, 2003).

Eisner (2003) suggests that the rise of the nation state may have played some role in the dramatic declines in homicide. Judges and sovereigns became increasingly involved in 'social disciplining,' including ordinances regarding feasts, child rearing, clothing, alcohol consumption and church attendance. At the same time, authorities began to regulate lethal interpersonal violence far more closely and concepts such as 'honorable manslaughter' fell out of favour. Nonetheless, growing efforts at state control alone cannot explain the decline in homicides given that police forces in Italian cities reached a considerable size (making up as many as one out of every 145 residents) at a time when homicides remained high. The role of a growing sense of community — of a *nation* state — which gave the state legitimacy to act to control public violence was an important element of the transition to lower homicide rates.

Using a global sample over more recent periods, manslaughter has actually risen faster in countries that have grown more rapidly over recent periods (Easterly, 1999). There is little evidence that the extent of hate crimes is linked in either direction to economic conditions (or levels of education, sadly) (Krueger and Maleckova, 2003). Across countries, survey evidence suggests that the percentage of people attacked or threatened with violence over the last five years ranged between twelve and twenty percent in the US, France, Canada, South Africa, Russia and Brazil, while the figures in Japan and India were only one percent (Human Security Centre, 2005). Indeed, differences in rates of violent crime between (rather than within) countries over long periods account for most of the global variation in violent crime.[29] This suggests that factors such as income or income growth must play a comparatively minor role in determining crime levels, although growth rates do appear to have some short-term impact. There

---

[29] Taking a sample of 44 countries over the period 1950–2000, 87 percent of the variation in homicide was accounted for by cross-country differences rather than differences over time within countries (LaFree and Tseloni, 2006).

is some evidence that inequality might be linked with greater rates of violent crime, although it is disputed. Levels of social capital may also play a role (Lederman et al., 2002 and Neumayer, 2004).

There are significant gender differences in the nature of crime. In early eighteenth-century Stockholm, women accounted for nearly half of all murder offenses. One major factor behind this appears to be that, for fear of eternal punishment in hell for suicide, desperate women would kill their children rather than themselves and then, after professing repentance for their crime, suffer the death penalty imposed on them by the judiciary. This extremely unusual calculus led to an extremely unusual outcome — women became almost as responsible for public violence as men, whereas through most of history they have accounted for 20 percent, or frequently far less, of total violent crime (Eisner, 2003).

Over time female victim homicides have decline considerably more slowly than male homicides. Related to this, violence within the family has become a growing issue, so that within-family homicides now account for around forty percent of the total (Eisner, 2003). More broadly, domestic violence against women appears to be the most common form of violent act worldwide. Rates across countries vary dramatically — with between three and 52 percent of women reporting physical violence by an intimate partner in the previous year (Watts and Zimmerman, 2002).

Violence against females frequently starts early. In the latest Indian census, there were only 93 women for every 100 men, suggesting that between 22 and 37 million girls and women are 'missing' due to sex-selective abortion, infanticide or fatal neglect. Amartya Sen (2000) cites results from India which suggest that the female labor force participation rate and female literacy both reduce the gap between male and female child mortality rates. Conversely, higher income levels (amongst other factors) can even increase the gender bias in child survival, while doing little if anything to reduce overall levels of child mortality. Furthermore, it is worth noting that the country with the highest male/female sex ratio at birth is South Korea, where 117 boys are born for each 100 girls. For third children, the ratio is 185 boys for each 100 girls, suggesting considerable early termination of female fetuses (Watts and Zimmerman, 2002).

Rates of violence against females do not appear to be closely correlated with average levels of income or income growth at later stages, either. A WHO survey (2005) of 24,000 women in ten countries found that one half of the women had been subject to physical or sexual violence. Women in Butajira province in Ethiopia had the lowest rate of non-partner violence, but one of the highest rates of partner violence, suggesting that complex causal mechanisms may be at work. Furthermore, despite high rates of domestic violence amongst women in this, one of the poorest countries of the World, it appears that the link between domestic violence and income across countries is weak. The region of Cusco, in Peru (a considerably richer country) saw even higher rates of domestic violence. Heise, Ellsberg and Gottmoeller (2002) argue that there are small-scale societies such as the Wape of Papua New Guinea where domestic violence is virtually unknown. They suggest that violence against women is a social phenomenon more common in societies where gender roles are rigidly defined and enforced and where cultural norms tolerate violence.

## Conclusion

Income can be used to promote welfare. Some level of income is required to consume enough calories and nutrients to live. Income is required to buy vaccines and procure the services of a skilled midwife. Far greater income is required to purchase a heart bypass operation or other advanced surgery. At the same time, the amount of income required to purchase the most cost-effective technologies that have driven the morbidity revolution is very small. And greater production and consumption can at times be a force for declining welfare.

As a result, the debate is no longer between those who see income as of central importance in the battle to improve global health outcomes and those who see income as one significant factor amongst many. The debate is between those who see income as one significant factor amongst many and those who see it as marginal or insignificant beyond some comparatively low level (see Jamison, 2006 and Jamison et al., 2001). For the great majority of countries, it is likely that the causal link from welfare improvements to economic growth is considerably stronger than the causal link from economic growth to improvements in welfare.[30]

Furthermore, it is worth emphasizing that while GDP per capita growth is not significantly correlated to a number of welfare outcomes, it is significantly related to a number of bad things—not least the expanded output of pollutants (including waste paper, carbon dioxide, sulfur dioxide and nitrogen oxides) (Easterly, 1999).[31] Pollution can have an immediate impact on welfare outcomes in terms of lead poisoning from petrol or lung damage from particulates. Environmental destruction which denudes species and habitats might be considered an assault on dignity. And whilst the status of the global environment is not a theme of this book, the threat which greater income growth in already wealthy countries poses to sustainable global welfare may be a real and significant one.

Rather than income, technology and the growing power of the state appear to have been the driving forces for improved welfare across countries. And evidence of rapid global convergence in welfare suggests they have been very powerful forces. At the same time, as the section on violence makes clear, if the beneficial leviathan turns malign, its power for harm has been similarly amplified. Institutional structures that control the state's potential for destruction have become ever more important, and these structures appear to be related to civil and political rights.

---

[30] See Easterlin, 2004, Wagstaff, 2005 and Lorentz et. al. 2005. Wiel's estimate of the health-to-growth relationship estimates that differences in health performance can account for between 10 and 23 percent of the global variation in GDP per worker.

[31] Mishan (1967) notes that 'bringing the Jerusalem of economic growth to England's green and pleasant land has so far conspicuously reduced both the greenness and the pleasantness.'

# PART THREE

## DIGNITY

# Chapter 5

# Choice, Worth, and Prestige

### Dignity

Of the elements of well-being, dignity is the most complex and the most contentious to analyse. It is related to each of the other two elements, welfare and contentment. A fundamental element of human dignity is the individual's awareness of his or her level of welfare. Dignity is related to contentment in that one's state of contentment may depend on one's assessment of the degree of dignity of one's condition.

Deliberately to keep people in ignorance of their absolute and relative condition of welfare is an affront to their dignity, even if it may increase their contentment. To balance dignity against contentment is a crucial and difficult task for those with responsibility for other people's welfare. Nowhere is this more obvious than when we are considering the situation of the terminally ill. Should one tell the patient candidly that her condition is desperate, thus depriving her of any contentment the hope of recovery might give her? If one leaves her in ignorance, is it an affront to her dignity to allow her to die amid a conspiracy of deceit?

The issue arises in the case of societies as well as individuals. The spread of television in the underdeveloped world has made members of poorer countries more aware of their position in relation to richer ones. No doubt the communication of this information gives them a greater insight into their own condition, and to that extent increases their dignity. But it is very doubtful how far it has increased their contentment with their lot.

By 'dignity' in the present work, it should be explained, is meant an objective feature of one's situation in life. 'Dignity' may also mean a character trait — the virtue of fortitude and the behavioural comportment that goes with it — which enables a person to remain self-possessed in adverse circumstances. That is not our concern in this section.

Dignity as here understood has three elements, that we may refer to in shorthand as choice, value, and prestige. To possess dignity you must have a degree of choice and control over your life, the life that you lead must be a worthwhile one, and it must carry with it a degree of prestige. These three elements are not all on the same level; but all of them must be investigated if we are to explain the notion of dignity that is essential to the assessment of a person's well-being.

## Choice

Even the most downtrodden of us is constantly faced with choices in daily life; but obviously not all choices are significant. The freedom to choose between blue cheese or thousand island dressing on one's salad is not a valuable component of liberty or dignity. The three most important choices are the choice of one's cultural identity, the choice of one's social role, and the choice of the governance under which one lives.

It is an important part of dignity that key elements of one's cultural identity — such as one's religion or one's language — are not forced on one unwillingly from outside. Cultural identity is of course never the result of deliberate choice from a zero position: it is much more a matter of consent. Each of us is brought up as part of an ethnic group, with a certain language, religion, morality, and customs. We cannot decide in advance what is to be the culture into which we are born and educated.

What matters is that when we come of age to take responsibility for ourselves, we should willingly identify with that culture. To measure the degree of voluntariness of our acceptance we can ask whether the social institutions under which we live are such that if we do not identify with the culture of our birth, we should be able to alter or discard features of it, or to adopt a different one.

When it is not our cultural identity, but our social role, that is to be defined, then it is an element of dignity that actual choice, and not mere consent, should enter in. For that reason there is greater dignity in marriage to a partner of one's choice than in a marriage arranged by one's family and friends. This is so, whether or not an arranged marriage may lead in certain circumstances to more secure welfare and greater contentment. Here once more there is a difficult trade-off to be made between different elements of human well-being.

Again, there is greater dignity in working at a job that one has freely contracted to perform than in carrying out duties that are assigned to one, willy-nilly, by one's social status. This is true whether one's assigned condition is lowly or privileged. The hero of many a Victorian novel has to decide whether to accept the prestige and duties that are attached to the class into which he has been born, or to assert his own individuality by making his way in a different professional or business world.

A third constituent of the control of one's life that is an element in dignity is one's degree of participation in the political arrangements under which one lives. Someone who has control over the rulers who govern her, to the minimal extent that she can help to vote them out of office, clearly enjoys greater dignity than one who has no such control. A citizen of a democracy in which every person has equal rights before the law is in possession of more dignity than the subject of an autocratic monarch.

## A Worthwhile Life

We have so far identified three elements of the control over one's life that is one of the constituents of dignity. But such control, though a necessary condition, is not a sufficient condition of the kind of dignity that is an important element of human well-being. For a life may be totally under one's control, and yet neither internally satisfactory, nor deserving of respect, because dissipated in pointless activities. For the dignity that is of the essence of human well-being, a life must involve experiences and activities that are worthwhile in themselves and not merely devices to pass the time.

In deciding whether activities are worthwhile, there are both subjective and objective factors to take into account. Whether a particular type of work confers dignity depends both on the degree of job satisfaction of the person employed and on the value placed on the job by society. Obviously, many different types of job may provide satisfaction and earn esteem: but it is an essential element of well-being that the manner in which one provides for the welfare of oneself and one's dependents should not be mere drudgery, work that is tedious and repetitive.

Of course, leisure as well as work may be assessed on the scale of dignity, as it ranges from the creativity of an artist to the torpidity of a couch-potato. Indeed, some philosophers, of an aristocratic bent, have thought that it was only leisure activities that could confer dignity: paid work was of its very nature degrading. In our own time it is unemployment rather than employment that is an affront to one's dignity.

The arguments that Aristotle gives in the tenth book of the Nicomachean Ethics to show that the highest form of happiness consists in philosophical contemplation of truth are well worth studying, not because they are likely to convince anyone of his conclusion, but because they offer interesting criteria for distinguishing between activities in respect of their intrinsic worth. Happiness, he says, must consist in the exercise of our best gifts, it must be something permanent and durable, difficult to disrupt, it must be wanted for its own sake, and above all it must be pleasant.

In this passage Aristotle behaves like the director of a marriage bureau who is trying to match his client's description of his or her ideal partner. Philosophy, he says, has all the qualities necessary for happiness. It is the exercise of our highest capacities upon the finest objects of study. It is an activity which demands little by way of support and therefore is less likely than other activities to be disrupted or terminated by factors outside our control. It is pursued for its own sake, not in order to serve some further purpose (Aristotle, 2002, 1177a12).

Finally Aristotle assures us that its pleasures surpass all others. The reason he gives for that is that they are purer than others, that is to say, they are unmixed with pains. The pleasures of hunger, thirst and sex follow periods of deprivation, but in advance of philosophising there are no pangs to be felt. Scientific curiosity is not painful in the way that a craving for a drink or a cigarette may be.

There are, fortunately, many other human activities that satisfy Aristotle's criteria for worthwhile activities besides the exalted ones to which he devoted his own life. But his requirements remind us that it our happiness is vulnerable if our principal activities depend for their success on expensive apparatus and a large staff. The solitary scholar will not have to suffer the kind of withdrawal symptoms that the chief executive of a large corporation will experience on retirement. The ideal life is one in which there is no clear boundary between work and recreation.

There is a further reason for placing a high regard on a life devoted to the acquisition of knowledge, which was emphasized more by Aristotle's master Plato. If happiness is placed in material goods, then competition is inevitable, and wholesale satisfaction is impossible. In a world of limited resources, there will never be enough material goods for all to share, so that there will be competition for possession and A's gain will be B's loss. Something similar is true of the pursuit of political power: such power must be power over others and can only be obtained at the cost of diminishing the dignity of others.

But no such disadvantages attach to the pursuit and transmission of knowledge. If B learns something from A, then A is in no way diminished; and when B in turn teaches something to C, B loses nothing of the knowledge he possesses. The same is true of the exercise of an acquired skill: a doctor who uses his medical expertise to heal a patient is not parting with anything in the way that a merchant is when he sells an object to a customer. The doctor is, qua doctor, no worse off when he heals his hundredth patient than when he heals his first.

Of course, as Plato was well aware, there can be competition for money and power among physicians and academics no less than among politicians and businessmen. But the competition, he suggested, was not of the essence of their calling as it is in the other cases. Healing and money-making, he maintained, were two different arts, even if practiced by the same person. A man might be a good money maker and a bad physician, or again be a good doctor but be bad at making money (Plato, 1997, 341c).

## Respect and Prestige

In addition to choice and worthwhile activity, the third element to be identified in dignity is prestige. Unlike the other elements of dignity, prestige is not an essential constituent of well-being; but it can undoubtedly contribute to and augment it. Prestige is based on one's possession of goods that arouse the respect and envy of others. These need not be material goods but they are bound to be positional goods; goods that relate to one's position in society and which of their nature cannot be universally shared, since — in the words of W.S. Gilbert — when everyone is somebody, then no one's anybody.

Prestige is an ambivalent element in well-being. Aristotle indeed denied that it could really be a part of one's happiness; when we are given honour, he said, the honour is something that resides in the person honouring, not in the person honoured. But the more important drawback of prestige is its essential connection with competition. It is not something that could be maximised according to any greatest happiness principle. As we shall see in a later chapter, when incomes rise above a certain point, people attach more importance to relative rather than to absolute income. The reason for that is that in developed societies prestige attaches to income. But the consequence of tying prestige to income is that increases in income bring diminished returns. Perhaps one should say that it is respect, rather than prestige, that is the third essential element in dignity. But in practice, in a competitive world, it is difficult to separate respect from prestige.

There seems to be a paradox in utilitarian economics. Competition seems both to be an obstacle to the spread of happiness, and yet an essential element in the free market which many economists believe to be the most efficient way of creating utility. Many economists claim that a market operating in comparative freedom is the most effective agent for the production of national wealth. An effective market depends on effective government to maintain civil order and impartial courts to enforce commercial contracts. Hence the preference for capitalist democracy among economists concerned to promote wellbeing.

However, while the free-market economy may be the most efficient tool so far discovered to generate wealth, it does not necessarily follow that it maximizes dignity or contentment. There are several reasons for this. In the first place, once basic needs have been satisfied, many people are more concerned with dignity than with welfare, and the operation of the market may diminish rather than increase the dignity of those engaged in it. Members of traditionally dignified professions may feel insulted if their services are rated simply at market value. The great inequalities which the free operation of the market allows to build up may cause great discontent among those at the lower end of the scale, even if in absolute terms their income is enough to provide adequate welfare. Some economists, as we shall see, go so far as to claim that it is relative, not absolute, income that is the determinant of contentment.

Some philosophers regard inequality of wealth as being in and of itself an affront to human dignity. There is no reason, however, why someone with average wealth should feel degraded simply because some other people are very much richer. If the existence of billionaires is the price to be paid for an economic system that is the most efficient method of reducing absolute poverty, we should not oppose it simply because it may mean that a man with only two yachts will be unhappy because his neighbour possesses three.

What matters in judging the merits of societies and economic systems is not so much the spread of incomes, as the absolute level of those who are least well treated by the system. Of course, those with great wealth may use their economic power to bring other people into a condition where their welfare and dignity is genuinely compromised. They may also be seriously at fault by not using their wealth to improve the lot of the poorest. But heartlessness and exploitation are not necessary concomitants of riches.

Dignity, as we have defined it, is not at all restricted to people occupying positions of wealth and power in economically advanced societies. St Simeon Stylites was a hermit who spent his life in prayer at the top of a pillar, revered by pilgrims who flocked to assist in his devotions. He was living a life of his choice, spent in an activity that he and his society regarded as the most worthwhile of all activities, and he enjoyed the esteem of his contemporaries. He possessed each of the three elements of the dignity that is a constituent of well-being.

Chapter 6

# The Economics
# of Dignity

This chapter is about the role that income plays in dignity but also about the relationship between economic development and dignity more broadly. It is hard to be dignified – or indeed to care much about dignity – when one is starving, or picking over garbage heaps to make a 'living.' For a society, a minimum level of welfare is surely a constituent of sustainable dignity. Furthermore, a minimum level of income is required to achieve that welfare, as we have seen. At the same time, as noted in an earlier chapter, the level of income required to achieve such welfare is, in global terms, low and falling, and the relationship between economic growth and welfare growth is very weak. Is the relationship between economic growth and the growth of dignity any stronger?

According to a number of measures that might be considered connected to dignity, the world has seen considerable improvement over the past 30–50 years. Measures of civil and political rights have gone up on average worldwide. The percentage of children aged 10 to 14 in the labour force declined from 24 to 10 percent 1960–2000. Between 1950 and 1999, the percentage of the world's population that was literate increased from 52 to 81 percent. Income inequality within the average country declined slightly 1960–90, while gender equality, measured as a percentage of female literacy as a proportion of male literacy increased from 59 to 80 percent between 1970 and 2000. As significant, and as with health measures discussed in a previous chapter, countries that were further behind on these measures of dignity have improved more rapidly than those which began further ahead — a result distinctly different from that for income per capita (C. Kenny, 2005b).

Nonetheless, it has been argued that widespread economic growth may be one factor behind a spread of dignity. This might be because income growth allows people to focus more on how much better they are doing than they were in prior years, rather than how they are doing compared to their peers. In turn, it has been argued, this creates a favourable environment for inclusive policies that aid the poor and disadvantaged (Friedman, 2005).

Of course, ensuring that incomes rise over each individual's lifetime does not require a growing GDP per capita. Indeed, there was no significant GDP per capita growth for most of the world over most of history, yet it is very likely that many individual people saw rising incomes over their lifetimes. As long as the young earn less than average, and the old more, a stagnant economy can preserve income progress for each individual.

This fact might help to account for the limited evidence in favour of the theory that faster economic growth increases contentment, as we will see in a later chapter. It may also help to explain the weak empirical relationship between developments that might be thought 'pro-dignity' and rates of economic growth. For example, Easterbrook (2005) points out that the thesis that economic growth leads to more inclusive societies faces some challenges from US history. The recession beginning in 1893 did not dampen the pressure for suffrage, Social Security was born in the midst of the Great Depression, and the last three decades have seen reduced evidence of discrimination in the workplace despite periodic episodes of low growth. Conversely, the Ku Klux Klan surged in the Roaring Twenties.[1]

---

[1]   Furthermore, as noted by Friedman (2005) '[m]ost of the people who favor either increased or reduced school funding, or a more or a less progressive tax system, rarely if ever change their attitude.' This suggests

This chapter discusses measures of choice, value and prestige and their determinants. Choice might most closely be measured by indicators of overall civil and political rights. Value is connected to the manner in which one provides for the welfare of oneself and one's dependents. This is perhaps best illustrated by indicators regarding the nature of employment over time. Finally, prestige is connected with the ownership of 'positional goods' and will be significantly related, at the lower end of the scale, with the capacity to appear in public without shame.

## The Global Growth of Choice

There has been a dramatic extension of the rights of mankind over time. The proportion of the world's countries that might be broadly defined as fully democratic according to the United Nations Development Program's *Human Development Report* has risen from effectively zero in 1000 AD to 52 percent in 2002. About one third of the population of ancient Greek states was enslaved, and a similar proportion in Roman Italy in 28 BC. The US southern states saw a slightly higher proportion of slaves in 1750 (about 38 percent of the population). In the Caribbean, the proportion reached as high as 90 percent at times. Legal slavery died out in 1970, with the final emancipations on the Arabian peninsula (Engerman, 1995).

It should be noted, however, that there remain significant numbers of people living under regimes with little respect for human rights and others who are in situations of bonded labour or effective enslavement. Women, in particular, frequently lack liberty. Somewhere between 700,000 and 2 million women and girls are still trafficked across international borders each year (Watts and Zimmerman, 2002). The previous chapter noted that dignity was linked to the ability to choose one's cultural identity and social role when one comes

---

factors that change over short periods (not least economic growth) are not the keys to such attitudes. Sweden stagnant in will be more generous in terms of progressive taxation and school funding than the US growing whatever the (recent) year, while the US in deepest depression in the last or next few years would be more generous than the US rampantly growing in 1887 in terms of taxation and schooling.

of age. Women in very many countries are denied that ability. Not least, over 100 million women worldwide are estimated to have suffered genital mutilation which, apart from significantly increasing the risks of future childbirth, including maternal blood loss and infant death (WHO, 2006), forces on girls a significant and irreversible decision on how to live.

The status of women's dignity might be further illustrated by the percentages of women who accept that a man has a good reason to beat his wife if she does not complete housework. In Butajira province in Ethiopia, two thirds of women agree with this statement, and in Cusco, Peru the proportion is 44 percent. These figures are reflected in very high rates of domestic violence against women in the two provinces. At the same time it is clear that dignity related to gender is a multifaceted concept which cannot be reduced to a single measure or set of causal agents. The World Health Organization's (2005) fifteen-site, ten-country survey of women's health and domestic violence found that despite high rates of violence, Butajira's relative performance in terms of the control exercised over women by their partners was comparatively positive. For example, only 6.5 percent of women in Butajira reported that their partners kept them from seeing friends, the second lowest figure in the sample sites, and compared to 31 percent in first-ranked Samoa.

Whilst discrimination on grounds of ethnicity is frequently outlawed this, too, persists in rich and poor countries alike. Ethnic minorities often find themselves at the lower end of measures of living standards. Forty-five percent of people living below the national poverty line in Guatemala belong to indigenous households and 93 percent of indigenous people are poor, for example. In the US, black infant mortality rates are more than twice as high as the rate for whites. In the Czech Republic, unemployment among the Roma is between 70 and 80 percent. And there is plentiful evidence that this difference in status reflects active discrimination, not merely an inherited disadvantage in terms of socio-economic environment. Discrimination is itself part of a broader exclusion from society including factors such as that textbooks frequently omit references to minority and indigenous histories and cultures (Stern et al., 2005).

There is significant evidence that, as with gender discrimination, ethnic discrimination can become self-reinforcing. This is suggested by a study of caste status on test performance in India. Mixed-caste and caste-segmented groups of Indian junior high school students were set the task of solving mazes for a small reward. In the first set of experiments, the caste of the participants in a mixed-caste group was not revealed to test-takers during the task. Performance did not vary by caste. In the second set of experiments the caste of the participants in a mixed-caste group *was* revealed prior to the task. The average number of mazes solved by the low-caste students fell by 23 percent. In a third set of experiments the group was made up purely of low-caste students, and this was revealed prior to the task. The average number of mazes solved fell even further (Hoff and Pandey, 2004). The way that people view themselves – their capacities and abilities, even the rights they feel entitled to – appears to be intimately related to the social status of their ethnic group or gender.

Whatever lies behind both the global spread of rights and remaining barriers to dignity of choice, it does not appear that income is central. As noted in a previous chapter, many writers throughout history have believed that greatly increased incomes were not required in order to ensure the dignity of choice for peoples. During the English Civil War, when incomes per capita averaged only a little above $1,000, Lilburn called for a republic with universal suffrage and equality before the law. John Stuart Mill called for a full range of liberties including women's equality, and was building on Mary Wollenscraft's *Vindication of the Rights of Women* written in the previous century. Outside of Europe, Akhbar, the Mughal emperor in power at the turn of the Sixteenth century, issued edicts codifying rights including religious freedom from his capital at Agra. Gandhi felt that India was quite capable of guaranteeing a full range of rights at a point when India's GDP per capita was around $600. More recently, a number of developing countries have developed and preserved systems that guarantee widespread civil rights at low levels of average income including Costa Rica, Botswana, South Africa and India itself.

Looking at global data, Ferguson (2001) cites statistics from the Polity III database which suggest that the world was growing steadily more democratic from 1800 to 1925, and then grew steadily less democratic from 1925 through 1950 and again from 1950 to 1975. The 1925-50 period did include the Great Depression, but Ferguson argues that eight of the fourteen dictatorships set up in formerly democratic regimes between the World Wars were set up before the onset of the depression. After 1928, he argues, 'there is simply no correlation between the severity of the Great Depression ... and the ease with which dictatorships were established in the 1930s; if there had been, then Czechoslovakia and France would also have turned fascist...'

Turning to the post-war period, using data from the 'Polity II' database which scores countries from -10 (most autocratic) to 10 (most democratic), for the 71 countries with data for 1950, 1970 and 2002, the average score was 0.3 in 1950, -0.6 in 1970 and 5.5 in 2002. This is a welcome sign of growing political rights across the globe, but provides little support to the centrality of income in that process — economic growth worldwide was more rapid 1950–70 when rights were receding than it was 1970–2002 when rights were rebounding (C. Kenny, 2005). In other words, worldwide, faster economic growth has been associated with greater authoritarianism and slower growth with democratization.

At the country level, Acemoglu et al. (2005a) find that the strong cross-country link between income and measures of democracy at any one time disappears when they control for historical determinants of economic and political development. They also find no significant link between changes in income and changes in measures of democracy over time (See also Easterly, 1999).[2] For example, one of the fastest growing countries in the world over the 1980–2000 period was China, where it is hard to argue that democracy was an immediate result.

---

[2]   A second paper finds education irrelevant using a similar technique — Acemoglu et al., 2005b.

Regarding political participation by women in particular, on average, the percentage of women in parliamentary bodies is slightly lower in low-income countries than in high-income economies. At the same time, the fact that South Africa has 30 percent women parliamentarians and Costa Rica has 35 percent female representation –far higher than the average for OECD countries – suggests that the relationship is a weak one.

As we have seen with welfare and as we shall see with measures of contentment, it is quite plausible to argue that any causal relationship between dignity and economic growth runs from dignity to growth, not the other way around. Early development theorists suggested that greater inequality and an authoritarian state might be necessary to promote rapid economic development. Looking at the post-war economic performance of the Soviet Union, for example, the general view amongst economists of Soviet planning was that 'it might be brutal, and might not do a very good job of providing consumer goods, but it was very effective at promoting industrial growth' according to Paul Krugman. More recent evidence suggests, however, that a basic level of rights and lower measures of inequality might actually spur faster growth, and the earlier they are introduced, the better.[3] Similarly, measures of education have appeared in numerous cross-country studies as an important determinant of economic performance (Easterlin, 1981). If the strength of the positive relationship is open to debate (Kenny and Williams, 2001), at least there is little evidence of a negative relationship between education, civil rights and GDP per capita growth, suggesting no sense of or need for a tradeoff between them.

## A Life of Value – the Dignity of Education and Dignity at Work

To the extent that education itself is part of the package of goods that might be thought to comprise value dignity, it is worth noting that here again the link with income growth is weak. There is no statistically significant relationship between

---

[3]  For example, Fay, 1993, Svensson, 1994, Clarke, 1995, Bourguignon, 1996, Seabright, 1997, Brunetti, 1997.

growth in gross primary or secondary enrollment and growth in income per capita globally or for a subsample of countries with incomes per capita below $3,000 over the 1975-2000 period. Over a longer timeframe but a smaller group of countries, there is no relationship between growth of literacy and income growth 1913-1999. Indeed, if anything, countries that have grown faster have seen slower rates of improvement in education (C. Kenny, 2006). Between 1950 and 1990, Angola, Nicaragua, Mozambique and Bolivia all saw declining real incomes per capita. Over the same period, they all saw dramatically increasing literacy and primary school enrollment. In Angola, where income per capita fell from $986 to $654 over the forty-year period, primary enrollment as a percentage of the population increased from 0.3 to 11.7 percent (it was 12.4 percent in the US in 1990) (Kenny, 2005b).

Conversely, the limited impact of education even in many of the richest countries suggests that even they have some distance to go in ensuring even a basic level of skills. One in four adults in the UK are functionally innumerate (they cannot figure out change from a simple shopping transaction) and one in five functionally illiterate — they cannot find the entry for plumbers in an alphabetical listing in the Yellow Pages (Westwood, 2002).

As with health, that per capita income increases are weakly related to improvements in levels and quality of education is likely to be connected to the fact that universal basic education is very cheap to provide. Budget scarcity is not a significant barrier to expanded enrollment rates, as suggested by Adam Smith in the *Wealth of Nations*, who noted that widespread education could be provided 'for a very small expense.' The barriers to enrollment, and learning once enrolled, are only in small part created by limited absolute income.

Child labour is an issue connected to dignity both directly and because it reduces opportunities for education. The International Labor Organization estimates that there were 206 million child labourers in 2000. But it appears that the relationship between economic growth and child labour rates is not straightforward. Indian state level data suggests that while child labour rates have been decreasing over time, states that saw faster growth rates over the 1982-93 period saw higher rates of child labour in 1994 (allowing for a range of other factors including income, education and religion) (Kambhampati and Rajan, 2006). A similar story can be told regarding trafficked children. Studies in Benin and Burkina Faso suggest that a range of factors beyond income are important. The presence of televisions and soccer clubs in the village, the death of a parent and the search for better educational opportunities all increase the supply of children for trafficking while the use of children for commercial sexual exploitation is one factor increasing demand (Fitzgibbon, 2003).

Regarding the dignity of work for adults, Amartya Sen (2000) notes the importance of employment itself to social dignity, an idea echoing Aristotelian concerns that the happy life is one of reason concerned with action. Beyond its impact on income, Sen notes that losing employment leads to social exclusion and fewer opportunities to make decisions as well as a weakening of social values including the growth of cynicism about the fairness of social relations. Concerns with dignity might help to explain why millions of legitimate welfare claimants in the UK do not make claims (Sen, 1995).

Over time, it appears that the social stigma attached to unemployment has changed considerably. As noted in the previous chapter, there have been times when the wealthy have found it demeaning to work. At the other end of the scale, views of pauperism and begging have also changed. The tax list of Augsburg for 1475 noted 107 taxpayers (out of a total 4,485) whose profession was listed as begging. Indeed, there was a widespread idea of the nobility of poverty and reliance on others, reflected most obviously in the life and following of St. Francis (although that example points out that the nouveaux pauvres were perhaps more worthy than the poor who had always been with us).

During the sixteenth century the view of begging began to change as the work ethic took root (Geremek, 1997). Porter (1999) argues that rocketing population growth combined with the spread of disease and famine after 1500 changed the view of beggars from 'God's holy ones' to dangerous rogues requiring discipline. The spread of pauperism overwhelmed traditional means of assistance, creating agitation against the 'undeserving poor'. Economic change which increased growth may, then, have worsened the social stigma of unemployment.

Edwin Chadwick, who ended his career convinced that poverty was the result of the declining health of poor people living in urban decay, had a prior incarnation as a key figure in the design of the new British Poor Laws during the Industrial Revolution as Secretary to the Poor Law Commission. At that point, he was a firm believer that the old system was too generous and encouraged waste and idleness (Porter, 1999). The Poor Law Amendment Act of 1834 was largely a result of his work. This stipulated that authorities should not give help to able-bodied individuals outside of a workhouse. Workhouse food, bedding and so on should be of a lower standard than those available to the lowest-paid labourer, and groups of paupers should be separated (including husbands and wives). Notices posted on workhouse doors suggested that 'By work I am nourished, by work I am punished' and that the building was 'For the Poor and the Wicked' (Geremek, 1997).

Regardless of the harshness of relief systems, the risk of being thrown into unemployment during the Industrial Revolution was considerably larger in growing urban areas than rural areas (Fernandez-Armesto, 2001) and partially as a result, pauperism expanded dramatically, as we have seen.

In the more recent past, official attitudes towards unemployment have softened with the introduction of unemployment benefit. But the link between low unemployment and income growth in wealthy countries has remained weak. Overall, employment rates were higher in the 1950s and 1960s in both the US and Europe when GDP per capita was considerably lower than it is today. And unemployment in the UK over the last twenty five years has remained stubbornly higher than in previous decades in times of high and low growth alike.

For those employed, Adam Smith was concerned that the simplifying of tasks by division of labour would cause the spread of work that was tedious in the extreme and far from what Aristotelians might consider rewarding employment:

> The man whose whole life is spent in performing a few simple operations... generally becomes as stupid and ignorant as it is possible for a human creature to become ... But in every improved and civilised society this is the state into which the laboring poor, that is the great body of the people, must necessarily fall, unless government takes some pains to prevent it (Smith, 1910).

Smith saw education as the primary policy remedy, but this does not seem to tackle the problem identified by him that tasks simplified by the division of labour make for tedious jobs. Smith himself noted that agriculture, where the division of labour was far more limited, made for considerably more interesting employment, suggesting that tedious work was a problem that the industrial revolution exacerbated. In 1700, agriculture accounted for 56 percent of British employment and industry for 22 percent. By 1890, agriculture accounted for 16 percent, and industry for 43 percent (Maddison, 2001). In 1848, Mill complained that the Industrial Revolution had developed as predicted by Smith: 'it is questionable if all the mechanical inventions yet made have lightened the day's toil of any human being. They have enabled a greater proportion to live the same life of drudgery and imprisonment' (Mill, 1985).

Since the 1700s we have also seen a dramatic rise in service jobs, which now account for over 70 percent of employment in the UK. These jobs, too, are increasingly made up of a series of frequently repeated, highly regimented tasks — not least after Ray Kroc brought assembly-line practices to the fast food industry. Approximately a third of the British workforce believes that their jobs require no skills or qualifications (Westwood, 2002). Overall job satisfaction in the UK, measured by the percentage of people completely or very satisfied with their jobs overall fell from 52 to 45 percent 1992–2000.

The 'new economy' does not appear to be creating many more of the types of jobs that Aristotelians would see as comparatively dignified, or that Marx imagined for the post-revolutionary period (where one would 'hunt in the morning, fish in the afternoon, rear cattle in the evening, criticize after dinner' according to the *German Ideology*). One example is the call center, where there is very high staff turnover and employees complain about monotony, frustration and stress. Indeed, measured levels of stress match those experienced by coal miners (Wallace et al. 2000). Three quarters of women in call centers have been victims of verbal abuse (Chappell and Di Martino, 2006).

Harassment remains a considerable problem across job types. 53 percent of all employees in the UK report having been a victim of bullying at work. Furthermore, many service jobs are particularly prone to incidents of harassment and bullying. In the European Union, hotel and catering workers are three time more likely than the average worker to suffer sexual harassment, and public administration workers are 50 percent more likely to suffer bullying (Chappell and Di Martino, 2000, 2006).

Across countries, using a measure of 'decent work' that encompasses employment status, pay, hours of work, gender equality in employment and pension measures, Ahmed (2003) concludes that while GDP per capita is related to these measures, 'high levels of decent work can be achieved without high incomes and ... high incomes do not guarantee high levels of decent work.'

## Non-Income Determinants of Choice and Value

We have seen that it is possible to achieve high school enrollment levels, civil rights and comparatively strong levels of dignity at work even in countries with low incomes, whilst high income or income growth are by no means a guarantee of progress in these areas. Instead of a close link to economic change, it may be that expansion of civil and political rights as well as educational opportunities is part of a process of social change. As a result, improvements appear to be a matter of long-term development. For example, it appears that one of the best predictors of democratic status in the future is democratic status in the past. This is an idea that Persson and Tabellini (2006) label 'democratic capital.'[4]

Similarly, Michael Clemens (2004) has found strong evidence of an 'adoption curve' regarding education. He shows that it is easy and accurate to predict how many children will be in school in twenty years time by looking at how many children are in school today. Across countries and over time, there appears to be a standard path of progress from low levels of enrollment to high levels. Initially slow rates of progress increase exponentially to an inflection point, and then the rate of increase in enrollment slows as education reaches ubiquity. One can imagine why this might be the case. It takes time to expand stocks of physical capital supporting education (schools, roads to schools). More importantly, parents who have been to school are far more likely to send their children to school. And a larger number of educated young adults provides for a larger pool from which to draw the next generation of teachers.

Amongst other causal factors, cross-country research suggests that urbanization and expanded civil and economic rights might both drive enrollments to some extent.[5] Given our discussion of the importance of relative income, it is also notable that income *inequality* correlates with lower measures of both educational attainment and democracy, as well as a number of other measures related to dignity across countries (Thorbecke and Charumilind, 2002, Gradstein and Milanovic, 2002).

Regarding liberty, at the same time as differing institutional determinants at the national level have played a role, it is clear that global change has played an important part, in a process akin to the technological advance that has propelled improvements in welfare. The global acceptability of totalitarianism has fallen, in part because of its atrocious record in improving welfare outcomes, in part because of the end of the Cold War.

The time at which governmental institutions started their development towards providing greater political and educa-

---

[4]  It should be noted that Persson and Tabellini do also find GDP per capita related to democratization in their study.

[5]  Esposto and Zaleski, 1999, Moore et al., 1999, Baldacci et al., 2004.

tional opportunities might in part have been determined by climate and disease burdens which shaped the initial nature of the institutions themselves. The physical and environmental conditions present in colonial areas had a significant impact on the nature and extent of colonial settlements and resulting political and economic structures. In the Southern colonies of the Americas, for example, soils and climates were better suited to lucrative crops grown on large farms with cheap labour (usually slaves). Tropical climates created disease burdens which deterred large settler populations and thereby encouraged extractive models of economic institutions (slavery, resource extraction) rather than models focused on local accumulation. In contrast, further North disease burdens were lower while climate and soils favoured mixed farming on smallholder plots better suited to large settler populations, frequently made up of immigrants that were already educated to some degree.

Areas dominated by small settler populations, in a desperate race to extract wealth before they succumbed to diseases, developed extreme economic, educational and political inequalities. Areas where settlers made up a considerable proportion of the population and where settlers intended to stay for the long term developed more equitable conditions. In the early 1900s, 75 percent of adult US males living in rural areas owned land, compared to 2.4 percent in Mexico. In 1870, over 80 percent of US adults were literate, compared to 16 percent in Brazil and Jamaica. Around 1880, three percent of Chileans had the vote compared to 18 percent of US citizens (Acemoglu et al. 2001, Engerman and Sokoloff, 2005). This 'institutional deficit' dating back to the colonial period might help to account for lower levels of institutional development today, due to the later start in terms of progress in liberty and educational outcomes.

At the same time, there are significant limits to such an interpretation. The differing outcomes we have seen between North and South Korea, Taiwan and mainland China, Haiti and the Dominican Republic, Botswana and Zimbabwe or East and West Germany all suggest the need for considerable caution in suggesting that climate is destiny in any strong sense. In some cases, climate may have been one factor in determining institutional development, but there are a number of others. Climatological determinism is a poor excuse for abuse of basic civil rights or denying educational opportunities.

## Income and Prestige in History

In 1714, Bernard Mandeville, in *The Fable of the Bees* discussed the nature of conspicuous consumption:

> The Druggist, Mercer, Draper and other creditable Shopkeepers can find no difference between themselves and Merchants, and therefore dress and live like them. The Merchant's Lady, who cannot bear the Assurance of those Mechaniks, flies for refuge to the other End of Town, and scorns to follow any Fashion but what she takes from thence. This haughtiness alarms the court ... the contrivance of fashion becomes all their Study, that they may have always new Modes ready to take up, as soon as those saucy Cits. shall begin to imitate those in being (quoted in Mason, 1998).[6]

The control of a fashion arms race between the classes was long an important area of public policy. Sumptuary laws were often introduced as a way to avoid widespread expenditures on fripperies, but increasingly they became a way to ensure that distinctions of social class were preserved in the face of the growing wealth of the lower orders. The express purpose of Elizabeth's sumptuary laws were to prevent 'the disorder and confusion of the degrees of classes' (although it is not clear to what extent limiting silk underwear to knights' wives controlled this disorder, at least in public) (Baldwin, 1926).

Adam Smith felt that the pursuit of riches was primarily driven by 'regard to the sentiment of mankind... to be observed, to be attended to, to be taken notice of...' (quoted in Hirschman, 1977). He found it 'a means most vulgar and most obvious' (Smith, 1910), but felt nonetheless that the pursuit of income was a good way of channeling men's desires in a manner that did more good (or at least less harm) than any other

---

[6]   Cf. Veblen (1987): 'A satiation of the average or general desire for wealth is out of the question ... no general increase of the community's wealth can make any approach to satiating this need, the ground of which is the desire of every one to excel every one else in the accumulation of goods.'

(Fitzgibbons, 1995). Because income was largely pursued as a source of regard, Smith noted that there was a tradeoff to be had between jobs with high income and those to which high honor was attached, independent of their pay scale. 'Honor makes a great part of the reward of all honorable professions. In point of pecuniary gain, all things considered, they are generally undercompensated' (Smith, 1910).

At the other end of the scale, as we have seen, Adam Smith felt that the minimum wage should cover the purchase of goods that 'the established rules of decency have rendered necessary.' Sadly, his idea was not adopted and the Industrial Revolution did little in the UK to improve the dignity of the working poor.[7] The income share of the top ten percent of the British population rose from 44 percent in 1688 to 49 percent in 1803 and to 53 percent in 1867 (it is about 27 percent today) (Lindert, 1986). The atrocious nature of life in British urban slums was a cause of the growing class divide—the *Communist Manifesto* was based in part on Engels' experience of Manchester.[8]

---

[7]  As a result of declining inequality and changing prices, it is worth noting one way that the rich at least in the UK are notably worse off than they were in mid-nineteenth-century Britain –today's pound doesn't buy you nearly as many butlers as it used to. In 1857, a household with an income of 500 pounds would tend to have a cook, house-maid, parlour-maid *and* a butler, according to Burnett (1974). 500 pounds translates to about 30,000 pounds in today's money (according to the CPI calculations at http://www.pierre-marteau.com/currency/indices/uk-02.html). Sadly, 30,000 pounds is no longer enough to hire even one decently experienced butler. The Prince of Wales' household staff (which includes two butlers, a master of the household, an assistant master of the household, a full-time and part-time equerry, a valet, four chefs, two chauffeurs and twenty three and a half other staff (in full-time equivalents) costs him approximately 73,000 pounds per person, for example (www.princeofwales.gov.uk/about/annualreview_2005.html).

[8]  British philanthropist David Urquhart blamed the growth of class antagonism on the fact that the rich had begun bathing while the poor increasingly stank. His prophylactic solution to revolution was to build Turkish baths in poor neighborhoods (A. Kenny, 1997). This was an interesting reversal of a previous trend. Public steam baths were in fact fairly widespread as early as the thirteenth century, but they were used for more than just personal hygiene and lost favour during the syphilis epidemic from the end of the fifteenth century (Porter, 1999).

## Income, Poverty and Prestige in the Modern World

The stigma attached to poverty and the regard attached to wealth has remained firmly in place. Frank (1997) argues that concerns with status help to account for wage distributions within firms that are more compressed than we would expect were it not for relative income concerns, and (echoing Smith) that there is a strong negative correlation between the extent to which an employee's occupation is viewed as being socially responsible and their annual earnings. The status importance of income is also demonstrated in people's responses to relative income concerns. A survey of Harvard students found that the majority of students asked if they would rather earn $100,000 while others got twice as much, or $50,000 while others got half as much, chose lower absolute income and higher relative income ($50,000 whilst others earned $25,000) (Dowling, 2005). Indeed, so important is relative income that in experiments where people can pay some of their own money to reduce the amount of money that other (richer) subjects have been given, two thirds of subjects will 'burn' richer subjects' money (Zizzo and Oswald, 2000). The (continuing) relative definition of wealth may help to explain why less than 0.5 percent of Americans are willing to label themselves as rich (Myers, 1992) and only 9 percent of those with a net worth between $1 to $4 million admit to being rich (Coniff, 2002).

The relative status of wealth and poverty is also clear from the relationship between perceptions of poverty and average incomes. 'Absolute' poverty lines are designed to measure the level of income necessary to avoid poverty in a manner supposed to take no account of the wealth of others or relative income concerns. Fisher (1995) notes that there is an impressive body of empirical evidence from the United States, Britain, Canada and Australia that successive poverty lines developed over time which were designed to be absolute in fact show a pattern of increasing as fast as average incomes were rising. These 'absolute' poverty lines tend to have remained roughly equal to a constant proportion of average incomes (an exception, of course, has been the official US poverty line since the 1960s). Over time, 'subsistence baskets' in the United States, for example, have expanded in both quantity and extent. The minimum acceptable weight of high-protein foods for a family of four per week increased from 22 pounds in 1908 to 55 pounds in 1960. In addition, between 1908 and 1960, allowances for electricity were added as well as the cost of 520 car journeys (all of this expanding basic needs to cover lighting, refrigeration, ironing and transport).

Popular definitions of what is required to 'get along' have been rising considerably, as well. Today, more than half of Americans say that they cannot afford everything that they really need (Graham et. al. 2004).[9] This is because the impression of what people 'really need' has been expanding. In the UK between 1983 and 1999, the percentage of people who thought that having a friend or family member visit for a meal was something that 'everybody should be able to afford' increased from 32 to 65 percent. The percentage who thought a telephone was a necessity rose from 43 to 72 percent. Other items increasingly seen as necessary included computers, video recorders, dishwashers, cars and going out for a meal (C. Kenny, 2005).

Similar findings hold around the world. Across countries, Cantril (1965) found an anecdotal definition of what was required for a decent standard of living that was highly correlated with income. Regular surveys asking Philippinos if they are poor have seen no downward trend as the Philippines gets richer (Ravallion and Lokshin, 2001). A survey of rural people living near six towns and cities in Tanzania provides some evidence of the relative nature of poverty even in a country where the majority of people subsist on less than two dollars a day. Survey respondents were asked to classify themselves into very poor, poor, average, rich and very rich. None classified themselves as very rich, although nearly one percent classified themselves as rich (a higher proportion than in the US).

Of the six districts, the area around Lindi had the lowest household income—around $330 per year. The areas around Arusha and Dar es Salaam had the highest average household

---

[9]    This despite the fact that between 1958 and 1999, personal disposable per capita income in the US rose 131 percent, and personal consumption expenditures increased 140 percent (Redmond, 2001).

incomes of the six regions — $2,000 for Dar es Salaam and $2,120 for Arusha. But the percentage of people who felt rich was almost exactly the same in Lindi and Arusha, and the proportion of people who felt poor was actually higher in Dar es Salaam than in Lindi. Perhaps unsurprisingly, when asked to categorize what counted as an average, rich or very rich income, the respondents in the area of Lindi suggested incomes that were about one half of those proposed by people living near Dar es Salaam.[10]

Indeed, even the global community's definition of 'what is a poor country' appears to change over time to reflect growing incomes worldwide. Rosenstein-Rodan's paper for the *Review of Economics and Statistics* in 1961 provided academic backing for the emerging consensus around a 0.7 percent aid target for rich countries. He calculated the investment needs of 'underdeveloped' countries in order to meet specific growth targets, the gap between current investment rates and those required to meet the growth target, and the percentage of 'rich world' income required in investment transfers in order to fill that gap. The figure came to approximately 0.7 percent of rich country GNP. The problems with such an approach are legion, but what is of more interest here is what Rosenstein-Rodan considered a 'rich' country — one that should be donating money in order to help 'poor' countries grow.

Rosenstein-Rodan suggested that any country with an income per capita of $600 ought to be a donor. He attempted to calculate internationally comparable measures of income allowing for the different purchasing power of a dollar in his potential donor countries, and calculated that in 1960 GNP per capita for Italy was around $900 in 1960 US dollars, for example. Using US inflation data, this is approximately equal to

---

[10]  C. Kenny, 2005c, see also Laderchi, Saith and Stewart, 2002, on Peru and related work by Pradhan and Ravallion, 2000 on Jamaica. It may be that who the comparators are changes over time, not least with the introduction of new communications technologies. Myers (1992) reports that there was a strong correlation between the introduction of televisions in US cities and the increases in rates of theft. Where TV became available in 1951, thefts jumped in that year, where it became available in 1955, thefts jumped then (although one wonders if it was only that people were stealing TVs).

$4,240 in 2000 US dollars. Given his suggested cut-off was two thirds of Italy's per capita income, this suggests that any country with an income per capita of above $3,000 in 2000 dollars should be considered a 'rich' donor country. If this standard were adopted today, the pool of donor countries would be significantly larger than it is. Amongst at least 74 new donors would be China, Indonesia, Nicaragua, Egypt, the Philippines, Cape Verde, Paraguay, Peru, Namibia, Brazil, Russia, Mexico and Malaysia. What it is to be poor isn't what it used to be at the international level, either.[11]

What drives changes in relative income across time within countries? Cross-country studies have some difficulty in determining robust relationships, in part because levels of inequality usually change so slowly (Dollar and Kraay, 2002). Having said that, at least in the case of wealthy countries, it may be possible to make a judgment based on patterns of change in inequality over the recent past. In the 1920s, the top 0.1 percent of the population in the US, the UK, France and Japan earned between 6–8 percent of total income. From 1950 to 1980, this share dropped to around two percent in all four countries. But in the next twenty years, the US top earner share climbed back to nearly eight percent while the UK rose above 3 percent (Piketty and Saez, 2006). This suggests that more generous welfare arrangements, progressive tax regimes and tougher labour laws may have played a role in holding down inequality.

At the same time, Krugman (1994) notes that more generous unemployment benefits correlate with higher unemployment rates across countries at any one time, suggesting that there may be some tradeoffs involved in preserving different elements of dignity. Krugman argues that different benefit packages do not help to explain far higher unemployment rates in Europe in the 1980s onward than these countries faced previ-

---

[11]  An alternate approach produces similar, if less dramatic results. The Penn World Tables suggest that Italy's purchasing power parity per capita GDP in 1960 was $6,890 in 2000 US dollars, and therefore suggests a 'cut-off' of $4,600 for developing countries. This still suggests that countries such as Paraguay, Colombia, Algeria, Tunisia, Iran and Belarus should be considered developed.

ously (in 1973, European Union average unemployment rates were below three percent). Instead, he suggests that rapidly growing inequality in the US and rapidly growing unemployment in Europe are both driven by technological change which has penalized unskilled workers. He suggests no easy fixes for this problem. Subsidized employment, that had apparently worked in Sweden until the 1990s, began to fail (and become ruinously expensive) after that, for example.

## Conclusion

There has been global progress in the spread of dignity. Civil rights, and in particular women's rights, may be more widespread today than at any point in history. Levels of child labour are falling, whilst levels of education are increasing, worldwide. Nonetheless, there remain many countries where basic civil rights are not respected. There are considerable gaps in gender and ethnic equality. The quantity and quality of work remains low in countries rich and poor. Significant numbers lack sufficient relative income to avoid social stigma. If the story of improvements in dignity is in considerable part an institutional one, however, this suggests that progress in such indicators is likely to be incremental, because institutions develop very slowly. Furthermore, at least in the area of employment and relative income, it may be that we lack the policy tools to achieve considerably better results, at least without facing tradeoffs.

# PART FOUR

# CONTENTMENT

# Chapter 7

# *Mental States and their Measurement*

## Introduction

Do people know when they are happy? If the most important elements in happiness are welfare and dignity, then individuals are not necessarily the best authorities on their own condition. We may be mistaken about the state of our bodily health, and our acquiescence in our social status may be the result of ignorance and lack of imagination. But surely each person is in the best position to say whether he or she is contented or not? If that is so, then while an Aristotelian may tell me that other people may know better than I whether I am truly happy, a Benthamite will surely allow me to have the last word on the topic, since happiness, for him, is essentially the same thing as contentment.

Contentment is undoubtedly a psychological state, and since the time of Descartes it has been very widely accepted that individuals are the ultimate authority on their own mental states, even though they may be dependent on trainers and doctors for the best information about their bodily states. But the matter is not simple, because there is more than one way of drawing the boundary between mind and body. For Aristotle and his successors prior to Descartes, the mind was essentially the faculty, or set of faculties, that set off human beings from other animals. Dumb beasts and human beings shared certain abilities and activities: dogs, cows, pigs and humans could all see and hear and feel, they all had in common the faculty or faculties of sensation. But only human beings could think abstract thoughts and take rational decisions: they were marked off from the other animals by the possession of intellect and will, and it was these two faculties that essentially constituted the mind. Intellectual activity, according to this tradition, was in a particular sense immaterial, whereas sensation was impossible without a material body.

### Cartesian Consciousness

For Descartes and many others after him, the boundary between mind and mater was set elsewhere. It was consciousness, not intelligence or rationality, that was the defining criterion of what is mental rather than corporeal. The mind, on this view, is the realm of whatever is accessible to introspection. It included therefore not only human understanding and willing, but also human seeing, hearing, feeling, pain and pleasure. For Descartes as for Aristotle, the mind was what distinguished humans from other animals, but the grounds of the distinction were different. Aristotelians thought that while only humans had intellects, animals no less than humans had sensations; Descartes denied that animals had genuine sensation because he denied that they were conscious. The bodily machinery that accompanies human sensation might, he agreed, occur also in animal bodies. But a phenomenon like pain, in an animal, was a purely mechanical event unaccompanied by the sensation that is felt by humans in pain.

Not many thinkers imitated Descartes by denying genuine sensation to animals. But many philosophers in the seventeenth, eighteenth, and nineteenth centuries followed him in accepting consciousness, rather than rationality, as the defining mark of the mind. The effect of this was to confer a special authority upon first-person expressions of mental experiences, activities, and states. Mental life, on this view, was something especially private (A. Kenny, 1968).

The intellectual capacities which distinguish language-using humans from dumb animals, and which were seen by the Aristotelians as the essential features of the mind, are not marked by any particular privacy. Whether Smith understands quantum physics, or whether his philanthropy is motivated by political ambition, is something that a third party may be in a better position to judge than Smith himself. In matters such as the understanding of scientific theory and the pursuit of long-term goals the subject's own sincere statement is not the last possible word.

On the other hand, if I want to know what sensations someone is having, then I have to give his utterances a special status. If I ask him whether he is in pain, or feels hungry, or what he is seeing in his mind's eye, what he says in reply cannot be mistaken. Of course it need not be true — he may be insincere, or misunderstand the words he is using — but it cannot be erroneous. Experiences of this kind have a certain indubitability, and it was this property that Descartes took as the essential feature of thought. Such experiences are private to their owners in the sense that while others can doubt them, they cannot.

Of course Descartes did not deny that we are often mistaken about what we see — in the dark mistaking a tree for a man, for instance, or being misled about something's colour because of a trick of the light. But in such a case, he said, we are misinterpreting a datum of consciousness which, considered purely in itself, cannot be doubted. If I ask someone what she seems to see, or what she seems to hear, then I have to take her word for it. With regard to these basic data of consciousness the conscious subject is in a position of special authority.

Among the private experiences that enjoy this status Descartes gave a special place to what he called 'the passions of the soul', by which he meant sentiments such as joy, fear and anger. These experiences, he maintained, were received into the soul in the same fashion as the objects of the exterior senses, and were known by us in exactly the same manner. But they were marked out by the greatest degree of infallibility, because unlike other experiences they were incapable of misleading us. We may be deceived, he said, by perceptions referred to external bodies, as in the examples above. We can also be deceived by perceptions referred to our own bodies, such as feelings of hunger and pain: we may feel hungry when we are not really in need of food, and we may feel pain in a phantom limb. But we cannot be deceived in the same way by our passions. 'They are so close and so interior to our soul' Descartes wrote 'that it is impossible that they should be felt without their being in reality just as they are felt ... Even if a man is asleep and dreaming, it is impossible that he should feel sad, or feel moved by any other passion, without it being strictly true that such a passion is in the soul' (A. Kenny, 1963, 2).

In the present context it has been worth dwelling on Descartes' account of the mind, because those who identified happiness with utility, or pleasure, or contentment, clearly thought of it as a 'passion of the soul' of the kind he describes. Such a concept is also at the root of the idea that the best way to find out whether people are happy is to ask them. Their first-person response will have a special authority that no other evidence could claim or challenge.

## Wittgenstein on Mental Events and States

In the twentieth century Wittgenstein offered a radical criticism of the whole Cartesian system. It is wrong, he argued, to suppose that each of us has access to a private realm of consciousness, from which we have to think our way out to a public world. Even in our most secret thoughts we are using a language that only makes sense in the context of social activities shared with other beings like ourselves.

To understand the nature of our different feelings and emotions we have to take account of the context of environment and activity in which they find their expression. If we do so we will find that rather than indubitability being a universal feature attaching to mental experiences of all kinds, the degree to which we enjoy first-person authority in expressing our mental states and activities varies from case to case. There is a wide spectrum ranging from dreaming at one extreme to sincerity at another. A person's authority in reporting a dream is absolute; her assurance of sincerity, on the other hand, may be worthless in the face of her actual behaviour (Wittgenstein, 1953).

Wittgenstein's denial that there are private and incommunicable experiences does not mean that he is a behaviorist: he is not identifying experience or emotions with behaviour, or even with dispositions to behave. However, he insists that there is a more than contingent connection between experiences of various kinds and capacities, or dispositions, to behave in certain ways. Wittgenstein makes a distinction between two kinds of evidence that we may have for the obtaining of states of affairs, namely *symptoms* and *criteria*. Where the connection between a certain kind of evidence and the conclusion drawn from it is a matter of empirical discovery, through theory and induction, the evidence may be called a *symptom* of the state of affairs; where the relation between evidence and conclusion is not something discovered by empirical investigation, but is something that must be grasped by anyone who possesses the concept of the state of affairs in question, then the evidence is not a mere symptom, but a *criterion* of the event in question. A red sky at night may be a symptom of fine weather tomorrow: but when tomorrow comes the shining of the sun and the clearness of the sky are not symptoms, but criteria, for the weather's being fine.

Exploiting the notion of *criterion* enabled Wittgenstein to steer between the Scylla of dualism and the Charybdis of behaviorism. He agreed with dualists that particular mental events could occur without accompanying bodily behaviour; on the other hand he agreed with behaviourists that the possibility of ascribing to people mental acts and states depends on such mental items having, in general, a behavioural expression. Each basic emotion, for instance, is related to a particular type of expression in behaviour.

The dualist picture was that one learned the names of particular emotions by observing in one's own private experience the occurrence of a sample of that emotion. The problem with this view is that one would never know that the experience one called by the name of a particular emotion was the same as that which others called by the same name. In its place, Wittgenstein offered a different account of the learning of meanings. In the case of sensations, for instance, words are connected with their primitive and natural expressions, and then used in the place of those expressions. Thus a child hurts herself and she cries; adults talk to her and teach her exclamations and later sentences, replacing primitive pain-behaviour with linguistic response (Wittgenstein 1953, I, 244).

## The Criteria of Emotions

In a similar way we learn the meaning of words for emotions. The child runs to his mother and she says 'don't be frightened!' or he trembles, and she asks: 'What are you afraid of?' But the emotions are connected not only with appropriate behaviour, but also with appropriate contexts. If a child cries we will know whether it is pain-behaviour or emotional behaviour only if we know whether he is crying because, say, he has bumped his head or because he has been left alone. The language of the emotions must therefore be taught in connection not only with emotional behaviour, but above all in connection with objects of emotion. It is in connection with fearful objects, pleasant tastes, and annoying circumstances that the child learns the verbal expression of fear, pleasure and anger.

The concept of each emotion is linked with non-emotional concepts in three ways. The concept, for example, of fear, stands on three struts: fearful circumstances, symptoms of fear, and action taken to avoid what is feared. In the standard case of fear, which is both the paradigm for learning and the most easily intelligible, all three factors will be present. The man-eating lion advances roaring; the defenceless planter screams, pales, and take to his heels. His later report 'I was terrified' is as fully intelligible as such a report can be. But the verbal expression of fear remains intelligible when one, or even two, of these factors is absent but the third remains. People suffering from claustrophobia or agoraphobia show symptoms of fear and take avoiding action in circumstances that are not dangerous and not frightening to most people. In other cases, in fearful circumstances the victim shows symptoms of fear but takes no avoiding action—rooted to the spot, perhaps, as he watches the uncoiling cobra. Thirdly, we have the cases where there is danger, and avoiding action, but no symptoms of fear: the tranquil taking of a prophylactic against some disease, for instance.

In these cases, two out of the three listed features have been present to render intelligible any verbal expression of fear which occurs in their context. There are also cases where only one of the props remains to support the admission of being afraid. The soldier marches resolutely into battle, with upper lip stiff and no thought of running away. Symptoms and avoiding action are absent, but the circumstances alone render intelligible any later admission of fear. Or a man makes a policy of never travelling in trains, at whatever cost of inconvenience. Trains are in fact, we are reliably informed, the least dangerous form of transport, and because our neurotic never goes near a train we never catch him trembling or whimpering. Still, his perseverance in his policy is itself enough to render intelligible his coy admission 'I am afraid of trains'.

However, if all three of the features we have identified are missing, there seems to be no foothold at all for fear. If a man says that he feels frightened, but is in no danger, shows no sign of fear and takes no particular action, we will be puzzled; and our puzzlement will turn to complete incomprehension if, when asked why he is afraid, he says 'because it is five to three and I always feel like this at five to three'. Would we not wonder why, whatever he felt, he called his feeling 'fear'? If he regularly used the word in this way, it would clearly lose all meaning. Any word in an unknown language which was regularly so used would clearly not mean 'fear' (A. Kenny, 1963, 45).

In the present context the point of these general considerations about the expression of mental states such as emotions is to stress that we are not dealing with a matter of a simple report on a private phenomenon. The very intelligibility of the expression of emotions depends upon their behavioural and environmental context. This must be particularly borne in mind when we are considering the role of mental states in the good life, and the value to be placed on self-ascriptions of them. So let us now turn directly to the topic of contentment — the mental state that for some philosophers is identical with happiness, and for all philosophers is one ingredient of happiness.

## Contentment and Pleasure

Rather than speaking of contentment, Bentham and his utilitarian followers spoke of pleasure, which they identified with
happiness. In our view Bentham was mistaken both in identifying happiness with pleasure, and in his conception of pleasure itself. Contentment is a much more enduring state than
pleasure. One can feel moments of genuine pleasure — sexual,
say, or gustatory — in the middle of a long period of misery;
and one may be genuinely content without, at a particular
moment in time, being aware of any pleasant sensation. One
can feel pleasure for a brief instant, no matter what went
before or followed that instant, but there could not be a tiny
period of sheer contentment in abstraction from of any preceding or subsequent context. One can feel intense pleasure while
realising that the pleasure will shortly cease; one cannot similarly be fully content while realising that the contentment is
about to come to an end. To be sure, a happy life will include
many pleasures, and a happy person is one who enjoys his life.
But that does not mean that contentment and pleasure are
identical.

Pleasure itself, however, is not a simple matter. Enjoyment
may be thought of as being distinct from, or as being identical
with, what is enjoyed. Bentham took the former view, and
regarded pleasure as a particular sensation which might be
caused by the most diverse objects. Aristotle, on the other
hand, offered the following argument to show that pleasure is
not a single uniform sensation. Actions are performed better if
accompanied by pleasure than if not: the more we enjoy doing
philosophy the better we philosophise. But if pleasure is
always the same, then an action will be improved by pleasure
derived from whatever source. On the contrary, Aristotle
maintained, activities are hindered by pleasures taken in other
activities: it is difficult to philosophise while having sex, and
flute-lovers cannot follow an argument if the flute is being
played next door. And in general, music while you work is a
poor substitute for enjoying your job (A. Kenny, 1963, 92).

It is, in fact, a mistake to think that what makes an activity or
experience pleasant is its being accompanied by a particular

sensation or class of sensations, in the way in which the writing of an essay may be made painful by its being accompanied with a headache. On such a view, the connection between the particular sensations and the objects that produce them would have to be learnt by experience. It would be a contingent matter that the pleasure of drinking did not occur while one was eating, nor the pleasure of climbing the Matterhorn while toasting crumpets.

Seeing the impossibility of defining pleasure as a sensation accompanying the action enjoyed, some philosophers have decided that it is actually identical with the action. Thus Ryle suggested:

> To say that a person has been enjoying digging is not to say that he has been both digging and doing or experiencing something else as a concomitant or effect of the digging; it is to say that he dug with his whole heart in the task, i.e. that he dug, wanting to dig, and not wanting to do anything else (or nothing) instead. His digging was a propensity fulfilment. His digging was his pleasure, and not a vehicle of his pleasure (Ryle, 1949, 108).

On this view, instead of asking 'When something is enjoyed, what happens that does not happen when it is not enjoyed' we should ask 'when something is enjoyed, what does not happen that does happen when it is not enjoyed?' A voluntary activity, we might say, is enjoyed unless there is some specific reason to the contrary; it is innocent of unpleasure until proved guilty. Thus Aristotle in one place defines pleasure as 'unimpeded operation'.

Neither the Benthamite nor the Aristotelian doctrine of pleasure seems altogether complete. Neither provides an explanation of why it is that pleasure is a motive for action, or why it is silly to ask someone why she wants pleasure. Like both of them, we may take these features as given, and observe that in any case contentment seems in fact more closely related conceptually to desire than to pleasure. To be contented is to feel that, broadly speaking, one's wants are being satisfied.

## Contentment and Desire

But if we are to fill out this sketch of a definition, we have to make at the outset a distinction between two kinds of wants. There are some wants where what is wanted is wanted for *now*, and the desire is unsatisfied, and perhaps grows, until what is wanted is obtained. Such wants include hunger, thirst, itching, sleepiness, and sexual desire. Other wants look forward to a perhaps remote date; as one can now want to go to Greece next summer, or to marry a certain woman once one has found a job.

Such wants are not frustrated every moment until the awaited day arrives; in one sense they are satisfied as soon as one has certainty that they will be realised. All animal wants are of the first, immediate, variety; long-term wants are peculiar to language users.

The enemy of contentment is unsatisfied desire: and some philosophers and religious thinkers have concluded that, given the limitations on human power, the way to contentment is to cut back desire. Epicurus, it will be remembered, distinguished between necessary and unnecessary desires. Some Hindu and Buddhist sages thought that desire should be altogether eliminated, so far as possible, and they have been echoed in the West by Schopenhauer. Even to the best of humans, Schopenhauer holds out no great hope of contentment. We are all creatures of will, and will of its nature is insatiable. The basis of all willing is need and pain, and we suffer until our needs are satisfied. But if the will, once satisfied, lacks objects of desire, then life becomes a burden of boredom. 'Thus life swings like a pendulum backwards and forwards between pain and ennui' (Schopenhauer, 1966, 312). All happiness is really and essentially negative, never positive.

The only sure way to escape the tyranny of the will, we are told, is by complete renunciation. What the will wills is always life; so if we are to renounce the will we must renounce the will to live. The mark of a good man, for Schopenhauer, is resignation, but a truly good man will gradually move beyond mere goodness to asceticism. He will abandon the will to live, which is the kernel of this miserable world. He will do all he can to disown the nature of the world as expressed in his own body: he will practice complete chastity, adopt voluntary poverty, and take up fasting and self-chastisement.

From the alternation between desire and satisfaction, Schopenhauer decided that life was a history of suffering and boredom; from the same premise he might with equal justification have concluded that it was a history of excitement and contentment. He provided no convincing reason, other than a prejudice in favour of pessimism, why we should adopt the ascetic programme with which he concludes. To be sure, the more philanthropic a person is, the more she will identify with the lives of others: but why should she identify only with their sufferings and not also with their joys? St Francis of Assisi mortified his flesh as severely as any Hindu mystic, and yet his prayer was that he would replace despair, darkness, and sadness with hope, light, and rejoicing.

Surely the path to happiness lies somewhere between the frenzied pursuit of every passing want and the total renunciation of desire. Contentment is perfectly compatible with having short-term animal wants that are unfulfilled. A healthy appetite and a level of sexual hunger may indeed contribute to contentment at a given time. It is not the actual non-fulfilment of desire, but the impossibility of its fulfilment, that destroys contentment. Not only Schopenhauer, but more sober philosophers such as Descartes, urged that when the world does not match our desires, it may be that the mismatch is to be remedied not by changing the world but by altering our desires. But a temperate control over our animal wants is itself a means to the satisfaction of longer term, overarching desires; and it is the satisfaction of those desires that is at the heart of contentment.

## First-person Reports

Contentment is not so much a feeling as a belief or judgement; a judgement that one's life, considered overall, as a whole, is going well, and that one's major desires are either satisfied or on the way to satisfaction. It is a judgement on these issues that the pollster wishes to elicit when he asks 'taking your life as a whole, would you consider yourself very happy, somewhat happy, or not happy at all?'

What value should be attached to the responses to these questions? Three issues arise; authority, sincerity, and consistency. Let us consider these in turn.

First, is each person in a position to pronounce accurately about his or her own contentment? The first person is certainly in a position of greater authority on the topic of contentment than she is on either the topics of welfare or of dignity. On the other hand, because an expression of contentment is a judgement about a long-term state, a person uttering it does not have the overriding authority that she would have if she were reporting a pain or narrating a dream. It is possible for a claim to contentment to be mistaken, and a person may well come to revise her own past estimates of her contentment. 'In those days I thought I was happy. Now I know better.' Or 'I wish I had realised how happy I was'. Again, if someone gives a positive answer to an inquiry about his contentment, but is regularly irritable, frequently quarrels with family and friends, is constantly trying to change his job, and often exhibits symptoms of psychosomatic illness, it may not be unreasonable to discount his evidence even if given in good faith.

But not all evidence is given in good faith: people may not always give a sincere answer to an inquiry about their state of contentment. Self-ascriptions may be misleading because a person may be too proud to reveal discontent, or too superstitious to boast of happiness. One may belong to a culture, or occupy a status, which is hostile to whingeing or fearful of hubris. Or one may refuse to give the answer that springs to mind, or any answer at all, because one regards the query as futile or impertinent.

The contentment that is a constituent of well-being must be an enduring, not a momentary state like a mood. But human beings are not necessarily good at predicting their own future contentment. We are not always clear in our minds what we really want, and even if we are, the satisfaction of our wishes does not always lead to happiness. St Teresa once said that more tears were shed over prayers that had been granted than over prayers that had not been answered. For this reason, if answers to happiness questionnaires are to be reliable sources of evidence, they need to show consistency over a period. Any method of inquiry that regularly produces answers that vary at different times of the day or different days of the month is measuring not stable contentment, but swings of mood.

When we compare answers to questionnaires, and conjoin them to make overall assessments, we may wonder whether all of the respondents mean the same thing by the word 'happy' in the question. It is, surely, very unlikely that they do. The problem is not simply that of the linguistic equivalence of synonyms for 'happy' in various languages; that is something that is easy enough to control for. Rather, as we have seen, philosophers and other thinkers using the same word in the same natural language have differed greatly in their understanding of happiness. Indeed, to make sense of the whole institution of happiness questionnaires, we have had to assume that they employ the word 'happy' in the sense of 'content'. And a positive or negative response to such a question is surely going to depend not so much on the linguistic competence of the respondent, as on his or her imagination, ambition, and character.

The problem is compounded when respondents are asked not just whether they are happy or not, but where they would place themselves upon a scale of happiness from one to five, or give themselves marks out of ten for well-being. Accuracy in answering here surely depends not just on unbiased introspection, but some estimate of an overall standard and of the position of other human beings relative to it. (One cannot answer the question 'are you very tall, tall, or not tall at all?' unless one has some idea of the height of people other than oneself.)

Despite all these problems, which will receive more detailed consideration in the following chapter, self-ascription does provide a rough and ready measure of contentment, which even if not particularly reliable in the individual case, can contribute to statistical studies of the well-being of large populations. We do, after all, place a degree of cautious reliance on political opinion polls, even though people are often unsure about their voting intentions and may give tactical rather than straightforward answers to the pollsters.

Avowals, however, whether spontaneous or solicited by researchers, are not the only expressions of contentment. Laughter, smiling, scowling, weeping, posture, comportment and other forms of non-linguistic bodily behaviour give us indications of other people's contentment or discontent. So too does the style and energy of their application to their daily tasks, and the spontaneity and cheerfulness of their social relationships. Such behavioural indications provide, to some extent, an objective check on the sincerity and reliability of linguistic expressions of subjective contentment.

Contentment, we have argued earlier, is only one element in well-being. Of course contentment is a valuable thing, and for individuals in many circumstances it may be well to aim at nothing more. Through no fault of my own the other elements in well-being may be beyond my reach. If I am going to remain poor and powerless for the rest of my life, I do best to trim my desires to those that can be satisfied in practice and count whatever blessings I have. But if this is a reasonable attitude to take with regard to one's own life, it is surely an inadequate one for those with power over and responsibility for the well-being of others. As far as possible we have to ensure not just that others are resigned to their narrow lot, but that they have appropriate options and wide horizons. 'They are perfectly happy as they are' is the slogan of the exploiter throughout the ages, whether it is slave-owners exploiting slaves, races exploiting races, or males exploiting females.

# Chapter 8

# *Subjective Well-being and its Correlates*

Throughout history, it is perhaps fair to say that the majority of people the majority of the time have been very conservative in their desires. People have wanted little more than adequate sustenance and the chance for a peaceful life as part of a community of family and friends. This perhaps helps to explain why the peasantry has that tended to make up revolutionary cannon-fodder were usually so reactionary. Skocpol (1976) argues that:

> When peasants 'rose' during historical social revolutionary crises, they did so in highly traditional rebellious patterns: bread riots, 'defense' of communal lands or customary rights, riots against 'hoarding' merchants or landlords, 'social banditry'. Peasants initially drew upon traditional cultural themes to justify rebellion. Far from being revolutionaries through adoption of a radical vision of a desired new society, 'revolutionary' peasants have typically been 'backward-looking' rebels incorporated by circumstances beyond their control into political processes occurring independently of them.

Similar worldviews appear to be reflected in many of the findings from the subjective well-being literature. People are highly risk averse. A stable life with family and friends, a good marriage and participation in a community of faith appears to be 'worth' many multiples of average incomes per capita amongst respondents to surveys in terms of impact on their self-reported happiness. Overall, the subjective happiness literature is not a good basis from which to build calls for a new world order. Nor, however, does it provide much comfort to those who see ever greater income as the key to global contentment.

## What Do Subjective Well-being Polls Measure?

Subjective well-being polls ask questions of the type 'taking your life as whole, would you consider yourself not happy, somewhat happy or very happy?' Such polls vary widely — sometimes respondents are asked to rank themselves on a ten point scale, sometimes they are asked about satisfaction with life rather than happiness per se, for example, but there are strong and reliable correlations between different instruments used to measure life satisfaction.

One should clearly treat the results of such surveys with caution. Elsewhere, we discuss why 'self-reported' happiness might be different from other conceptions of the term, but even ignoring such issues, 'happiness polls' suffer from the same weaknesses as any other poll. Surveyors can intentionally or unintentionally bias results by 'anchoring' questions. For example, if the pollster asks a group of students how happy they are, and then asks how many dates they went on last week, there is no correlation between the answers. If they reverse the question order (asking about dates first) there is a clear correlation in answers, as respondents focus on the 'number of dates' question while thinking about their level of contentment (Strack, Martin and Schwarz, 1988).

People can interpret polls in different ways. For example, the word used in many happiness studies in Slavic languages is usually restricted to rare moments of profound bliss rather than general contentment. Culture will also matter — Americans may smile more and say they are happy because it is expected of them. For similar reasons, people can also lie. It may be that certain groups of people or certain cultures find it inappropriate to respond that they are very happy or miserable, which could bias or bunch responses (Wierzbicka, 2004). Indeed, language enters significantly as a correlate with subjective wellbeing in cross-country studies (Dorn et al., 2005), which may reflect such biases.[1]

Nonetheless, the correlation across different survey instruments measure above is one reason to believe that subjective well-being surveys do capture an underlying 'psychological reality.' There are a number of other reasons. Representative well-being surveys conducted in quick succession report very similar levels of satisfaction and open-ended questions which probe the areas of life most relevant to answers regarding subjective well-being consistently point up the same areas — most importantly, family and friends. Those who say they are happy smile more than the average person, they more frequently express positive emotions, and they appear happier to friends, family and psychologists observing them. They sleep better, have higher self-esteem, feel more in control of their lives, are comparatively infrequent visitors to psychotherapists and are less likely to commit suicide. Those who report happiness have higher than average levels of activity in the left prefrontal region in the brain, which is rich in receptors for the neurotransmitter dopamine, and they also register higher concentrations of dopamine itself. At the same time, they register considerably lower levels of cortisol, an adrenal hormone related to the risk of obesity, hypertension and autoimmune conditions. In US surveys, cortisol levels are 32 percent lower in the highest self-reported happiness quintile than in the lowest.[2]

The voluminous evidence that subjective well-being responses are connected with physiological, psychological and third-party indicators of good feeling or well-being, and the fact that answers are correlated over time suggests some use for these responses as an indicator of contentment. In par-

---

[1]   It should be noted that subjective wellbeing surveyors go to considerable lengths to minimize the language problem, having one set of translators render the question into a second language and then a second set retranslate into the original to ensure accuracy, for example. A number of works suggest that such approaches do minimize potential problems. See the collection in Gullone and Cummins (eds) (2002).

[2]   Results from Cummins, 2002, Frank, 1997, Myers and Diener, 1996, Kahneman and Krueger, 2006, Helliwell, 2004.

ticular, it appears plausible to imagine such poll responses at least proxy as a measure of the stock of individual utility itself, as thought of by utilitarians or, indeed, by economists. This is also suggested by the fact that an increasing number of distinguished economists are using poll responses precisely as such a proxy.[3]

## Correlates with Subjective Well-being

A number of personal characteristics appear associated with subjective well-being responses. The self-professed happy have a higher degree of social interaction — they are more likely to initiate contact with friends, more likely to respond to requests for help and more likely to trust strangers. At the same time, they are less likely to be absent from work or to be involved in disputes when at work (McGill, 1967, Frank, 1997). Individuals who contribute to the public good of environmental protection report higher levels of satisfaction (Videras and Owen, 2006). In addition, those who score themselves as happy also see themselves as being more moral than the average person (Myers and Diener, 1996).

A sense of control appears to matter both for happiness and for health. Plous (1993) reports a study of residents of a nursing home in which one floor of patients were reminded by the administrator that they had control over how they spent their time, how they arranged their rooms and so on, and were given a plant to care for. On another floor, patients were told that the staff were there to take care of them and were given a plant that the nurses would take care of. Three weeks after this communication, 71 percent of residents who were told that the staff were there to take care of them were rated (by themselves and the staff) as having become more debilitated, while 93 percent of those told that they had decision-making power were rated as seeing an overall improvement in functioning. The importance of a sense of control is also reflected in findings of a negative correlation between subjective well-being

[3]     For example, Easterlin, 1974, Blanchflower and Oswald,1992, Helliwell, 1996, Kahneman et. al. 2004, Layard, 2005.

and alcoholism, incarceration, and living under an oppressive regime (Myers and Diener, 1996).

Beyond personality traits and a sense of control, there are a range of life conditions that appear to correlate with subjective well-being. Helliwell and Huang's (2006) study finds that the ability of government to deliver services, general levels of trust between people and trust in the police force, the importance of religion in people's lives, marital status, education, income and employment are all significant determinants of subjective well-being. Together these factors are related to about 17 percent of the variation in subjective well-being between people.[4] Employment status is amongst the stronger determinants found in the literature, it has an impact out of all proportion to its effect through income, and an impact larger than divorce, for example. Frey and Stutzer (2002) find that unemployment reduces self-reported happiness by 1.65 points on a ten-point scale. The effect is particularly noticeable amongst the first-time unemployed.

The particulars of what makes people subjectively happy vary by culture, ideology and location. Unemployed people suffer less unhappiness if they live in areas where many other are unemployed, and suffer more in communities where there is a strong social norm to live off one's own income. Self-esteem is more closely correlated with subjective well-being in individualist versus collectivist cultures. Right-wingers are made more upset by inflation and left-wingers by unemployment (Frey and Stutzer, 2002). Obese people in Russia report greater happiness, in the US they report lower levels of happiness than the non-obese (Graham and Felton, 2005). Nonetheless, it appears that status, control, and levels of social interaction are universal determinants of subjective happiness across cultures.

## Income and Subjective Well-being

Within countries at any one time, rich people report marginally higher subjective well-being than poor people. Across

[4]   This as measured by the R-squared of a regression analysis containing these variables.

countries at any one time, richer countries have higher average self-reported happiness than poor countries. Variation in incomes in the United States at any one time is correlated with about two to five percent of the variation in subjective well-being between people (Ahuvia and Friedman, 1998). Put another way, two to five percent of the differences in subjective well-being between people is related to differences in incomes between them. There appears to be a considerable declining marginal utility to income in terms of subjective well-being – in other words, the impact of an extra dollar on the subjective well-being of a poor person is considerably higher than the impact of the same dollar on a millionaire.

At the same time, US and European data make clear that differences in income between people in the same country are a comparatively minor source of variation in self-reported happiness in that country. The considerable differences in US income (the lowest ten percent of the population share two percent of total income, the richest ten percent share 30 percent of total income) are associated with a maximum of five percent of the differences in subjective well-being between individuals. In a recent study of German self-reported happiness, an individual would need an income increase of over 800,000% in order to increase their subjective well-being by one on a ten point scale (Carbonell and Frijters, 2004). Similarly, the differences of wealth between nations at any one time can only 'explain' (issues of causality and omitted variables aside) two to three percent of the variance between individuals across countries in terms of subjective well-being (Royo and Velazco, 2005). Overall, Blanchflower and Oswald (2000) note that 'one of the interesting conclusions, from an economist's point of view, is how influential non-financial variables appear to be' in their comparative impact on subjective well-being responses. In their study, for example, a lasting marriage is correlated with the same incremental increase in subjective well-being as is an additional $100,000 in income.[5]

---

[5]  Why doesn't wealth bring much greater contentment? Conniff (2002) asked a beneficiary of a large trust-fund set up by his wealthy parents why the rich weren't happier and the response was a litany of woes: '... social isolation, resentment from peers, rich-bashing from society,

This limited impact of income on contentment can be seen in the context of earlier chapters which suggested that, especially in wealthy countries, the impact of greater domestic product on welfare and dignity is likely limited. To the extent that contentment builds on a basis of welfare and dignity, it is likely that any impact of GDP growth on overall levels of subjective well-being in wealthy countries will be connected with economic disruptions that change relative status. For example, Galbraith (1987) notes that

> [d]uring the severe recession of the early 1980s in the United States and elsewhere in the industrial world, the production of goods and service declined over a broad range. No one was thought, however, to suffer because of what was not produced... All suffering was identified with the interruption in the flow of income — with unemployment or loss of employment... In the modern industrial economy production is of first importance not for the goods it produces but for the employment and income it provides.

It is perhaps unsurprising, then, that what limited impact income does have on subjective well-being appears to be largely the result of relative income differences rather than absolute income increases. What promotes contentment is not being rich, but being richer than others. We can see this by looking at the impact of increased average incomes in subjective well-being across countries over time. Japan is a prime case, where GDP per capita increased three and a half times between 1962 and 1987 and subjective well-being stayed level. Again, taking a sample of US citizens born between 1941 and 1950, their average 1972 income was worth about $12,000 in 1994 US dollars, compared to $27,000 in 2000. Yet this cohort saw average happiness remain unchanged (Easterlin, 2004). Between 1952 and 1989, US GDP per capita approximately doubled, and average subjective well-being slightly declined.

---

betrayal or exploitation by friends, unrealistic expectations from family and society, unequal financial status in marriage, and the absence of all the usual factors (like worrying about the rent) that cause the rest of us to drag ourselves out of bed most mornings in search of bread and a modicum of self-worth.'

Table Six presents data on average subjective well-being (on a scale of 1–3), GNP per capita and the Gini coefficient for the US and UK over recent periods. The Gini coefficient is a measure of income distribution where 0 is perfect equality — where incomes are the same for every person — and 100 is perfect inequality — all income is received by one individual with everyone else getting none. The table demonstrates the weak relationship between income growth and subjective wellbeing growth, as well as some evidence for the importance of income equality. A positive (if weak) relationship between average levels of contentment and equality of income is also found between two settlements in Israel by Morawetz (1979) and between countries by C. Kenny (1999).

| Country | Year | GNP per Capita US$ | Gini | Subjective Well-being |
|---------|------|--------------------|------|-----------------------|
| UK | 1965 | 7,679 | 24 | 2.5 |
| | 1986 | 11,726 | 28 | 2.1 |
| USA | 1952 | 9,074 | 35 | 2.4 |
| | 1989 | 18,095 | 38 | 2.2 |
| Source: C. Kenny (1999) | | | | |

*Table Six*

It would be a reason to question the value of measures of subjective well-being if absolute income increases from extremely low initial levels did not correlate with improvements in self-reported happiness scores — but there is some evidence that they might. In the case of the slums of Calcutta, a subjective well-being survey revealed both average family incomes of around $60 per month and an average level of subjective well-being which was considerably lower than usually found in such surveys (Biswas-Diener and Diener, 2000). A similar result holds in the poorer parts of Africa. Ravallion and Lokshin (2005) find that the average subjective well-being poll answer in Malawi, one of the World's poorest countries (with a GDP per capita one third the average for Sub-Saharan Africa), is considerably lower than averages in rich and middle income countries. Ravallion and Lokshin find that subjective well-being is strongly and positively related to income in Malawi. They also find that higher income amongst friends and neighbours makes poorer Malawians more content. Relative deprivation does become a concern for the well-off Malawians, but for poorer groups relative concerns are not an issue.[6]

In other words, Malawi provides some evidence that at absolute levels of deprivation the impact of increased income on contentment is not entirely a phenomenon of relative concerns. 'Within the boundaries of this low-income country' argue Ravallion and Lokshin, 'we find economically well-off people who essentially care about relative position, side-by-side with a large number of poorer people (by far the majority) who appears to care far more about their absolute [income].'[7] A survey in Thailand suggests one reason why one would expect that, at low enough levels of GDP per capita, contentment would have to be related to income. The survey, while replicating other middle-income country results in many areas, did find that shortages of staple foods were linked to lower subjective well-being (Royo and Velazco, 2005). When income is low enough that basic needs required for welfare cannot be met, contentment is reduced.

Nonetheless, even in the Malawi case, the percentage of variation explained by measures of absolute and relative economic welfare, household characteristics, education and geographic location all together remained at only around 4 percent of total variation.[8] And even in the Malawi case, relatively rich respondents (who would remain relatively poor on any global standard) are concerned with relative income.[9] The top quintile of the population in Malawi sees income in the

---

[6] Although it should be noted that this finding has been replicated in rich countries as well (Ahuvia and Friedman, 1998) – it may be at a level of aggregation larger than the neighborhood that the negative externalities connected with other people's incomes is present.

[7] Similarly, survey evidence in South Africa suggests that absolute income did matter to the subjective well-being of the poorest third of respondents (Kingdon and Knight, 2003, 2004).

[8] This is the R-Squared of the regression result.

[9] Similar results hold for rich South Africans – Kingdon and Knight, 2004.

range of $1,697 (estimated from UNDP, 2005), which gives them about the same income as the average person in Senegal, or less than five percent of the income of the average citizen of the US. Again, even in the case of the slums of Calcutta discussed earlier, the authors concluded 'scores were not as low as one might expect based on living conditions' and 'even in the face of adverse circumstances these people find much in their life that is satisfying' (Diener and Diener, 1995).

Matching this finding, other evidence suggests that absolute income becomes unimportant for contentment very early on in the transition from least developed to industrial country status. Suicide rates have been found to be significantly correlated at the national level to average levels of subjective well-being (Helliwell, 2004). The results of an analysis of suicide rates in Western countries over the past 150 years are not those that would be expected were there a close link between income growth and subjective well-being even from fairly low levels of initial income. Chesnais (1995) reports that in the middle decades of the last century, no country outside of the German cultural area of Central Europe had an annual suicide rate of above 10 per 100,000 inhabitants. Today, most countries in the Western World see suicide rates between 10 and 20 per 100,000 people.[10] This is over a period when per capita incomes in Western Europe have risen from less than $2,000 to above $17,000.

More recent evidence comes from surveys on subjective happiness from developing countries which are slightly more wealthy than Malawi. For example, real incomes per capita in China increased by a factor of 2.5 between 1994-2005, and this was associated with rapid increases in the ownership of goods — color television ownership increased from 40 to 82 percent of households, telephones from 10 to 63 percent, for example. Incomes started at a very low level, averaging $2,604 per capita. Nonetheless, the percentage of people satisfied with life declined (Kahneman and Krueger, 2006). Suicide rates in China are also very high — the country accounts for 44

[10] Data quality will certainly be an issue here — at a time when suicide was considerably less socially acceptable, suicides may have been rarer, but so will reports of suicide, with cause of death frequently reclassified.

percent of the World's total annual suicides (Buvinic and Mor-rison, 2000). Similar results regarding income growth and con-tentment have been found for groups of (income) successful but unhappy people in Latin America that Graham and Pettinato (2002) label 'frustrated achievers'.

So early does the transition from absolute to relative income concerns develop that a number of studies have found that the cross-country relationship between subjective well-being and income is even weaker in samples of poor countries than amongst samples of rich countries (Schyns, 1998, Vitterso et al., 2002). A survey of subjective well-being in Kyrgyzstan finds the usual results that marriage and employment are pos-itively associated with self-reported happiness, but finds actual income is not robustly associated with subjective well-being (Namazie and Sanfey, 2001). Results suggesting a relationship between income and subjective well-being as weak or weaker as that in OECD countries have also been found in surveys of countries in Latin America (Graham and Felton, 2004) and Russia (Graham, 2004).[11]

Overall, Graham (2004) concludes that for the most part, the determinants of subjective well-being are the same in develop-ing and advanced economies. As with richer countries, there is some evidence that greater inequality and greater instability leads to dips in subjective well-being (Sanfey and Teksoz, 2005). And, as with rich country samples, income, health, mar-riage status and other factors all together only correlate with about four to seven percent of the variance in subjective well-being.[12]

Indeed, there is some evidence that income is a bigger deter-minant of subjective well-being in rich countries than in poor, with slightly larger and more significant relationships

---

[11]   A survey of eight developing countries with a number of subjective well-being polls could find a positive and significant relationship between GDP per capita growth and changes in average subjective well-being in only two of them. Taking 21 developing countries and using a different statistical technique, the study could find no significant link between changes in income and changes in subjective well-being (C. Kenny, 2005c).

[12]   See also Cummins et al., 2002, Rojas, 2002, Vitterso et al., 2002, Graham et al., 2002.

between income and subjective happiness in some wealthy country samples than in poor country samples (C. Kenny, 2005c). This may be because income becomes a more important measure of status as countries get richer. This tentative result would fit with a growing concern with making money in the United States over time — where the proportion of college freshmen who thought being well off financially was a very important or essential life goal increased from 39 to 74 percent between 1970 and 1995, making it the most important life objective and beating out raising a family (Myers and Diener, 1997).

At the same time, it may be that the global spread of television will homogenize worldwide judgements regarding the levels of income that constitute 'wealthy' or 'poor.' If this happens, an ever greater percentage of people in developing countries may see themselves as very poor in a way that may reduce their contentment. This would fit with evidence suggesting that television viewing is correlated with lower levels of subjective well-being (Bruni and Stanca, 2006).[13]

## Valuing Non-Rival Goods over Positional Goods

In earlier chapters we have seen why we should expect these results. Once basic needs are assured, poverty and wealth are relative concepts with social meanings. The extent to which we are social animals is clear from numerous experiments that make people do unusual things in order to fit in with a group of people they have never met who are doing the same — they strip, ignore smoke pouring out of a vent or call a long line 'short,' for example (Pinker, 2002). Given this, it is not surprising that adaptation to income levels is such a powerful force –if everyone else has a television and a car, we will only be satisfied if we have both also.[14]

---

[13]  This correlation may also reflect the passive, isolating nature of television viewing compared to other potential uses for leisure time.

[14]  Friedman (2005) argues that faster economic growth should lead to greater contentment. It appears, however, that rates of economic growth are not related to increases in subjective well-being across nations. This suggests that increases in income are adapted to very rapidly.

In wealthy countries, subjective well-being correlates far better with subjective evaluations of peoples' income levels than it does with objective comparisons (Ahuvia and Friedman, 1998). It is frequently the case that those with money worries are not objectively amongst the poorest but those who *feel* poor. This might help to explain why a greater concern for possession of material goods is correlated with lower subjective happiness across individuals (Furnham and Argyle, 1998).

Money concerns in rich countries frequently reflect personality more than penury. A US survey which asked people who were concerned with their financial situation and compared the top quarter of respondents on this question with the bottom quarter found that 59 percent of the most concerned felt they had less money than most of their friends compared to 17 percent in the least concerned category. But the same study also found that the people most concerned with their financial situation were more afraid of a number of non-pecuniary negative life events – 56 percent were concerned about the loss of a loved one compared to 43 percent of those unconcerned with their financial situation, 51 percent of the financially concerned were worried about becoming ill compared to 41 percent of those unconcerned by their financial situation. The proportion who felt 'constant worry and anxiety' was 50 percent amongst those concerned with their financial situation compared to 7 percent amongst those not concerned (reported in Furnham and Argyle, 1998). Some of that may be accounted for by truly more distressing financial situations, but it appears that much may be accounted for by differences in a general susceptibility to worry.

This same finding applies to developing countries. Ravallion and Lokshin (2001) find a correlation between perceived and actual changes in economic welfare 1994–96 in Russia, but they note that the link between income growth and growth in subjective economic welfare, while statistically significant, is also weak in terms of the percentage in variation in responses it can explain (less that one percent). They conclude that there is 'clearly a lot more to changing perceptions of economic welfare than measured income growth rates.'

In rich countries, the chase for more income is largely a chase for status. And this is a race that very few can win. Indeed, as we have seen, concern with wealth-related status appears to affect even those who by any global or historical standard rank with Croesus — less than 0.5 percent of Americans are willing to label themselves as rich (Myers, 1992). Relatively richer people will always have greater access to positional goods, which have value in considerable part because only some can have them. These are goods which no amount of income can allow us all to have (waterfront property in downtown Manhattan, or two servants each). There is experimental evidence from Sweden that demonstrates this effect with cars. One only gets pleasure out of one's Ford if everyone else drives a Skoda, or out of one's BMW if everyone else is driving a Ford.

Luckily, however, the same is not true of all goods. Swedish people do not value leisure time and car safety in positional terms. They want more holidays, they do not want more holidays than their neighbor (Carlsson et al., 2003). A similar finding comes from the survey of Harvard students cited earlier. As we saw, the majority of students, when asked if they would rather earn $100,000 while others got twice as much, or $50,000 while others got half as much, chose lower absolute income and higher relative income ($50,000 whilst others earned $25,000). Conversely, when asked if they would rather have two weeks of holiday when others only got one or four weeks when others got eight, the majority chose absolutely more, but relatively less holiday (four weeks).

This suggests that, unlike income, holidays are not considered in relative terms (Dowling, 2005), and provides an insight to policymakers from the subjective well-being literature — average contentment might be increased by taxing or discouraging the pursuit of positional goods (income or cars) while subsidizing or otherwise encouraging the pursuit of goods valued in an absolute rather than relative sense (insurance and holidays).[15] One might also want to support access to some of the other variables found significantly correlated with subjec-

[15] People are naturally highly risk averse. Nearly 75 percent of people offered the choice of a one in one thousand chance of winning $5000 or a

tive wellbeing—health, education, low inflation and full employment. Furthermore, the limited benefit in terms of contentment of being very much richer than average suggests that taxing the wealthy to provide better employment, education, health, insurance and leisure outcomes for all might provide a significant net gain in average levels of contentment.

A second lesson is the overall importance of the honest, efficient operation of government itself. The comparative importance of institutions over income to subjective well-being is clear from Helliwell and Huang (2006), who show that the significant correlation between cross-country income and subjective well-being at any one time disappears if a measure of the quality of government is added to the analysis.[16] In other words, it appears likely that the link between subjective well-being and GDP per capita across countries at any one time is similar to the link between welfare and dignity outcomes and GDP per capita. It is driven by the underlying impact of institutions on both GDP per capita outcomes and subjective well-being. Helliwell (2002) had earlier concluded that 'those who have the highest levels of subjective well-being are not those who live in the richest countries, but those who live where social and political institutions are effective, where mutual trust is high, and corruption is low.'

## Problems with Subjective Well-being as a Measure of the Good

We have seen that subjective well-being does capture elements of what might be called contentment — with self-reportedly happy people smiling more, experiencing elevated levels of dopamine and so on. At the same time, we have seen that subjective well-being does vary with objective life circumstances — the absolutely poor, the imprisoned and the unem-

---

sure gain of $5 take the gamble on $5000 compared to nearly 80 percent of people who opted for a sure loss of $5 over the one in a thousand gamble of losing $5000 (Plous, 1993). This, along with findings on the negative impact of inflation on subjective wellbeing, suggests the importance of economic stability to contentment.

[16] Using the Freedom House index of democracy, the result is sometimes reversed — income remains significant while the index of democracy drops out (Dorn et al., 2005).

ployed are, as a rule, low scorers on subjective well-being measures. Happiness polls may be a useful tool for estimating what might be plausibly though of as levels of utility, then. It can also provide some useful information about policy tools that might increase contentment. Nonetheless, there are significant problems with using subjective wellbeing as an overarching measure of the good.

## Little Variation in Subjective Well-being Due to Objective Quality of Life Factors

We have seen that, at least since the Enlightenment, thinkers have imagined it quite possible to for entire peoples to be content. Furthermore, there appears to be little evidence that the majority of people were miserable throughout history. As emphasized above, this was despite the fact that the great majority of people were very poor indeed by modern standards. But it is also despite the fact that health outcomes were desperately weak. To take the example of the Dutch Republic in the seventeenth century, life expectancies were in the low 30s. This historically weak connection between apparent levels of contentment and objective measures of quality of life is strongly echoed in modern survey evidence attempting to link objective measures of the quality of life to the results of happiness surveys.

At the international level, it would be expected that cross-country data might over-emphasize the role of national characteristics because of the potential impact of cultural factors on answers to subjective well-being questions (which are likely to artificially exaggerate cross-country differences). Given that, it is surprising how low is the amount of variation in satisfaction with life accounted for by cross-country as compared to within-country variation. Using average country subjective happiness scores, about two thirds of countries are within a ten point range on a 100-point scale of life satisfaction. Within countries, about two thirds of people are within a much larger 36 point range on a 100-point scale.[17] Similarly,

---

[17]  Average country scores for subjective well-being are 75 with a standard deviation of 5 across 44 countries. This suggests a coefficient of variation

Vitterso and colleagues' (2002) 41 country study, including economies from the US to Zimbabwe, found that 87 percent of the variation in satisfaction with life scores was due to within-country, rather than across-country factors. This contrasts significantly with most measures of objective quality of life (health, for example) where within-country differences are dwarfed by cross-country differences. In short, despite all of their objective differences, countries are very similar in their average levels of life satisfaction and the role for cross-country differences in explaining life satisfaction is very small compared to the role for within-country differences.

At the same time, measurable within-country factors can apparently explain little of the variation in subjective well-being at the individual level. For example, a recent study of life satisfaction in transition economies including income, age and gender was able to explain less than four percent of the variation in individual subjective well-being (Sanfey and Teksoz, 2005). The survey of subjective well-being in Kyrgyzstan cited earlier found that, excluding subjective measures, less than seven percent of variation in subjective well-being could be explained by data including income, age, sex, marital and employment status, education, location and ethnicity (Namazie and Sanfey, 2001).[18]

Combining the two approaches (cross-country and within-country factors), we saw that Helliwell and Huang's (2006) study was able to find correlates associated with about 17 percent of the variation between individual levels of subjective well-being in a multi-country study. This is a comparatively successful result. Dorn et al. (2005) use measures of income, employment, marital status, household size, religion, gender, age, education and the status of democracy across survey populations in 28 countries and could find correlating factors associated with only eight percent of the variation in individual

---

of 0.07, compared to a 73-country estimate (from C.Kenny, 2005b) of 0.85 for GDP per capita, for example. Average within-country standard deviation for subjective well-being for a Western sample of countries is 18 – three and a half times larger than cross-country variance in subjective happiness (Cummins and Nistico, 2002).

[18]  See also Graham and Felton (2004) for a similar result for Latin American countries.

subjective well-being, about one half of the variation accounted for by Helliwell and Huang.

Most variation in subjective well-being occurs at the individual rather than national level, then—but our ability to explain subjective well-being differences at the individual level using external objective factors is very weak. Neither factors that vary considerably across nations (such as health or income) nor those that vary more within rather than between nations (such as age, marital status, parental status, or employment) explain much of the variation in subjective well-being between individuals. There appear to be two major reasons for this—the importance of inherited factors in determining subjective well-being and the role of adaptation in minimizing long-term subjective well-being impacts of life events.

## The Role of Inheritance

We have seen that subjective well-being is fairly stable across time within individuals. This should not come as a surprise. It is at least in part a character trait, and character traits tend to be fairly set. Indeed, character traits are to some significant degree inherited. Happiness joins a long list. 'Autism, dyslexia, language delay, language impairment, learning disability, left-handedness, major depressions, bipolar illness, obsessive-compulsive disorder, sexual orientation, and many other conditions run in families, are more concordant in identical than fraternal twins, are better predicted by people's biological relatives than by their adopted relatives, and are poorly measured by any measurable feature of the environment' according to Pinker (2002). He argues that 40–50 percent of the variation in basic personality types across a given population at a given time are tied to differences in genes (including introverted versus extroverted neurotic or stable, incurious or open to experience, agreeable or antagonistic, conscientious or undirected). Furthermore, causes that are not directly related to the home shared environment account for the great majority of personality differences not accounted for by genetic factors. As a result, '[a]dult siblings are equally similar whether they grew up together or apart … adoptive siblings are no more similar than two people plucked off the street at random …'

With regard to subjective well-being in particular, based on a study of twins, Lykken and Tellegren (1996) conclude that 80 percent of the differences in life satisfaction were heritable, while less than three percent were explained by socio-economic status, education, income, marital status and religious commitment.

This is not to say social and economic factors have no role. Nature and nurture interact in forming persons and personalities. By way of illustration, US twin samples suggest height in any one generation is substantially heritable: nearly 90 percent of height variation between individuals appears to be genetic. At the same time, that average heights have changed considerably over time suggests that even heritable states are sensitive to environments. It is only because nearly everyone in the US is well fed and free from childhood illness that the genetic factor is so predominant a cause of height differences today.

Looking at the interaction of nature and nurture in the area of personality, lying, stealing, and starting fights are also partially predicted by heritability but also determined by the acceptability of such behavior in different milieus.[19] Furthermore, whilst measured personality traits may not be influenced too significantly by home environment, we know that health and education, for example, *are* significantly impacted by decisions by parents early in the life of a child and so, partially as a result, is income. Bowles and Gintis (2002) conclude that 'the determination of the genetic component in a transition process says little by itself about the extent to which public policy can or should level a playing field.'

---

[19] There is also a difference between personality types, values and skills. For example, Pinker reports a Danish adoption study which found the biological children of convicts were slightly more likely to get into trouble than the biological children of law-abiding citizens, but that the chance of criminal activity was far, far greater if the children were adopted by people who were criminals themselves and who lived in a large city (often in high-crime neighbourhoods).

## Adaptation to Objective Circumstances

The interaction of nature and nurture aside, the strong role of inheritance and the weak role of objective factors in explaining answers to happiness polls suggests that people have a considerable ability to adapt to circumstances (both positive and negative) in terms of their contentment. We have seen this earlier in the case of income, but it also applies to other domains of the objective quality of life. This suggests strongly that contentment can be present absent acceptable levels of welfare and dignity.

Barbara Tuchman (1978) argues that the most noticeable difference between the medieval and modern character was 'the comparative absence of interest in children.' She notes the almost complete absence of children in illustrations or of books of advice on raising children (compared to numerous sources on etiquette, housewifery, deportment and home remedies, for example). She argues that very high infant mortality may be one cause of this lack of interest. Mortality rates were indeed very high—Tuchman notes that by her death in 1378, only three of the eight children born to Jeanne de Bourbon, Queen of France were still alive.[20] Similarly, Clark and Hulme (2005) note that in some of the poorer *favelas* of Brazil, poor mothers expect their weaker children will die as a matter of course, doing little to save them and treating them as transient visitors –'little angels'. This is a sign that adaptation can even occur in the case of something as wrenching as the loss of a child.

With regard to people's own health, Myers (1992) reports a University of Illinois survey of able-bodied students which found that the average student was happy 50 percent of the

---

[20] Tuchman does report cases where child death caused considerable upset. The death of two of the Dauphin's children, aged three and one, within two weeks of each other in 1360, left him 'so sorrowful as never before he had been' according to chronicles. Nonetheless, the dominant attitude towards death does seem to have been different –according to Aries (1974) it was treated without great fear or awe. He notes that the habit of hiding away the dying expanded in the second half of the Nineteenth Century. Today, he suggests, 'technically we admit that might die; we take out life insurance on our lives to protect our families from poverty. But really, at heart we feel we are non-mortals. And surprise! Our life is not as a result gladdened!'

time, 22 percent of the time unhappy, and 29 percent of the time neutral. The numbers were the same—within one percent—for surveyed disabled students. Cummins et al. (2002) report returns towards 'set' levels of subjective well-being for people who have received a diagnosis of cancer, people who have become paraplegic and those who have received burns. Again, self-reported ratings of health correlate far better with subjective well-being than objective measures by physicians (Cummins et al., 2002, Zautra and Hempel, 1984, Frey and Stutzer, 2002).[21]

In developing countries, Nussbaum (2001) studies evidence of Indian women in abusive and discriminatory households who live their lives and make choices without feeling oppressed. Amartya Sen has noted that Indian women rank themselves as more subjectively content with their health than do Indian men, despite suffering from considerably worse overall health status (cited in Gasper, 2004). Earlier, Hadly Cantril's work enumerating *The Pattern of Human Concerns* (1965) noted that good health was a very low aspiration in India, despite it being the country in his study with by far the worst objective health conditions.

Adaptation also plays a role in weakening the strength of relationships between low income, unemployment and contentment. We have seen that it is plausible that the largest impact of relative income on subjective well-being may be in the wealthiest countries, whilst the impact of inequality is larger in (comparatively egalitarian) Europe than the (comparatively unequal) United States. The impact of unemployment on subjective well-being also depends very much on where one is unemployed. If the unemployed person is in a household or region where unemployment is high, the amount of subjective well-being they lose from being unemployed is reduced (employment, then, is to some extent a posi-

---

[21] Related to this, patients expressing 'satisfaction' with treatments can be feeling resignation, helplessness and the feeling that the treatment is useless. Satisfaction with health is rarely significantly related with self-reported happiness, and while self-reported health does tend to enter significantly, this is primarily due people's perception of their *mental* health, where questions of causality must be at their most significant (Camfield, 2003).

tional good) (Clark, 2003). Again, political and personal freedoms are correlated with subjective well-being more strongly in wealthy countries where they tend to be already comparatively high (Frey and Stutzer, 2002).[22]

In many cases, adaptation is not complete. Easterlin (2005) suggests the evidence is in favour of some long-term negative impact on contentment from adverse health shocks. He also argues that a relationship between subjective well-being and marriage (positive) and divorce, separation or widowhood (negative) remains over the long term. He concludes that 'while there may be complete hedonic adaptation with regard to income, this does not mean that there is complete hedonic adaptation with regard to all sources of happiness.' Where social comparison is not the primary driver of desire and satisfaction, hedonic adaptation is perhaps not complete.[23] Nonetheless, it does appear to be considerable, to the extent that a person's initial 'set point' of subjective well-being is a far better predictor of their current and future responses to happiness surveys than objective measures even when these measures include dramatic life events.

Sen (1985) argues that a person in poverty is disadvantaged whatever they think about it: 'can we possibly believe that he is doing well just because he is happy and satisfied? Can the living standard of a person be high if the life that he or she leads is full of deprivation?' The answer to this question must depend on the nature of the deprivation. Nonetheless, the potential for contentment in the face of physical abuse, the loss of a child or severe physical disability is a sign that the human ability to adapt to a range of circumstances in terms of subjec-

---

[22]    An interesting case of correlational relationships changing sign is that of obesity. In the United States, the obese are made less content by their condition while in Russia obesity and subjective well-being are positively correlated. Perhaps obesity is still seen as a sign of prosperity in Russia, despite the fact that the average Russian has long been able to afford excess calories (indeed during the Soviet era, Russia had the highest obesity rates in Europe) (Graham and Felton, 2005).

[23]    Frank (1997) uses the analogy of traffic noise to the impact of events to which we cannot completely adapt. Even though a large increase in background noise which then continues at a constant, steady level is experienced as less intrusive as time goes on, prolonged exposure still produces lasting elevations in blood pressure.

tive well-being may be greater than the extent to which we would like to see *objective* circumstances vary. That people can adapt to loss does not mean that no harm is done by the loss, and evidence of adaptation to circumstances that reduce welfare and dignity emphasizes the problems with subjective well-being as a single measure of the good life.

## Causality Between Objective Circumstances and Subjective Well-being

The extent of adaptation and the strength of a set-point level of contentment raises the possibility that many of the objective variables correlated with subjective well-being may be so correlated because contentment is a causal factor in the objective outcome rather than vice-versa. Ravallion and Lokshin (2001) note that strong personality correlates with subjective well-being include extraversion, social competence, collective self esteem, comfort with intimacy, emotional stability and lack of anxiety, self-confidence and self respect. Conversely, those who are nervous, apprehensive, irritable, excessively emotional and over-sensitive also tend to be those who report low scores on subjective well-being (Cummins et al., 2002). Such positive character traits associated with happiness are likely to be independently and positively associated with outcomes including employment and income.

Indeed, cross-country studies suggest that if there *is* a causal relationship between changes in average subjective well-being and income in wealthy countries, it runs from self-reported happiness to GDP growth rather than the other way around. Contented countries grow rapidly rather than growing countries becoming more content (C.Kenny, 1999), and contented individuals become richer as much as richer individuals gain contentment (Graham et al., 2004)

It seems likely that traits of happy people may also increase the likelihood of marriage and of close friendships. Furthermore, there is evidence to suggest that happy people may be healthier because they are happy (Steptoe et al., 2005). If this is the case, an increase in employment, health or friendships may have less impact on subjective well-being than suggested by coefficients from the cross-sectional regression analyses cited above — analyses that already had very low explanatory power.

It is also interesting to note that people who score highly on subjective well-being polls are those who have the *least* clear grasp of objective reality regarding their situation. We do indeed live in Lake Woebegone (a town where everyone is above average). Ninety percent of the US population, for example, consider that they experience above-average levels of life quality. People appear to have an in-built bias to feel good about themselves and their situation — with people consistently rating themselves more cheerful, enthusiastic and confident than their peers, and more likely to live long and have a better job. Only the depressed are comparatively accurate in their self-perception (Cummins and Nistico, 2002).

## Centrality of Subjective Well-being as a Motivation

A final problem with subjective well-being as a measure of the good life is that, unlike the theoretical notion of utility, it does not appear that our sole motivation in life is maximization of subjective well-being. Take the amount of time most people spend on earning income. That we expend so much effort on achieving income increases, which apparently bring us so little contentment, may in part be a sign of relative income concerns. But that even relative income increases tend to have little impact suggests that the hope of a status change is not adequate motivation for all of that effort. Instead, could this be a sign that we do much of what we do for reasons other than maximizing our subjective well-being? Perhaps we earn income in part to provide for our present or future offspring. These offspring bring us absolutely no benefit in terms of subjective well-being, according to the survey data (see Carbonell and Frijters, 2004),[24] but surely they are a source of motivation for many of our actions.

---

[24] Apart, possibly, from the intimate relations which create them — see Kahneman and Krueger, 2006.

## Conclusion

The subjective well-being literature does a good job of uncovering the fragile link between income and utility (contentment). However, the literature also suggests a weak link between utility (so measured) and measures of the good life more broadly defined. Adaptation theory explains both of these results. People get used to more income, but also to worse health, for example. As a result, the policy implications of the subjective well-being literature are perhaps not as clear-cut as we would like.

First, the fact that so much of the cross-country variation in subjective well-being remains unexplained by the raft of objective influences that have been put into regression analyses suggests a distinct limit to policy or other interventions in increasing average subjective well-being scores. This problem looms especially large given the importance of reverse-causality. It may be that some of the robust correlates between contentment and objective situations that we do see are robust because contented people have characteristics that make them more likely to achieve those objective situations. Contented, confident, outgoing people are likely to have more friends or gain employment, for example. Even if we find strong policy measures to improve objective circumstances, we may be disappointed by the returns to contentment, then.

Second, whilst some correlates with subjective well-being are disconnected with status (health and leisure, perhaps), it is clear that much of the variation in happiness which we can explain is connected to variation in status. This applies to employment and, potentially, even marriage. Even if we push down inequality in one measure of status, it is surely likely that we will become more sensitive to variation in this or another status measure.

Third, there can be significant problems with implementing policies in many of the non-status areas where we may see subjective well-being returns. We lack evidence of the causal mechanisms (let alone mechanisms that can be influenced by public policy) that determine objective outcomes linked to subjective happiness. What are the proven policy measures that the state can introduce to encourage overall rates of happy marriage, or even of employment, for example?

Given what we know of its strong genetic determinants, if the only aim of public policy was to increase average or total subjective well-being over time, the best course of action would be to force those who score highly on such polls to mate and produce many children. At the same time, those who scored average or below on contentment would be sterilized and filled full of drugs so that they felt nothing but the maximum happiness of which they were capable. In the short term, we might sacrifice some of the five or six percentage points of contentment scores that are connected with factors such as liberty, but at what great long-term gain to the 50-80 percent of subjective well-being which is inherited?

Of course, this is a dystopian nightmare, but one which follows from too singular a focus on utilitarianism based on subjective well-being. If we are trying to maximize average subjective well-being as measured on a three-point scale, we are likely to be attempting to change something over which the usual (and proper) domains of public policy have only limited influence. And so whilst the results of subjective well-being studies do show that fixation with income as a good measure of utility is misplaced, they also suggest that utility so measured is only a partial tool for policy determination.

The subjective happiness literature does provide one more reason to doubt the centrality of income to the good life. To the extent that subjective happiness is a measure of utility, it appears that utility is little connected with income even among the great majority of people in 'developing' countries. What little impact income does appear to have beyond a low absolute minimum is through status effects rather than the joy of access to more goods and services themselves. The literature points to some elements of life where subjective well-being might be raised for all through the greater provision of goods not purely valued in a relative sense. Insurance against (the impact of) negative life events such as unemployment or, indeed, sudden loss of income are examples. At the same time, there are limits to the extent we can expect such changes to increase contentment. It appears that the largest potential and plausible return to government policy in terms of impact on contentment would be to ensure welfare and dignity for all citizens. Beyond this, the role for policy may be marginal, with contentment largely the result of the character and actions of the individual.

# PART FIVE

# CONCLUSIONS

# Chapter 9

# Happiness and Morality

In this final section we ask what conclusions can be drawn from our investigation of happiness for private morality and public policy. In this chapter we will concentrate on issues of individual morality, and in the next chapter we will consider matters of national and international policy.

## Morality: Community, Values, and Code

We have seen that different philosophers have had widely differing views of the nature of happiness. They have likewise had widely differing views of the nature of morality, and on the relationship between morality and happiness. To set these disagreements within a framework, let us begin by observing that there are three elements essential to a moral system. There must be a moral community, a set of moral values, and a moral code.

All three are necessary. First, it is as impossible to have a purely private morality as it is to have a purely private language, and for very similar reasons. Secondly, the moral life of the community consists in the shared pursuit of non-material values, such as justice, truth, freedom and love. It is the non-material nature of the values pursued that distinguishes morality from pure economics. Thirdly, this pursuit is carried out within a framework which excludes certain prohibited types of behaviour. It is this that distinguished morality from aesthetics, which is also a pursuit of non-material values, (e.g. beauty and harmony) but without a framework of prohibitions. 'Who does the prohibiting?' it may be asked. The answer is that it is the members of the moral community: membership of a common moral society involves subscription to a common code. The moral community creates moral laws in a manner similar to that in which the linguistic community creates the rules of grammar and syntax. Moral rules, like linguistic rules, may change as society changes; but unless a set of such rules is in operation society collapses into anarchy as language collapses into incoherence.

This conception of the origin of moral rules was picturesquely sketched by Immanuel Kant in his *Groundwork of the Metaphysic of Morals*. Every human being, he said, is a member of a kingdom of ends, a union of rational beings under common laws. My own will is rational only in so far as its maxims — the principles on which it makes its choices — are capable of being made universal laws. The converse of this is that universal law is law that is made by rational wills like mine. A rational being is 'subject only to laws which are made by himself and yet are universal'. In the kingdom of ends, we are all both legislators and subjects.

Just as philosophers have disagreed about the nature of happiness, so they have disagreed about each of these elements of morality. For Aristotelians only human beings are members of the moral community and possess moral rights, because only they are capable of the rational intersubjective discourse that is the medium of moral suasion and sanction. Though it is wrong to mistreat them pointlessly, animals do not have rights. Only those can have rights who can have duties, and animals have no duties, for duties like rights presuppose the possibility of rational intercommunication. For Benthamites, on the other hand, there is no reason in principle to exclude animals from the moral community, since morality is defined in terms of pleasure and pain which the higher animals undoubtedly share.

Among the non-material values that morality pursues, both Aristotle and Bentham give a supreme place to the value of happiness. In the context of morality, the most important difference between the two is that the happiness that is paramount in Aristotle's ethics is the happiness of the individual, whereas he happiness paramount in Bentham is the general happiness. Whatever the difficulties in making the notion of 'general happiness' precise, Bentham is surely to be preferred here to Aristotle.

Perhaps the most important practical difference between Aristotle and Bentham concerns the moral code. If a code is a set of absolute prohibitions, then for a utilitarian the content of the code is zero.

We may divide moral philosophers into absolutists and consequentialists. Absolutists believe that there are some kinds of action that are intrinsically wrong, and should never be done, irrespective of any consideration of the consequences. Consequentialists believe that the morality of actions should be judged by their consequences, and that there is no category of act which may not, in special circumstances, he justified by its consequences. Prior to Bentham most philosophers were absolutists, because they believed in a natural law, or natural rights. If there are natural rights and a natural law, then some kinds of action, actions that violate those rights or conflict with that law, are wrong, no matter what the consequences.

Bentham rejected the notion of natural law, on the grounds that no two people could agree what it was. He was scornful of natural rights, believing that real rights could only be conferred by positive law; and his greatest scorn was directed to the idea that natural rights could not be overridden. 'Natural rights is simple nonsense: natural and imprescriptible rights, rhetorical nonsense – nonsense upon stilts' (Bentham, 1843).

If there is no natural law and there are no natural rights, then no class of actions can be ruled out in advance of the consideration of the consequences of such an action in a particular case.

This difference between Bentham and previous moralists is highly significant, as can be easily illustrated. Aristotle, Aquinas, and almost all Christian moralists believed that adultery and murder were always wrong. Not so for Bentham: the consequences foreseen by a particular adulterer or murderer must be taken into account before making a moral judgement.

A believer in natural law, told that some Herod or Nero has killed five thousand citizens guilty of no crime, will say without further ado 'that was a wicked act'. A thoroughgoing consequentialist, before making such a judgement, must ask further questions. What were the consequences of the massacre? What did the monarch foresee? What would have happened if he had allowed the five thousand to live?

## Moral absolutes

On this issue, we take sides against Bentham. We believe that there are some actions, such as rape and torture, which should be ruled out without consideration of consequences. We accept that there can be disagreements among intelligent and upright people about which particular classes of acts are intolerable (capital punishment? abortion?), but we believe that in the absence of some code of prohibitions morality collapses into crude cost-benefit analysis.

It is the code of prohibitions that generates the natural human rights — or rather, those human rights that are negative, such as the right not to be murdered or tortured. Among human rights we agree with the founding fathers of the United States that there is a right to pursue happiness. In the declaration of independence happiness was most likely conceived as a mental state of satisfaction, and the rights to life and liberty are separately specified. We prefer to interpret the right to pursue happiness not just as a right to pursue contentment, but as a right to pursue well-being in the broad sense that we have defined it, as including welfare and dignity.

The pursuit of happiness, however, is a right, not a compulsion or an obligation. We disagree with those who maintain that every human being, in every action, pursues his own well-being willy-nilly. We also disagree with those who believe that there is an obligation to pursue one's own well-being that overrides all other considerations. We believe that it is possible, and may often be admirable, to cease from the quest for one's own happiness in favour of the pursuit of some altruistic goal. Society rightly values and respects callings (such as that of the firefighter) that carry with them a professional duty, in the appropriate circumstances, to place the welfare of others above one's own welfare and contentment. Moreover, the fact that the pursuit of different elements of happiness can conflict, and that there is no simple metric to make comparisons across the elements, is itself sufficient to show that there cannot be any simple obligation to pursue happiness.

It was observed by John Stuart Mill that the explicit pursuit of one's own happiness was not necessarily the best way to achieve it. 'I never,' he tells us in his autobiography

> wavered in the conviction that happiness is the test of all the rules of conduct, and the end of life. But I now thought that this end was only to be obtained by not making it the direct end. Those only are happy (I thought) who have their minds fixed on some object other than their own happiness; on the happiness of others, on the improvement of mankind, even on some art or pursuit, followed not as a means but itself as an ideal end. Aiming thus at something else they find happiness by the way (Mill, 1969, 85).

## Work and Play

For most of us the pursuit of happiness consists not in the single-minded pursuit of some overarching Aristotelian goal, but rather in a number of separate fundamental choices: the choice of a career, the selection of our friends, the decision whether to marry and have a family. The very nature of these choices rules out a single minded focus on one's own individual happiness. The goodness of a marriage depends on what it has to offer to two partners, not one; having a family is a boon only if the family is a happy family. A career which brings benefits to other members of society is more rewarding than one which gives pleasure only to the careerist.

Among the choices that are relevant to happiness are the ways we adopt of spending our leisure. Leisure, is indeed, a significant element in the good life, as is made clear by the constant debate on achieving a work-life balance. Aristotle himself, in spite of his monistic view of happiness, attached great importance to the concept of leisure. He used it in one of his many arguments to show the uniquely satisfying nature of philosophy. A warrior, he said, makes war only to have peace, and a businessman works only in order to have leisure, but for the philosopher work and leisure coincide. He was helped to give plausibility to his argument by the fact that the Greek word for 'leisure' and the Greek word for 'academy' are the same, namely *schole*. But he undoubtedly has a point that the happiest career is one in which there is no clear division between work and play, between business and leisure. Fortunately there are many other careers besides that of the philosopher of which this is true: the artist, for instance, the writer, the sportsman.

## Individual and General Happiness

We have agreed with Bentham against Aristotle that morality demands a care for happiness other than one's own. But it is perhaps a mistake to regard the alternative as an undifferentiated concern for the general good. The ancient Stoics were better inspired when they said that each of us stands at the centre of a series of concentric circles. According to the Stoic theory, the first circle contains my body and its needs, the second contains my immediate family, and the third and fourth contain extensions of my family. Then come circles of neighbours, at various distances: my city, my nation, the world and the cosmos. Our concern with the inner circles was naturally greater than that for the outer circles: but moral progress consisted in reaching out and making ever wider circles into parts of one's home environment. If I am virtuous, the Stoics said, I will try to draw these concentric circles closer together, treating cousins as if they were brothers, and constantly transferring people from outer circles to inner ones.

The Stoics called this process 'oikeiosis', which means home-making. A Stoic, adapting himself to the nature of the cosmos, is making himself at home in the world he lives is; but he is also making other people at home with himself, taking them into his domestic circle.

Religious thought followed a development parallel to the philosophical universalism of the Stoics. The Biblical injunction to love one's neighbour as oneself already proclaimed a morality more inclusive than that of Aristotle. It was however compatible with a distinction between neighbours who were, and gentiles who were not, members of God's chosen people. It was the parable of the good Samaritan which fostered the ideal that a neighbour was to be defined in terms of need rather than of ethnic origin.

It is surely unrealistic to think that everyone can bestow the same affection on the most distant foreigner as on one's own family and friends. Justice must be for all: but love cannot help but be selective. Stoic universalism had its pragmatic side in recognizing the distances between the different concentric circles. But in the contemporary world it is more difficult to decide what counts as 'my city' and 'my nation' than it was in the palmy days of the Roman Empire, and it is not clear how sensible it is to defined levels of obligation of care by civic and national boundaries, many of which are accidents of history. It may be questioned whether it is reasonable to ask the Chinese to have a special care for one quarter of the planet's population while the special obligation of the Andorrans extends only to their 70,000 nearest neighbours.

In general, when we turn from matters of individual morality or global aspiration to practical matters of public policy, there is little guidance to be had from ancient and classical writers, since the social institutions in which they lived were so different from our own. Thomas More's Utopia is perhaps the earliest philosophical text in which we can recognize policy concerns that are at all similar to those of the present day. But even that work is, unsurprisingly, Utopian. Its proposal to maintain the family as the primary unit of society while abolishing all privacy and private property has never been taken, and perhaps was never meant, to be a blueprint for an actual commonwealth.

Utopia is one of the first texts in the early modern age to raise the issue of population size as a matter of public policy. As we saw earlier, the greatest happiness principle gives no guidance on this matter. For much of the Christian era it was not regarded as a policy issue: couples followed their instincts, and then accepted 'as many children as God sends'. Overpopulation was not seen as an issue, since God took away by infant mortality so many of the children he sent. When contraception was seen as a moral option after the nineteenth century discussions of population control by Malthus and Mill, it was still seen as a matter of individual, not societal choice: it was family planning, not state planning. Only in the twentieth century, with incentives in fascist states for larger families, and enforcement of smaller families in communist states, has the actual number of persons whose well-being is to be maximised been seen as a matter of governmental policy.

It has to be said that philosophers have had little success in setting out principles that should guide decisions about population size. Philosophers of a conservative bent have focussed their attention not on the optimum number of inhabitants of the globe, but rather upon the morality of different methods of population control (abstinence, use of the safe period, male and female contraceptive devices, abortion). Utilitarians have found difficulty in reaching a consensus on the optimum size of the population because of disagreement whether the greatest happiness principle should aim at maximum total happiness or highest average happiness.

In the nineteenth century, Sidgwick attempted to combine the two measures.

> [S]trictly conceived, the point up to which, on Utilitarian principles, population ought to be encouraged to increase, is not that at which average happiness is the greatest possible ... but that at which the product formed by multiplying the number of persons living into the amount of happiness reaches its maximum (ME 415-16).

His recommendation has not been found very helpful, particularly as he used it, in combination with the thesis that civilised life was happier than uncivilised life, in order to promote the cause of imperial emigration and colonization.

At the present time the whole gamut of possible opinions on optimum population size can be found in the writings of philosophers, including the thesis that human life is so miserable that it is wicked to bring a child into the world, and that all existing foetuses should be aborted. Fortunately, this is not a widely held opinion, and in the face of it one finds it comforting to learn from the subjective well-being polls that most of the human race seem to be more happy than not.

## The Paradox of Happiness

Once it has been decided, on whatever basis, who are those whose interests are to be taken into account in the distribution of well-being, what should be the goal of public policy? One thing is clear from our analysis. Once one has identified and individuated the disparate elements of happiness, with the best will in the world, no one will ever achieve a policy that will maximise everything that is included in our intuitive notion of happiness or in the constructs of philosophers or economists.

Some years ago, in an essay on individual happiness which drew a contrast between satisfaction and fulfilment, one of us wrote:

> In assessing happiness we have regard not only to the satisfaction of desires but also to the nature of the desires themselves. The notions of contentment and of richness of life are in part independent, and this leads to paradox in the concept of happiness, which involves both. Plato and Mill sought to combine the two notions, by claiming that those who had experience of both inferior and superior pleasures would be contented only with the superior pleasures of a rich intellectual life. This, if true, might show the felicity of Socrates satisfied, but will not prove that Socrates dissatisfied is happier than a fool satisfied. The greater a person's education and sensitivity, the greater his capacity is for the 'higher' pleasures and therefore for a richer life. Yet increase in education and sensitivity brings with it increase in the number of desires, and a corresponding lesser likelihood of their satisfaction. Instruction and emancipation in one way favour happiness and in another militate against it. To increase a person's chances of happiness, in the sense of fullness of life, is to decrease his chances of happiness, in the sense of satisfaction of desire. Thus in the pursuit of happiness, no less than in the creation of a world, there lurks a problem of evil (A. Kenny, 1973, 61).

Using a threefold rather than a dual analysis of the elements of happiness and concentrating on the happiness of groups

rather than individuals does not lead one to contradict the conclusion that there can be no simple recipe for the maximization
of happiness, and indeed that such maximization is a chimerical goal for moral or political policy. But this does not mean
that we cannot seek ever better systems of trade-offs to protect
and promote the well-being of the inhabitants of the planet.
The following chapter will make some suggestions as to how
this may best be done.

# Chapter 10

# *Policies for Happiness*

## Introduction

As McMahon (2006) notes, and as discussed in the opening chapters, 'If human beings were moved solely, as the utilitarians argued, by sensations of pleasure and pain, then why individuals should sacrifice the one and endure the other for the sake of their fellow men was not at all clear.' Rare is the thinker who believes self interest, unconstrained, is the key to the dignified life. Scotus and Kant surely are correct that we need something other than individual happiness however defined to judge the morality or justice of actions. One needs to believe that others have a right to a certain level of some goods or freedoms, or at least that one has a duty to act towards others in a particular way.

Adam Smith, for example, saw the need for more than self-love in the conduct of the individual, demanding a self-interest that allowed for virtue. 'In the race for wealth, for honors, and preferments, he may run as hard as he can... But if he should justle, or throw down any of them ... it is a violation of fair play...' (*Theory of Moral Sentiments*). Justice was the foundation of society, he felt, required to constrain greed and self-love (Fitzgibbons, 1995).

For Smith, the institutional constraints of a fair market system were an effective tool to channel self-interest in ways that would improve outcomes for all. But justice was part of the institutional model required for the 'free' market to play this role. In a system of welfare economics based in part on Smith's thinking an attractive but ultimately unsatisfactory solution to the dilemma posed by utilitarianism was that individuals motivated by their own desires would, under a set of market institutions (which impose a particular kind of justice), act in ways that maximized the desire fulfillment of all.

One challenge was and remains that there are numerous theoretical and practical exceptions to that rule, involving not only the problem of comparing utilities, but also the nature of goods and exchange within the market. Non-rival and non-excludable goods, different advantages to scale and to monopoly, the complexities of exchange where those involved know different amounts about the goods in question; the list of exceptions to the rule is long and significant.

Partially as a result of this problem, and depending on one's imperfect model, the answer to most practical policy questions regarding welfare economics is 'that depends' (Greenwald and Stiglitz, 1986). Furthermore, by abstracting from issues of distribution, welfare economics has abandoned the tools to examine both issues of welfare as we have defined them and issues connected with dignity and contentment related to relative status. The somewhat sullied version of utilitarianism that is modern welfare economics is frequently a weak guide to morality or policy, then.

Regarding overall income growth, policy based on past empirical regularities might provide a somewhat better basis for action than the theoretical writings of welfare economists, but this too has significant limits. Even the data mined as hard as statistics measuring economic growth have produced few hard and fast policy recommendations. For example, the role of education, investment or trade policies in promoting past economic growth all remain topics of heated debate (Kenny and Williams, 2001).

Regardless, basing future policies on past correlates of a poorly measured proxy (income) weakly related to the outcomes we would like to see improved is a strategy that carries some significant risk. Indeed, aggregate income appears a particularly blunt proxy for anything beyond (or perhaps including) measures of revealed preferences satisfied. If increases in

GNP per capita were closely correlated with improved average health, or reduced crime and warfare, or improved human rights, or subjective well-being, it would surely be a good thing to increase it. But the evidence is against such a close link in all but the poorest communities. It is the failure of income to significantly raise contentment, dignity *or* welfare which makes it an irrelevance for perhaps the majority of the World's countries.

More broadly, Max Weber despaired of social or natural sciences providing definitive answers to the question of how to live and condemned the politics of happiness as 'flabby eudaimonism.' 'We must renounce human happiness as the goal of social legislation' he argued. Instead, we should 'cultivate and support what appears to us *valuable* in man: his personal responsibility, his deep drive towards higher things, towards the spiritual and moral values of mankind ...' (quoted in McMahon, 2006).

As suggested by the chapters on contentment, 'flabby eudaimonism' might in fact point us towards some of the policies which Weber would have supported on the grounds that they cultivated what he found valuable in man. Nonetheless, a broader conception of happiness than one focused on revealed preferences satisfied or (even) earlier notions of utility would suggest different policy approaches. A broader view of development which takes into account welfare, dignity and contentment changes what we might view as suitable targets and policy priorities.

The 'self evident truth' contained in the US Declaration of Independence that all men have the unalienable right to life, liberty and the pursuit of happiness is perhaps as good a guide to the role of the state as any. The state has a primary duty to ensure what is absolutely necessary to life (peace, shelter, food, sufficient measures for public health), it has a secondary duty to ensure freedom from captivity and extortion as well as sufficient means to be free to take part in society as an equal and, as a tertiary responsibility, it should put in place other conditions that allow all the possibility for achieving individual happiness (broadly defined).

## Enhancing Welfare and Dignity Within Countries

A basic package of goods that help to ensure a minimal level of welfare for all (access to housing, nutrition, basic health care and security) combined with a certain minimum level of income and education to ensure that the individual can take part in society without shame is achievable by the great majority of countries. In fact, many countries already go most of the way towards providing such a package. Given what we know of the welfare, dignity and contentment costs of living without that package, the declining contentment returns to additional income, and the minimal benefits to the constituent elements of happiness provided by very high relative wealth in rich countries, the reasons for denying such a package to all through direct and indirect transfers from rich to poor appear very weak.

In addition, Frank (1997) argues that relative concerns are responsible for a number of socially sub-optimal outcomes. For example, status concerns drive the quest for ever-larger houses even while the greater the tract, the lower the density and the longer a society's average commute. As people do not fully adapt to the stress of commuting and the time wasted, he argues, individual desires to live in larger houses create social losses. This provides a double rationale for taxing the construction of large houses. Not only are such houses largely valuable to the purchaser because they redistribute a set stock of societal status (in other words, the construction is the source of a negative externality to owners of smaller houses), but construction has negative externalities in terms of wasted time in commutes and additional pollution. Similarly, families competing to buy houses in good school districts bid up house prices without increasing the number of places in good schools. One could imagine improved outcomes if these resources were used instead to improve the condition of school buildings or teacher pay.

A reorientation towards welfare, dignity and contentment as policy goals would suggest considerably less government intervention in some areas. If we stop thinking of faster economic growth on its own as being a suitable goal for government in the majority of countries, a number of policies lose their rationale. The (already wobbly) leg that investment subsidies, excessive intellectual property rights and other forms of corporate welfare rely on would be removed. At the same time, the case for forcibly evicting people from their homes in the name of development, or for government bureaucracies designed to stimulate output, would also disappear. One might imagine that this was a set of outcomes that both liberals and conservatives could unite behind.

A tax regime that was relieved of the burden of supporting corporate welfare programs and related investment subsidies while provided with additional resources from the taxation of positional goods, environmental bads and the incomes of the rich would be quite likely to have the ironic feature of being more economically efficient. In other words, it is quite possible that removing corporate welfare programs and taxing negative externalities would actually improve economic performance by removing a considerable source of transactions costs and ameliorating a number of market imperfections.

At the same time, such a regime could generate additional resources for the provision of public and private goods which form a necessary (if insufficient) basis for the good life. If we accept that the state should have multiple goals as part of its efforts to increase welfare, dignity and contentment, then it should use multiple tools. We know that poor people in rich and poor countries alike do not spend their incomes in ways that maximize their potential levels of health or education or future earnings. They, like the non-poor, are concerned with leisure, with current consumption and with issues of status. Indeed, even in developing countries, poor and rich alike spend a good deal of money on items that are positively harmful for their health, including excess calories, cigarettes and alcohol. If we decide that other things than satisfying revealed preferences are part of our targets for society, additional tools beyond income transfers will be required. This provides a rationale beyond perceived economic externalities for universal and free access to basic education and health care as well as universal and cheap access to basic infrastructure including water and sanitation, for example. It also provides an additional rationale for improved provision of public goods — not least in terms of adequate policing in areas of high crime.

The general finding that non-rival goods such as insurance and time off may be under-supplied compared to rival goods suggests a further rationale for state sponsorship of insurance mechanisms covering events such as unemployment and ill-health. The importance of insurance would be recognized by Aristotle, who (as we have seen) argued that a happy life should, as far as possible, be invulnerable to bad luck. For similar reasons, a regard to stability suggests that the state should remain concerned with keeping inflation low (high inflation both reflecting and causing significant turbulence in income levels). A focus on non-rival goods suggests a rationale for public policies mandating generous leave policies because status concerns within firms frequently deter individuals from taking holidays.

Regarding dignity, as suggested by earlier chapter, it is likely that the precise constituents of 'necessary dignity' will vary by country, culture and time. Nonetheless, this is undoubtedly an important area where the state has a role as guarantor, but also fetters on the state are important to limit a major source of constraints on choice. Isaiah Berlin (1969) attacked the notion that different peoples have different needs for different types of freedom. While Berlin notes that 'to offer political rights, or safeguards against intervention by the state, to men who are half-naked, illiterate, underfed, and diseased is to mock their condition' he still argues that 'the minimum freedom he needs today, and the greater degree of freedom that he may need tomorrow, is not some freedom peculiar to him, but identical with that of professors, artists, and millionaires.'

Furthermore, given the poor showing of abusive dictatorships in furthering more rapid provision of clothing, education, food and medicine it appears that offering political safeguards even in advance of the half-naked and starving person's ability to fully utilize them carries little risk. Of course, negative rights may only have full value in a situation where the Leviathan has already won — where one won't get shot, or starve, before one has exercised one's right to speak.

But the Leviathan can win at very low levels of income, and states can do considerable harm at that level, too — Rwanda and Cambodia provide two recent examples. Because the evidence is against a strong tradeoff between basic human rights and economic growth or welfare there is no justification for such a tradeoff (even were it a good one to make). Indeed, because what evidence we have points the other way — civil rights improving the state's provision of welfare — we should encourage development of such rights most particularly in the poorest countries.

Looking at the issue of economic dignity, if we accept that there is a role for government in ensuring access to a level of income that allows such dignity, we have to accept that there will never be a definitive list of items that this requires. In Adam Smith's Scotland, such a list might not have included shoes. In Adam Smith's England, it did. For Alfred Marshall it also involved a frock coat and silk hat. More recently, we have seen that popular conceptions of goods that all should be able to afford include having a friend over for dinner, for example. The cost of the consumption basket involved in such lists tends to rise in lock-step with average incomes. A poverty line within countries is better expressed not as an absolute dollar amount or indeed the dollar equivalent of an absolute amount of goods, but instead as a proportion of average incomes. It would be simple enough to calculate the cost of today's 'absolute poverty' consumption basket as made up of goods that people consider a necessity. This poverty line, expressed as a percentage of median incomes, would provide the target income that the state might attempt to ensure for all through minimum wages, earned income tax credits or unemployment insurance provisions.

There are a number of tools that might assist in promoting different elements of dignity and welfare simultaneously. The United States' earned income tax credit is apparently successful in increasing both the earnings and employment rates of poor people. In developing countries, conditional cash transfers providing families with income in exchange for employment training school attendance, vaccination, or prenatal visits can improve measures of welfare, dignity and contentment simultaneously. One such program in Cambodia involved a $45 annual cash transfer to families with girls in secondary schools. This program increased girls' enrollment and attendance at program schools by 30 to 43 percentage points (Filmer and Schady, 2006).

We have suggested the role of considerable taxation of the wealthy to fund programs designed to increase the welfare, dignity and contentment of the poor. What of property rights? It is simple enough to demonstrate that our stocks of property are only to some small extent the pure result of our own labors and therefore ours 'by right.' Not least, Bowles and Gintis (2002) find that intergenerational elasticities of consumption in the United States are as high as 0.68, and elasticities of income are as high as 0.65. This suggests that a one percent change in the relative income position of the parent is associated with a 0.65 percent change in the relative income position of the child. A second set of data reported by Bowles and Gintis suggest that children born to parents in the top income decile have a 23 percent chance of being in that decile themselves and a 41 percent chance of being in the top quintile — compared to a 3.7 percent chance of being in the top quintile to children born in the lowest decile. It is worth noting that estimates for the inter-generational earnings elasticities are about as large in the UK as in the US but only about half as large in Sweden and Canada (Solon, 2002).

As suggested by the notably greater chances of moving from poor to rich across generations in Sweden and Canada than the UK or US, it is not merely that the 'natural order' of the free market underpinned by property rights somehow determines little mobility in a way that is above the concerns of justice. There is no such thing as the 'natural order' of the free market. A vision of such a 'natural order' is as chimerical as Rousseau's state of nature. The free market is something that takes the awesome power of a leviathan to construct and maintain. Rather, it is a power that no actual state has ever fully achieved — the free movement of peoples, goods, ideas and money is hampered in myriad ways, not only at national borders but within them, in every country in the world. Even the most dogmatic political leaders intent on the liberty of the economy have managed at best a minor reduction in these barriers (and largely only those barriers previously created by the state itself).

Similarly, there is no such thing as a 'natural' absolute right to property, defended by a principal of non-interference. Absent others, we might be able to wander where we would, and absent others we would be free of the dangers of contagious disease, violence, captivity or extortion. Absent others, however, our 'property' would be significantly reduced. Absent others, we would not have banks to hold our money nor shops in which to spend it, nor indeed could we meaningfully have 'money' at all. We would have no-one to employ, nor would we have employment. Property is very much a construction of society. At the individual level, as we have seen, the amount of property we own is far more the result of where and when and to whom we were born rather than our individual effort. Any rights we choose attach to property are the result of a social compact and the formation of extremely *un*natural institutions.

## Policies in the Poorest Countries

We have seen that international conceptions of poverty versus non-poverty appear to move as much as do national levels. However, at least from the point of view of welfare, given the very weak relationship between improvements in objective and subjective indicators of the quality of life and income growth in all but the poorest circumstances, it may be that the original Rosenstein-Rodan cut-off between aid donors and aid recipients makes some sense. This cut-off suggests that a number of countries currently considered 'developing' might be more sensibly be viewed as 'wealthy' — and as a result might want to turn their attention away from a direct concern with absolute income to broader measures of development.

For the poorest countries, economic growth may remain an important element of achieving a sustainable basic quality of life. Having said that, economic growth appears to be a complex policy goal. Our understanding of how to increase growth in the short term is very weak (Kenny and Williams,

2001). At the same time, the last fifty years suggest some very positive conclusions about other elements of the quality of life, as we have seen. To wit, even at levels of income considerably below $2 a day, we can see dramatic progress in broader measures of the quality of life, and there is no necessary tradeoff between progress in the areas of dignity and welfare. Whatever it is that LDCs are doing with health and education, however inefficient and corrupt it might be, their performance is historically incredibly impressive. We did not have to see huge increases in income to see very impressive gains in infant survival, life expectancy and education rates. We will not have to wait for such increases to see continued improvements in the future.

As we have seen, improvements in welfare and dignity may also be causal factors behind increased growth rates. This suggests that perhaps the best pro-growth strategy in poor countries is one that targets elements of welfare and dignity. This would include the provision of basic health services, water and sanitation, education (especially to girls) and the basic infrastructure required to support access. It would also include a package of basic rights and a system of government that is transparent and responsive to the needs of citizens.

## Sustaining the Provision of Welfare Services in Poor Countries

As noted in previous chapters, there is considerable scope for improved delivery of services connected to welfare outcomes in developing countries at low cost. Redirecting health resources towards higher-impact services including, for example, those connected with maternal and infant health is one part of the story. Additional resources could be provided by diverting funding and resources from areas of government with negligible or negative social returns, or those where government involvement is unnecessary, to areas such as the provision of services connected to welfare where there is a vital, irreplaceable role for government.

 Military expenditures might be one source of resource transfers. Over the period 1988–2005, military expenditures in

Africa have increased 23 percent and in South Asia by 91 percent compared to a global decline of 4 percent. This suggests a growing misallocation of resources at a time of continued need for the basics of welfare in the World's poorest regions. In addition, there are a range of activities carried out by governments in developing countries that take up time and resources of both officials and citizens to little obvious benefit. Not least, governments in many developing countries own (and frequently subsidize) industries that can be run privately in a competitive environment. The rationale for public ownership of steel or car companies, let alone cheese factories (in Nepal) or shoe factories (in Ethiopia) is unclear. Taking the financial and bureaucratic resources applied to such industries along with the resources applied to enforcement of unnecessary regulations and controls and using them to expand access to vaccination or sanitation programs instead would surely improve welfare outcomes.

At the same time, the delivery of services central to welfare and dignity could be made significantly more efficient. Corruption and mismanagement in health care leads to grossly inflated prices and poor delivery of services, as we have seen. Improved governance will be central to ensure that any increased resources are effectively used. One key in this regard is the use of mechanisms of transparency. Uganda provides an example of the impact that information dissemination can have on the delivery of services. A three-fold increase in spending on primary schools in the country in the early 1990s showed no increases in children at school, according to official statistics. Data on grants per schoolchild showed only 2% of the additional spending was reaching schools in 1991. The government started to publish and broadcast the exact amounts transferred and required schools to maintain public notice boards, posting funds received. Funds reaching schools rose dramatically, from 2% in 1991, to 26% in 1995, to more than 90% in 1999.

Having said all of this, welfare conditions in many developing countries remain atrocious, with malnutrition, stunting and death by easily avoidable causes the lot of millions each year. And, especially in the short term, welfare improvements will be considerable more rapid in poor countries in the presence of improved policy programs including well-designed programs of assistance from rich countries.

## Maximizing Happiness — Global or Local?

Taking the global view, to what extent is the state of the villager in Guinea-Bissau poor because of choices that she made or because of factors outside of her control? The children of rich people are usually rich. Rich countries, by and large, remain rich. Thus, those born rich in rich countries almost always remain rich in global terms. The income of the richest quintile (20 percent of the population) in the United States is 528 times the income of the poorest quintile in Guinea-Bissau. The chance that someone born to a family in the poorest quintile of Guinea-Bissau would achieve an income equal to the richest quintile of those living in Guinea-Bissau is small. The chance that they might reach an income equal to those of the richest income quintile in the United States is infinitesimal.

If a person's wealth was really just about individual effort, one would expect there to be wealthy people evenly spread the world over (unless one really believes that all Asians and Africans are feckless layabouts, which is hard to sustain). One would expect one fifth of the people on the Forbes list of the World's 100 richest people to come from families that had got by on a dollar a day and half to be born of families subsisting on two dollars a day. One would expect none of them to come from the minutely small global stock of billionaire families. One would expect there to be only five Americans and 15 from all developed countries combined. Instead, 38 of the World's 100 richest people are from the United States, and 96 from developed countries. Of the World's 691 billionaires, Forbes claims over 42 percent largely inherited their wealth. Based on a random global distribution of wealth, one would expect that number to be closer to 0.00001 percent, or one three-point-six millionth of the actual figure.

A secondary question involves the extent to which a *country's* poverty is due to free choices made by that country's leaders. Different choices by leaders can clearly make a large difference. Robert Mugabe and Kim Jong-Il carry a heavy personal responsibility for driving their countries into ever-deeper poverty. At the same time, the reason that some countries are poor and others are not clearly has a considerable amount to do with differing geographic environments and a global history of economic relationships. Otherwise it would be hard to explain why the relative wealth of a country in 1870 is such a very powerful predictor of its relative wealth in 2000 (C. Kenny, 1999b).

Furthermore, even if it may be in some sense true that the fate of countries lies in their own hands, this is not the case for individuals. It may be that if only the country had the right institutions and the right policies and the right levels of education, it would be rich. But it is rather a lot to ask of the individual that she or he single-handedly ensure that her country builds up its institutions, changes its policies and educates its masses.

We have used the example of income to point out the limited power of the individual to change their status over time. The same applies even more strongly to measures of welfare. Can anyone really argue that differing rates of mortality before the age of one are based on an insufficient will to live on the part of the babies that die? And yet infant mortality across countries remains considerably unequal and does so largely for reasons that are simple to remedy.

Given this, the question arises, how much are those lucky enough to be born in healthy, wealthy countries morally responsible to help those who, through no moral failing of their own, find themselves in countries with limited resources and low welfare. The argument that property 'rights' are contingent ones frequently outweighed by the welfare needs of others is widely accepted within countries, this is a reason why the state is given the power to tax and redistribute wealth. But the argument is frequently challenged as to its applicability across countries. The communitarian position is that governments may only use force or the threat of force to take property and redistribute it if this is in the common interest of citizens under that government.

But this gives considerably primacy to wealth distributions and borders that are largely the accident of history and are hardly barriers of impenetrable strength. For example, virtually all Western states have governments which have, at one time or another, used considerable force to redistribute property not owned by its citizens and also to redraw borders themselves. The Berlin Conference of 1884 set the international borders for much of Africa with little input from Zambians or Congolese.

Pogge (1994) argues for a globalization of Rawls' difference principle, that to the extent social institutions create social or economic inequalities, they must be designed to the maximum benefit to those at the bottom of these inequalities.

> Why, after all, do liberals want the law of peoples to be supportive of the internal justice of all societies, if not for the sake of the persons living in them? ... why should we focus so narrowly on how well a law of peoples accommodates their interest in living under just domestic institutions and not also, more broadly, on how well it accommodates their underlying and indisputable interest in secure access to food, clothing, shelter, education, and health care, even where a reasonably developed liberal society is still out of the question?

Pogge's case for a moral responsibility to the least well-off at least in terms of their basic welfare wherever they are in the world appears strong.

We would argue that access to a minimum level of welfare is a global right and a global responsibility. We accept that both dignity and contentment, while involving universals, are at a practical level usually subjects of national policy as well as community and individual choices. Even with welfare, there are, of course, practical considerations with regard to giving all of the World's people access to the goods and services required to lead a life of good health, but they are *practical*, not moral. We should be bending over to make the moral practical, and at the moment we are far from doing that.

## The Case for Global Support

Whilst developing countries could use their own resources significantly better to deliver services central to welfare, improvements could be achieved far more rapidly with the assistance of resources from abroad. At the moment, however, large parts of the international economic system are instead set up to the considerable disadvantage of the World's poorest people. Movement across borders, which would allow poor people to sell their labor in countries where it is relatively scarce, is particularly constrained for those with the least resources. Trade in agricultural goods, which are the products produced by the majority of the World's poorest people (who are rural), is some of the least free. At the moment, OECD agricultural support is valued at $248 billion each year (six times the amount of official aid flows) (Stern et al., 2005). Intellectual property rights covering basic medicines raise their price beyond the reach of the global poor.

The extent of global inequalities today may make a policy of completely open borders impractical, but (once more) this is an issue of practicality, not morality. More open borders, and in particular increased avenues for migration from the World's poorest countries, can be a powerful force for increased welfare both for migrants and the families that they leave behind. Fewer restrictions on agricultural imports and reduced subsidies might increase the possibilities for export from some of the poorest countries in the developing world.

Globally we know that we are so far from equality even in access to basic goods, that the imperative of greater equality is surely greater than the risk of an attack on the liberty of Western consumers. We are a safe distance, still, from concerns that more forced giving from rich countries tramples rights out of all proportion to potential benefit. Which is likely to have a bigger impact on any of one's chosen measures of the good life? Taking an average citizen from Chad and doubling their income, or taking an average citizen from the United States and adding two percent to their income? In dollar terms (using purchasing power parity), the two actions require the same resources.

Good basic health care can be provided at a low and drop-ping level of GDP per capita if national institutions are in place to support such an effort. At the same time it is also true that many countries around the world such care is not provided. Whose *fault* that is might be considered somewhat irrelevant to a child dying of a measles infection or diarrhea. What is more to the point is that the global community can do some-thing about it, at very low cost. We know that the marginal impact of a dollar in terms of life, liberty or utility in wealthy countries is close to zero. We know that the impact of that dol-lar spent on delivering a measles vaccination or research into a vaccine for malaria may be considerably higher. It is difficult to understand the moral case against moving that dollar.

Thirty-five years ago, Samuel Huntington (1970) laid out the different degrees of ethical strength behind different types of assistance:

> The moral obligation to feed the hungry in India is fairly obvi-ous. The moral obligation to insure that India's economy grows at 6 percent per annum is considerably less obvious. The moral obligation is further weakened by the nature of the public aid-giving process. This typically involves the transfer of resources or credit from one government to another gov-ernment. The moral obligation, however, is to help the poor *people* of poor countries …

This rings true. Our moral obligation is to individuals in the developing world, and it is to promote some basic, sustain-able, minimum level of well-being, not ever more rapid growth. Furthermore, looking at the three elements of welfare, dignity and contentment, it appears the case for international intervention weakens from welfare to dignity and from dig-nity to contentment. It is surely hard to resist the moral power of calls for an international response to famine or mass murder (much though issues of practicality might provide legitimate or illegitimate cover for inaction). Beyond some of the most egregious violations (slavery, or mass arrests, for example), the elements of dignity may vary by considerably by country. In particular, we have seen that the minimum level of goods required to go out in public without shame will vary by time and community. Furthermore, the patchy record and grim human cost of the international community's efforts to impose civil and political rights through force suggests the need for considerable caution in using the most desperate measure of military intervention. At the same time, the limited efficacy of international attempts to build institutions in developing countries suggests the need for modesty in expectations. Contentment appears to be almost completely a matter of domestic policies and of individual choice and character.

Having said that, Huntington's conclusion demands caveats. Especially in the poorest countries of the world, rapid growth is likely to be part of the package needed to promote basic well-being. And governments are likely to be a vital partner in ensuring the sustainable delivery of public goods such as clean water and vaccinations that should be part of that package. Without states, we are unlikely to be able to meet our moral obligation to individuals.

This leaves a practical question of the efficacy of aid. Development assistance does not appear to have been a terribly effective tool of improving economic growth in the very countries where we would most like to see it work (Easterly et al., 2003). At the same time, economic growth does not appear to be a terribly powerful tool in improving quality of life even in the countries where we would most like it to be. The aid-growth-quality of life channel is doubly inefficient, then.

But it is a weakness of imagination to argue that because traditional models of aid have had many failings and see declining returns especially in terms of income growth, there is no way to spend additional resources in a manner that will improve the quality of life in developing countries. Aid has had a significant impact if we take a broader view of its purpose—not least as part of the global efforts to eradicate smallpox and polio. The argument about aid amongst those convinced of the imperative to improve outcomes in the poorest countries should not be about more or less aid, but about how it should be delivered. It is quite possibly the case that more aid as currently delivered to many developing countries would do little to improve outcomes. But this is an argument for aid reform, not aid stagnation.

For example, because poor people are an unlikely consumption group for $100 pills, the sad result is that more money goes to inventing a new way of beautifying the noses of Hollywood than goes towards a cure or a vaccine for malaria. Schemes such as that recently created by the UK government to guarantee a purchase pool for a malaria vaccine when it is invented bypasses developing country governments but will still have a dramatic impact on the lives of those in developing countries if and when a vaccine results. Programs to provide conditional payments to suppliers who roll out access to services and consumers who use them have both been successfully supported by aid agencies in numerous developing countries with considerable results in terms of welfare.

## Conclusion

This chapter has only gone a part way in exploring the policy implications of a broader focus on welfare, dignity and contentment. It has left largely unanswered questions about tradeoffs between elements of the good life and levels of welfare that can or should be expected as a global minimum. It has said little about policies for expanding dignity or minimizing welfare losses due to violence.

Nonetheless, policy conclusions do emerge. Focusing the efforts of governments on the constituents of happiness rather than the chase for greater GDP per capita would relieve them of a number of responsibilities. Their already questionable role in industrial policy or widespread industry ownership would fade, for example. Instead, there would be enhanced priorities focused around the provision of health, education and basic infrastructure services, mechanisms to ensure against negative life events, and tools to reduce negative externalities related to positional goods. Transfer mechanisms can be designed that both ensure a level of income sufficient to go out in public unashamed while simultaneously encouraging improved welfare outcomes. All of these services can be better provided in an environment of transparency and participation that better flourishes where civil rights are protected. Such rights are, regardless, a key constituent of dignity and one of the few effective tools against violence.

While the primary responsibility rests with countries themselves, there is a considerable role for international cooperation to provide improved welfare outcomes. The happiness of those in rich and poor countries alike would be significantly increased if that cooperation were forthcoming.

# Bibliography

Abadie, A. (2006) Poverty, Political Freedom and the Roots of Terrorism, *American Economic Review* 96, 2.

Acemoglu, D. S. Johnson and J. Robinson (2001) The Colonial Origins of Comparative Development: An Empirical Investigation *The American Economic Review* 91, 5.

Acemoglu, D., S. Johnson, J. Robinson and P. Yared (2005a) Income and Democracy, NBER Working Paper 11205, March.

Acemoglu, D., S. Johnson, J. Robinson and P. Yared (2005b) From Education to Democracy? NBER Working Paper 11204, March.

Adams, P. (1949) The Social Responsabilities of Science in Utopia, New Atlantis and After, *Journal of the History of Ideas*, 1949, pp. 374-398

Ahmed, I. (2003) Decent Work and Human Development *International Labor Review*, 142, 2.

Ahuvia, A. and D. Friedman (1998) Income, Consumption and Subjective Wellbeing *Journal of Macromarketing*, Fall, 1998.

Alesina, A. and R. Wacziarg (1998) Openness, Country Size and Government *Journal of Public Economics*, 69, 305-321.

Annett, A. (2001) Social Fractionalization, Political Instability, and the Size of Government *IMF Staff Papers* 48, 3.

Aquinas, T. (1993) *Selected Philosophical Writings* selected and translated by Timothy McDermott, Oxford: Oxford University Press.

Aries, P. (1974) *Western Attitudes Toward Death: From the Middle Ages to the Present* Baltimore: Johns Hopkins.

Aristotle (1962) *The Politics*. Harmondsworth: Penguin.

Aristotle (1992) *Eudemian Ethics, Books I, II and VIII* Oxford: Clarendon Press.

Aristotle (2002) *The Nicomachean Ethics* S. Broadie & C. Rowe. Oxford: Oxford University Press.

Augustine, St (1963) *The Trinity* Washington DC: Catholic University of America Press.

Augustine, St (1972) *The City of God* Harmondsworth: Penguin Books.

Augustine, St (1992) *The Confessions* Oxford: Oxford University Press.

Baldacci, E. B. Clements, S. Gupta, Q. Cui (2004) Social Spending, Human Capital, and Growth in Developing Countries: Implications for Achieving the MDGs, IMF Working Paper 04/217.

Baldwin, F. (1926) Sumptuary Legislation and Personal Regulation in England *Johns Hopkins University Studies in Historical and Political Science* 44(1) 1-282.

Banister, J. and X. Zhang (2005) China, Economic Development and Mortality Decline *World Development* 33, 1, 21-41.

Bentham, J. (1843) *Works* reprinted 1962, New York: Russell and Russell.

Bentham, J. (1982) *Introduction to the Principles of Morals and Legislation* London: Routledge.

Berlin I. (1969) Four *Essays on Liberty* Oxford: Oxford University Press.

Bernstein, W. (2004) *The Birth of Plenty* New York: McGraw Hill.

Besley, T. and M. Kadamatsu (2006) Health and Democracy *American Economic Review*, 96, 2.

Bhattacharya, S. (2005) WHO Reports Steep Rise in Obesity in Poorer Countries *New Scientist* 16:26, 23 September.

Biswas-Diener, R. and E. Diener (2000) Making the Best of a Bad Situation: Satisfaction in the Slums of Calcutta, mimeo, University of Illinois.

Blanchflower, D. and A. Oswald (1992). Entrepreneurship, Happiness and Supernormal Returns: Evidence from Britain and the US. NBER Working Paper No. 4228.

Blanchflower, D. and A. Oswald (2000) Well-Being Over Time in Britain and the USA, NBER Working Paper 7487.

Bloom, D. and J. Sachs (1998) Geography, Demography and Economic Growth in Africa, mimeo, HIID, Harvard.

Bourguignon, F. (1996) Equity and Economic Growth: Permanent Questions and Changing Answers? Background paper for the 1996 Human Development Report, UNDP.

Bourguignon, F. and C. Morrisson (2002) Inequality Among World Citizens: 1820-1992 *American Economic Review* 92, 4.

Bowles, S. and H. Gintis (2002) The Inheritance of Inequality *Journal of Economic Perspectives* 16, 3, 3-30.

Brecke, P. (2001) The Long-Term Patterns of Violent Conflict in Different Regions of the World Paper prepared for the Uppsala Conflict Data Conference on 8-9 June 2001, Uppsala, Sweden.

Bronk, R. (1998) *Progress and the Invisible Hand: The Philosophy and Economics of Human Advance* London: Warner Books.

Brunetti, A (1997). Political Variables in Cross-Country Growth Analysis, *Journal of Economic Surveys*. 2: 163-90.

Bruni, L. and L. Stanca (2006) Income Aspirations, Television and Happiness: Evidence from the World Values Survey *Kyklos*, 59, 2.

Buvinic, M. and A. Morrison (2000) Living in a More Violent World *Foreign Policy* 118 (Spring) 58-72.

Camfield, L. (2003) Using Subjective Measures of Wellbeing in Developing Countries, mimeo, ERSC Research Group on Wellbeing in Developing Countries, University of Bath.

Cantril, H. (1965). *The Pattern of Human Concerns* New Brunswick: Rutgers.

Carbonell, A. and P. Frijters (2004) How Important is Methodology for the Estimates of the Determinants of Happiness *The Economic Journal* 114, 641-659.

Carlsson, F., O. Johansson-Stenman and P. Martinsson (2003) Do You Enjoy Having More than Others? Survey Evidence of Positional Goods, Goteburg University Working Papers in Economics No. 100.

Chappell, D. and V. Martino (2000) *Violence at Work*, Geneva: ILO.

Chappell, D. and V. Martino (2006) *Violence at Work, Third Edition*, Geneva: ILO.

Chesnais, J. (1995) Worldwide Historical Trends in Murder and Suicide in Julian Simon (ed.) *The State of Humanity* Cambridge US: Blackwell

Claeys, G. and L. Sargent (1999) *The Utopia Reader* New York: New York University Press.

Clark, A. (2003) Unemployment as a Social Norm: Psychological Evidence from Panel Data *Journal of Labour Economics* 21, 2.

Clark, D. and D. Hulme (2005) Towards a Unified Framework for Understanding the Depth, Breadth and Duration of Poverty ERSC Global Poverty Research Group Working Paper 020.

Clark, G. (2005) *The Economics of the Ascent of Man: A Brief Economic History of the World* Princeton University Press.

Clarke, G. (1995) More Evidence on Income Distribution and Growth *Journal of Development Economics* 47: 403-427.

Clemens, M., C. Kenny and T. Moss (2005) The Trouble with the MDGs: Confronting Expectations of Aid and Development Success, Center for Global Development Working Paper, No. 40.

Clemens, M. (2004) The Long Walk to School: International education goals in historical perspective, Working Paper 37, Center for Global Development, Washington, DC.

Collier, P. and A. Hoeffler (2004) Greed and Grievance in Civil War, mimeo, Center for the Study of African Economies, Oxford.

Comin, D. B. Hobijn and E. Rovito (2006) Five Facts You Need to Know About Technology Diffusion NBER Working Paper 11928.

Conniff, R. (2002) *A Natural History of the Rich* New York: Norton.

Cummins, R. (2002) The Validity and Utility of Subjective Quality of Life: A Reply to Hatton and Ager *Journal of Applied Research in Intellectual Disabilities* 15 261-268

Cummins, R. and H. Nistico (2002) Maintaining Life Satisfaction: The Role of Positive Cognitive Bias *Journal of Happiness Studies* 3: 37-69.

Cummins, R., E. Guillone and A. Lau (2002) A Model of Subjective Well-Being Homeostasis: The Role of Personality in E. Guillone and R. Cummins eds. *The Universality of Subjective Wellbeing Indicators: A Multi-Disciplinary and Multi-National Perspective* London: Kluwer.

Cutler, D. and G. Miller (2004) The Role of Public Health Improvements in Health Advances: The 20th Century United States, NBER Working Paper 10511.

Cutler, D., A. Deaton and A. Lleras-Muney (2006) The Determinants of Mortality NBER Working Paper 11963.

Das, J. and J. Hammer (2005) Money for Nothing: The Dire Straights of Medical Practice in Delhi, India, World Bank Policy Research Working Paper 3669.

Deaton, A. (2004) Health in an Age of Globalization, Paper for the Brookings Trade Forum, Brookings Institution, Washington DC, May 13-14, 2004.

Deaton, A. and C. Paxson (2004) Mortality, Income and Income Inequality Over Time in Britain and the United States in D. Wise (ed.) *Perspectives on the Economics of Aging* Chicago: University of Chicago Press.

Diamond, J. (1987) The Worst Mistake in the History of the Human Race *Discover Magazine*, May, pp 64-66.

Diener E, and C. Diener (1995) The Wealth of Nations Revisited: Income and Quality of Life *Social Indicators Research* 36: 275-286.

Diogenes Laertius (1972) *Lives of Eminent Philosophers*, Cambridge, MA: Harvard University Press.

Dollar, D. and A. Kraay (2002) Growth Is Good for the Poor *Journal of Economic Growth*, 7, 3.

Dorn, D., J. Fischer, G. Kirchgassner, A Sousa-Poza (2005) Is It Culture or Democracy? The Impact of Democracy, Income and Culture on Happiness, University of St Gallen Discussion Paper 2005-12.

Dowling, M. (2005) Decision Making, Neuroeconomics and Happiness, mimeo, Center for Institutional Performance, Reading University.

Dreze, J. and A. Sen (1989) *Hunger and Public Policy*, Oxford, Clarendon.

Easterbrook, G. (2005) The Capitalist Manifesto, Review of The Morla Consequences of Economic Growth by Benjamin Friedman, *New York Times Review of Books*, November 27, 2005.

Easterlin, R. (1974) Does Economic Growth Improve the Human Lot? in: P. David and M. Reder (eds) *Nations and Households in Economic Growth* New York: Academic Press.

Easterlin, R. A. (1981) Why Isn't the Whole World Developed? *Journal of Economic History* 1, 41, 1-19.

Easterlin, R (1995) Industrial Revolution and Mortality Revolution: Two of a Kind? *Journal of Evolutionary Economics* 5: 393-408.

Easterlin, R. (1998) How Beneficent is the Market? A Look at the Modern History of Mortality, mimeo, University of Southern California.

Easterlin, R. (2004) Diminishing Marginal Utility of Income? A Caveat, University of Southern California Law School: University of Southern California Law and Economics Working Paper Series C04-6.

Easterlin, R. (2004) *The Reluctant Economist* Cambridge: Cambridge.

Easterlin, R. (2005) Explaining Happiness, mimeo, USC, California.

Easterly, W. (1999) Life During Growth *Journal of Economic Growth* 4: 239-275.

Easterly, W. and R. Levine (2003) Tropics, Germs and Crops: How Endowments Influence Economic Development *Journal of Monetary Economics* 50.

Easterly, W., R. Levine, and D. Roodman (2003) New Data, New Doubts: Revisiting 'Aid, Policies and Growth', CGD Working Paper 26, Center for Global Development, Washington DC, February.

Eisner, M. (2003) Long-Term Historical Trends in Violent Crime *Crime and Justice* 30 83-142.

Engerman, S. (1995) The Extent of Slavery and Freedom Throughout the Ages, in the World as a Whole and Major Subareas in Julian Simon (ed.) *The State of Humanity* Cambridge US: Blackwell.

Engerman, S. and K. Sokoloff (2005) Colonialism, Inequality and Long-Run Paths of Development, NBER Working Paper 11057.

Ersado, L. (2005) Small-Scale Irrigation Dams, Agricultural Production, and Health: Theory and Evidence from Ethiopia, World Bank Policy Research Paper 3494, January.

Esposto, A. and P. Zaleski (1999) Economic Freedom and the Quality of Life: An Empirical Analysis *Constitutional Political Economy* 10, 2, 185-97.

Fay, Marianne (1993) Illegal Activities and Income Distribution: A Model with Envy, mimeo, Columbia University.

Ferguson, N. (2001) *The Cash Nexus: Money and Power in the Modern World 1700-2000* London: Allen Lane.

Ferguson, N. (2003) *Empire: The Rise and Demise of the British World Order and the Lessons for Global Power* New York: Allen Lane.

Fernandez-Armesto, F. (2001) *Civilizations: Culture, Ambition and the Transformation of Nature* New York: Touchstone.

Filmer, D and L. Pritchett (1997) Child Mortality and Public Spending on Health: How Much Does Money Matter? mimeo, World Bank.

Filmer, D. and N. Schady (2006) Getting Girls into School: Evidence from a Scholarship Program in Cambodia World Bank Policy Research Working Paper 3910.

Filmer, D., J. Hammer and Lant Pritchett (2000) Weak Links in the Chain: A Diagnosis of Health Policy in Poor Countries *World Bank Research Observer* 15, 2.

Fisher, G. (1995) Is There Such a Thing as an Absolute Poverty Line Over Time? Evidence from the United States, Britain, Canada and Australia on the Income Elasticity of the Poverty Line. Mimeo, US Census Department.

Fitzgibbon, K. (2003) Modern-Day Slavery? The Scope of Trafficking in Persons in Africa *African Security Review* 12, 1.

Fitzgibbons, A. (1995) *Adam Smith's System of Liberty, Wealth and Virtue: The Moral and Political Foundations of the Wealth of Nations* Oxford: Clarendon.

Fogel, R, (2004) *The Escape from Hunger and Premature Death, 1700-2100* Cambridge: Cambridge University Press.

Fogel, R. (1995) The Contribution of Improved Nutrition to the Decline in Mortality Rates in Europe and America in Julian Simon (ed.) *The State of Humanity* Cambridge US: Blackwell.

Frank, Robert (1997) The Frame of Reference as a Public Good *The Economic Journal* 107, November: 1832-1847.

Frey, B. and A. Stutzer (2002) *Happiness and Economics* Princeton: Princeton University Press.

Friedman, B. (2005) *The Moral Consequences of Economic Growth* New York: Knopf.

Furnham, A. and M. Argyle, (1998) *The Psychology of Money* London: Routledge.

Galbraith, J. (1987) *A History of Economics: The Past as the Present* London: Penguin.

Gasper, D. (2004) Subjective and Objective Well-Being in Relation to Economic Inputs: Puzzles and Responses, ERSC Research Group on Wellbeing in Developing Countries Working Paper 09.

Geremek, B. (1997) *Poverty: A History* Oxford: Blackwell.

Gilbert, G. (1997) Adam Smith on the Nature and Causes of Poverty *Review of Social Economy* 55 (3) 273-91.

Gradstein, M and B. Milanovic (2002) Does Liberte = Egalite? A Survey of the Empirical Links Between Deomcracy and Inequality. World Bank Policy Research Working Paper 2875, August 2002.

Graham, C. (2004) Can Happiness Research Contribute to Development Economics? paper presented at the Massachusetts Avenue Development Seminar, February 2004.

Graham, C. and A. Felton (2004) Does Inequality Matter to Individual Welfare? An Initial Exploration Based on Happiness Surveys from Latin America, mimeo, the Brookings Institution.

Graham, C. and A. Felton (2005) Variance in Obesity Across Cohorts and Countries: A Norms-Based Explanation Using Happiness Surveys Brookings Institution CSED Working Paper 42.

Graham, C., A. Eggers and S. Sukhtankar (2004) Does Happiness Pay? An Exploration Based on Panel Data from Russia forthcoming in *Journal of Economic Behavior and Organization* 55.

Graham, C. and S. Pettinato (2002) Frustrated Achievers: Winners, Losers, and Subjective Well Being in New Market Economies *Journal of Development Studies* 38, 4.

Greenwald, B. and J. Stiglitz (1986) Externalities in Economies with Imperfect Information and Incomplete Markets *Quarterly Journal of Economics* 101: 229- 264.

Gribbin, J. (2002) *Science: A History* London: Penguin.

Gullone, E. and R. Cummins eds (2003) *The Universality of Subjective Wellbeing Indicators* London: Kluwer.

Hanmer, L. and H. White (1999) The Impact of HIV/AIDS on Under-Five Mortality in Zambia and Zimbabwe in *Human Development in Sub-Saharan Africa: The Determinants of Under-Five Mortality* The Hague: ISSAS.

Hanmer, L., R. Lensink and H. White (2003) Infant and Child Mortality in Developing Countries: Analysing the Data for Robust Determinants *Journal of Development Studies* 40,1.

Hayek, F. (1944) *The Road to Serfdom* London: Routledge.

Hegre, H. and N. Sambanis (2005) Sensitivity Analysis of the Empirical Literature on Civil War Onset, Paper for the 13th Norwegian National

Conference in Political Science, Hurdalsjoen, Norway, 5-7 January, 2005.

Heise, L., M. Ellsberg and M. Gottmoeller (2002) A Global Overview of Gender-Based Violence *International Journal of Gynecology and Obstetrics* 78 Suppl. 1.

Helliwell, J. (1996) Economic Growth and Social Capital in Asia, NBER Working Paper 5470.

Helliwell, J. (2002) How's Life? Comparing Individual and National Variables to Explain Subjective Well-Being, NBER Working Paper 9065.

Helliwell, J. (2004) Well-being and Social Capital: Does Suicide Pose a Puzzle? NBER Working Paper 10896.

Helliwell, J. and H. Huang (2006) How's Your Government? International Evidence Linking Good Government and Well-Being, NBER Working Paper 11988.

Hermann, M. and C. Kegley (1996) Ballots, a Barrier Against the Use of Bullets and Bombs: Democratization and Military Intervention *The Journal of Conflict Resolution* 40, 3, 436-59.

Hertz, E., J. Hebert and J. Landon (1994) Social and Environmental Factors and Life Expectancy, Infant Mortality and Maternal Mortality Rates: Results of a Cross-National Comparison *Social Science and Medicine* 39, 1, 105-114.

Hill, C (1991) *The World Turned Upside Down: Radical Idea During the English Revolution* London: Penguin.

Hill, K. (1995) The Decline in Childhood Mortality in Julian Simon (ed.) *The State of Humanity* Cambridge US: Blackwell.

Hill, K., R. Pande, M. Mahy and G. Jones (1998) Trends in Child Mortality in the Developing World 1960-1996, mimeo, Johns Hopkins University.

Hirschman, A. O. (1977) *The Passions and the Interests: Political Arguments for Capitalism Before Its Triumph* Princeton: Princeton University Press.

Hobbes (1996: 1651) *Leviathan* Cambridge Revised Student Edition, Tuck.

Hoff, K. and P. Pandey (2004) Belief Systems and Durable Inequalities: An Experimental Investigation of Indian Caste, mimeo, World Bank.

Human Security Centre (2005) *Human Security Report* University of British Columbia, Canada.

Huntington, S. (1970) Foreign Aid for What and for Whom *Foreign Policy* 1, 161-189.

IMF (International Monetary Fund) and World Bank (2005) *Global Monitoring Report* Washington DC: World Bank.

Jamison, D. and Colleagues eds (2006) *Disease Control Priorities in Developing Countries, Second Edition* New York: Oxford University Press and World Bank.

Jamison, D. (2006) *Investing in Health* in D. Jamison et. al. *Disease Control Priorities in Developing Countries* New York: Oxford University Press.

Jamison, D., M. Sandbu and J. Wang (2001) Cross-Country Variation in Mortality Decline, 1962-87: The Role of Country-Specific Technical Progress, CMH Working Paper Series, WG1:4.

Jardine, L. (1999) *Ingenious Pursuits: Building the Scientific Revolution* London: Little Brown.

Johnson, D.G. (2000) Population, Food and Knowledge *American Economic Review* 90, 1.

Kahneman, D. and A. Krueger (2006) Developments in the Measurement of Subjective Wellbeing *Journal of Economic Perspectives* 20, 1 3-24.

Kahneman, D., A Krueger, D. Schkade, N. Schwarz, and A. Stone (2004) Toward National Wellbeing Accounts *American Economic Review* 94,2.

Kambhampati, U. and R. Rajan (2006) Economic Growth: A Panacea for Child Labor? *World Development* 34, 3, 426-445.

Kant, I. (1991) *Metaphysics of Morals* Ed. M. Gregor, Cambridge: CUP.

Kenny, A. (1963) *Action, Emotion and Will* London: Routledge.

Kenny, A. (1968) *Descartes* New York: Random House.

Kenny, A. (1973) *The Anatomy of the Soul* Oxford: Blackwell.

Kenny, A. (1992) *Aristotle on the Perfect Life* Oxford: Clarendon.

Kenny, A. (1997) *A Life in Oxford* London: John Murray.

Kenny, A. (2004) *Ancient Philosophy* Oxford: Oxford University Press.

Kenny, A. (2005) *Medieval Philosophy*. Oxford: Oxford University Press

Kenny, A. (2006) *The Rise of Modern Philosophy* Oxford: Oxford University Press.

Kenny, C. (1999) Does Growth Cause Happiness, Or Does Happiness Cause Growth? *Kyklos*, 52, 1.

Kenny, C. (1999b) Why Aren't Countries Rich? Weak States and Bad Neighborhoods *The Journal of Development Studies* 35, 5, 26-47.

Kenny, C. (2005a) There's More to Life than Money: Examining the Link Between Income, Health and Education, mimeo, World Bank.

Kenny, C (2005b) Why Are We So Worried About Income? Everything Else that Matters is Converging *World Development* 33, 1.

Kenny, C (2005c) Does Development Make You Happy? *Social Indicators Research* 73, 2.

Kenny, C. (2006) Were People in the Past Poor and Miserable? *Kyklos* 59, pp. 275-306.

Kenny, C. and D. Williams (2001) What Do We Know About Economic Growth? Or, Why Don't We Know Very Much? *World Development* 29.

Kingdon, G. and J. Knight (2003) Well-being Poverty versus Income Poverty and Capabilities Poverty? CSAE Working Paper 2003-16.

Kingdon, G. and J. Knight (2004) Community, Comparisons and Subjective Well-being in a Divided Society, CSAE Working Paper 2004-21.

Kirby, P. (1995) Causes of Short Stature Among Coal-Mining Children, 1823-1850 *The Economic History Review* 48, 4.

Klasen, S. (2005) Economic Growth and Poverty Reduction: Measurement and Policy Issues, OECD Development Center Working Paper 246.

Korenromp, E., F. Arnold, B. Williams, B. Nahlen and R. Snow (2004) Monitoring Trends in Under-5 Mortality Rates Through National Birth History Surveys *International Journal of Epidemiology* 33: 1293-1301.

Krueger, A. and J. Maleckova (2003) Education, Poverty and Terrorism: Is There a Causal Connection? *The Journal of Economic Perspectives* 17, 4.

Krugman, P. (1994) Past and Prospective Causes of High Unemployment *Federal Reserve Bank of Kansas City Economic Review*, Fourth Quarter.

Kupperman, K. (1984) Fear of Hot Climates in the Anglo-American Colonial Experience *The William and Mary Quarterly* 3, 41, 2.

Lacina, B. (2006) Explaining the Severity of Civil Wars *Journal of Conflict Resolution*, 50, 2, 276-289.

Lacina, B. and N. Gleditsch (2005) Monitoring Trends in Global Conflict: A New Dataset of Battle Deaths *European Journal of Population* 21: 145-166.

Laderchi, C., R. Saith and F. Stewart (2002) Everyone Agrees we Need Poverty Reduction, But Not What this Means: Does this Matter? mimeo, Oxford University.

LaFree, G. and A. Tseloni (2006) Democracy and Crime: A Multilevel Analysis of Homicide Trends in Forty-Four Countries, 1950-2000, *Annals, AAAPS*, 605, May.

Landes, D. (1998) *The Wealth and Poverty of Nations* New York: Norton.

Laxminarayan, R., J. Chow and S. Shahid-Salles (2006) Intervention Cost-Effectiveness: Overview of Main Messages in Health in D. Jamison et. al. *Disease Control Priorities in Developing Countries* New York: Oxford University Press.

Layard, Richard. (2005) *Happiness: Lessons from a New Science* London: Allen Lane.

Lederman, D., N. Loayza, A. Menendez (2002) Violent Crime: Does Social Capital Matter? *Economic Development and Cultural Change* 50, 3.

Leipziger, D., M. Fay, Q. Wodon, T. Yepes (2003) Achieving the Millennium Development Goals: The Role of Infrastructure, World Bank Policy Research Working Paper 3163.

Lena, H. and B. London (1993) The Political and Economic Determinants of Health Outcomes: A Cross-National Analysis *International Journal of Health Services* 23,3 585-602.

Levitt, S. (2004) Understanding Why Crime Fell in the 1990s: Four Factors that Explain the Decline and Six that Do Not *Journal of Economic Perspectives* 18, 1.

Lewis, M. (2006) Governance and Corruption in Public Health Care Systems, Center for Global Development Working Paper 78.

Lindert, P. (1986) Unequal English Wealth Since 1670 *The Journal of Political Economy* 94, 6, 1127-1162.

Loevinsohn B. and A. Harding (2005) Buying results? Contracting for Health Service Delivery in Developing Countries *Lancet* 2005, 366: 676–81.

Logan, T. (2005) The Transformation of Hunger: The Demand for Calories Past and Present, NBER Working Paper 11754.

Long, A. and Sedley, D. (1987) *The Hellenistic Philosophers* Cambridge: Cambridge University Press.

Lorentzen, P., J. McMillan and R. Wacziarg (2005) Death and Development, NBER Working Paper 11620.

Lucas, R. (1988) On the Mechanics of Economic Development *Journal of Monetary Economics* 22, 1.

Lykken, D. and A. Tellegen (1996) Happiness is a Stochastic Phenomenon *Psychological Science* 7, 3.

Maddison, A. (1995) *Monitoring the World Economy 1820-1992* Paris: OECD.

Maddison, A. (2001) *The World Economy: A Millennial Perspective* Paris: OECD.

Madon, G. (2003) Energy, Poverty and Gender: Impacts of Rural Electrification on Poverty and Gender in Indonesia, mimeo, World Bank.

Malthus (1798) *An Essay on the Principle of Population* London: J. Johnson.

Mason, R. (1998) *The Economics of Conspicuous Consumption: Theory and Thought Since 1700* Cheltenham, UK: Edward Elgar.

McGill, V. (1967) *The Idea of Happiness* New York: Praeger.

McGuire, J (2005) Basic Health Provision and Under-5 Mortality: A Cross-National Study of Developing Countries *World Development* 34, 3.

McGuire, J. (2001) Social Policy and Mortality Decline in East Asia and Latin America *World Development* 29, 10, 1673-1697.

McMahon, D. (2006) *Happiness: A History* New York: Atlantic Monthly Press.

Mill, J.S. (1889) *Three Essays on Religion* London.

Mill, J.S. (1962) *Utilitarianism* London: Collins.

Mill, J.S. (1971) *Autobiography* Oxford: Oxford University Press.

Mill, J.S. (1985) *Principals of Political Economy* London: Penguin.

Mishan, E. (1967) *The Costs of Economic Growth* London: Pelican.

Moore, M, J. Leavy, P. Houtzager and H. White (1999) Polity Qualities: How Governance Affects Poverty IDS Working Paper 99.

Morawitz, D. (1979) Income Distribution and Self-Rated Happiness: Some Empirical Evidence *The Economic Journal* 87: 511-522.

Myers, D. (1992) *The Pursuit of Happiness* New York: Harper Collins.

Myers, D. and E. Diener (1996) The Pursuit of Happiness *Scientific American* 272, 5, May: 70-2.

Myers, D. and E. Diener (1997) The Science of Happiness *The Futurist*, 31, 5 pp. S1-S7.

Namazie, C. and P. Sanfey (2001) Happiness and Transition: the Case of Kyrgyzstan *Review of Development Economics* 5 (3) 392-405.

Narayan, D. and L. Pritchett (1996) Cents and Sociability: Household Income and Social Capital in Rural Tanzania, mimeo, The World Bank.

Neumayer, E. (2004) Is Inequality Really a Major Cause of Violent Crime? Evidence from a Cross-National Panel of Robbery and Violent Theft Rates, mimeo, London School of Economics.

Nord, M., M. Andrews and S. Carlson (2003) Household Food Security in the United States, 2002 USDA Economic Research Service Food Assistance and Nutrition Research Report No. 35.

Nussbaum, M. (1999) *Sex and Social Justice* New York: Oxford University Press.

Nussbaum, M. (2001) *Women and Human Development: The Capabilities Approach* Cambridge: Cambridge University Press.

Nussbaum, M. (2003) Capabilities as Fundamental Entitlements: Sen and Social Justice *Feminist Economics* 9, 2-3.

Painter, G. (1922) The Idea of Progress *The American Journal of Sociology* 28, 3, 257-282.

Persson, T. and G. Tabellini (2006) Democratic Capital: The Nexus of Political and Economic Change, NBER Working Paper 12175.

Pigou, A. (1912) *Wealth and Welfare* London: Macmillan.

Piketty, T. and E. Saez (2006) The Evolution of Top Incomes, NBER Working Paper 11955.

Pinker, S. (2002) *The Blank Slate: The Modern Denial of Human Nature* London: Allen Lane.

Plato (1997) *Complete Works* Indianapolis: Hackett.

Plous, S. (1993) *The Psychology of Judgment and Decision-Making* New York: McGraw Hill.

Pogge, T. (1994) An Egalitarian Law of Peoples *Philosophy and Public Affairs* 23, 3, 195-224.

Porter, R. (1999) *The Greatest Benefit to Mankind: A Medical History of Humanity* New York: W.W. Norton.

Pradhan, M. and M. Ravallion (2000) Measuring Poverty Using Qualitative Perceptions of Consumption Adequacy *The Review of Economics and Statistics* 82,(3).

Preston, S. (1975) The Changing Relation Between Mortality and Level of Economic Development *Population Studies* 29, 2, 231-248.

Pritchett, L. (1997) Divergence, Big Time *Journal of Economic Perspectives* 11,3, Summer.

Pritchett, L. and L. Summers (1996) Wealthier is Healthier *Journal of Human Resources* 31, 4: 842-68.

Quah, D. (1993) Empirical Cross-Section Dynamics in Economic Growth *European Economic Review* 37, 426-3.

Ram, R. (1992) Intercountry Inequalities in Income and Basic Needs Indicators: A Recent Perspective *World Development* 20, 6 899-905.

Ranis, G. and F. Stewart (2001) Growth and Human Development: Comparative Latin American Experience *The Developing Economies* XXXIX-4 333-65.

Ravallion, M. and M. Lokshin (2001) Identifying Welfare Effects from Subjective Questions *Economica* 68, 335-357.

Ravallion, M. and M. Lokshin (2005) Who Cares About Relative Deprivation? Policy Research Working Paper, World Bank, No. 3782.

Rojas, M. (2002) The Multidimensionality of Poverty: A Subjective Well-Being Approach, mimeo, Department of Economics, Universidad de las Americas, Puebla, Mexico.

Rosenstein-Rodan, P. (1961) International Aid for Underdeveloped Countries *The Review of Economics and Statistics* XLIII, 2.

Rousseau, J-J. (1984) A *Discourse on Inequality* London: Penguin.

Royo, M. and J. Velazco (2005) Exploring the Relationship Between Happiness, Objective and Subjective Wellbeing: Evidence from Rural

Thailand, mimeo, ESRC Research on Wellbeing in Developing Countries, University of Bath, Great Britain.

Ruhm, C. (2006) A Healthy Economy Can Break Your Heart, NBER Working Paper 12102.

Ryle, G. (1949) *The Concept of Mind* London: Hutchinson.

Sanfey, P. and U. Teksoz (2005) Does Transition Make You Happy? European Bank for Reconstruction and Development Working Paper 61.

Schama, S. (1997) *The Embarrassment of Riches: An Interpretation of Dutch Culture in the Golden Age* New York: Vintage Books.

Schopenhauer, A. (1966) *The World as Will and Representation* New York: Dover Books.

Schultz, B. (2004) *Henry Sidgwick: Eye of the Universe*, Cambridge: Cambridge University Press.

Schyns, P. (1998) Crossnational Differences in Happiness: Economic and Cultural Factors Explored *Social Indicators Research* 43.

Seabright, P. (1997) The Effect of Inequality on Collective Action, mimeo, The World Bank.

Sen, A. (1985) *The Standard of Living* Cambridge: Cambridge University Press.

Sen, A. (1992) *Inequality Reexamined* New York: Russell Sage.

Sen, A. (1995) Rationality and Social Choice *American Economic Review* 85, 1: 1-24.

Sen, A. (1999) Democracy as a Universal Value *Journal of Democracy* 10.3 (1999) 3-17.

Sen, A. (2000) *Development as Freedom* New York: Anchor.

Shi, A. (2000) How Access to Urban Potable Water and Sewerage Connections Affects Child Mortality, World Bank Policy Research Working Paper 2274.

Sidgwick (1907) *Methods of Ethics* London: Macmillan.

Simon, J. (1995) Introduction in Julian Simon (ed.) *The State of Humanity* Cambridge, US: Blackwell.

Skocpol, T. (1976) France, Russia, China: A Structural Analysis of Social Revolutions *Comparative Studies in Society and History* 18, 2, 175-210.

Smith, A. (1910) *The Wealth of Nations* London: J.M. Dent.

Smith, A. (1982) *The Theory of Moral Sentiments* (Glasgow edition) Indianapolis: Liberty Press.

Smith A. (1993) *Wealth of Nations* Oxford: OUP.

Solon, G. (2002) Cross-Country Differences in Intergenerational Earnings Mobility *Journal of Economic Perspectives* 16, 3, 59-66.

Steptoe, A., J. Wardle and M. Marmot (2005) Positive Affect and Health-Related Neuroendocrine, Cardiovascular, and Inflammatory Processes *Proceedings of the National Academy of Sciences*, May 3, 102, 18 6508-6512.

Stern, N., J.-J. Dethier and H. Rogers (2005) *Growth and Empowerment, Making Development Happen* Cambridge, MA: The MIT Press.

Strack, F., L. Martin and N. Schwarz (1988) Priming and Communication: Social Determinants of Information Use in Judgments of Life Satisfaction *European Journal of Social Psychology* 18, 429-42.

Svennson, J. (1994) Investment, Property Rights and Political Instability: Theory and Evidence, mimeo, Institute for International Economic Studies, Stockholm.

Szreter, S. (1997) Economic Growth, Disruption, Deprivation, Disease and Death: On the Importance of the Politics of Public Health for Development *Population and Development Review* 23, 4.

Thorbecke, E. and C. Charumilind (2002) Economic Inequality and Its Socioeconomic Impact *World Development* 30, 9 1477-1495.

Tuchman, B. (1978) *A Distant Mirror: The Calamitous 14th Century* New York: Ballentine.

UNDP (United Nations Development Program) (2005) *Human Development Report* New York: UNDP.

United Nations (2002) *UN Statistical Database*, available at http://unstats.un.org/

Videras J. and A. Owen (2006) Public Goods Provision and Well-Being: Empirical Evidence Consistent with the Warm Glow Theory *Contributions to Economic Analysis & Policy*: Vol. 5: No. 1, Article 9.

Vitterso, J., E. Roysamb and E. Diener (2002) The Concept of Life Satisfaction Across Cultures: Explaining its Diverse Meaning and Relation to Economic Growth in E. Guillone and R. Cummins *The Universality of Subjective Wellbeing Indicators: A Multi-Disciplinary and Multi-National Perspective* London: Kluwer.

Wagstaff, A. (2001) Child Health on a Dollar a Day: Some Tentative Cross-Country Comparisons, mimeo, World Bank.

Wagstaff, A. (2005) The Economic Consequences of Health Shocks, World Bank Policy Research Working Paper 3644.

Waldmann, R. (1992) Income Distribution and Infant Mortality *Quarterly Journal of Economics* 107, 4 1283-1302.

Wallace, C., G. Eagleson, and R. Waldersee (2000) The Sacrificial HR Strategy in Call Centers *International Journal of Service Industry Management* 11, 2.

Wang, L. (2002) Health Outcomes in Low Income Countries and Policy Implications: Empirical Findings from Demographic and Health Surveys, World Bank Policy Research Working Paper 2831.

Watts, C. and C. Zimmerman (2002) Violence Against Women: Global Scope and Magnitude *The Lancet* 359, April 6.

Westwood, A. (2002) *Is New Work Good Work?* London: The Work Foundation.

WHO (World Health Organization) (2002) *The World Health Report*, Geneva: World Health Organization.

WHO (World Health Organization) (2005) WHO *Multi-country Study on Women's Health and Domestic Violence Against Women*, Geneva: WHO.

WHO (World Health Organization Study Group on Female Genital Mutilation and Obstetric Outcome) (2006) Female Genital Mutilation and Obstetric Outcome: WHO Collaborative Perspective Study in Six African Countries *The Lancet* 367, 1835-41.

Wierzbicka, A. (2004) Happiness in Cross-Linguistic and Cross-Cultural Perspective *Daedalus* Spring.

Williams, S. (2005) Poor Relief, Labourer's Households and Living Standards in Rural England c. 1770-1834: A Bedfordshire Case Study *Economic History Review* LVIII, 3.

Wittgenstein, L. (1953) *Philosophical Investigations*, Oxford: Blackwell.

World Bank (2003) *The Millennium Development Goals in Health: Rising to the Challenge* Washington, DC: World Bank.

World Bank (2004) *World Development Report* Washington, DC: World Bank.

World Bank (2005) *World Development Indicators* Washington, DC: World Bank.

World Bank (2006) *World Development Report: Equity and Development* New York: Oxford.

Younger, S. (2001) Cross-Country Determinants of Declines in Infant Mortality: A Growth Regression Approach, mimeo, Cornell University Food and Nutrition Program.

Zautra, A. and A. Hempel (1984) Subjective Wellbeing and Physical Health: A Narrative Literature Review *International Journal of Aging and Human Development* 19 (2).

Zizzo, D. and A. Oswald (2000) Are People Willing to Pay to Reduce Others' Incomes? mimeo, Brasenose College Oxford, January 22.

# Index

adaptation 168-71
adultery 181-2
agriculture 203
Ahmed, Ifthikar 122
aid 204-6
Anaxagoras 15
Angola 84, 118
animals 28, 136, 180
Aquinas, St Thomas 23-4, 48
Aristotle 13-17, 24, 34, 58-60,
   106-7, 142, 180-1
asceticism 31,42, 110
Augustine, St 21-3

Baille, Mathew 78
Bangladesh 82
behaviourism 38-9, 139
Benin 119
Bentham, Jeremy 25-30, 142-3,
   180-1
Berlin Conference 202
Berlin, Isiah 194
Blanchflower, David 154
Bolivia 92, 118
Botswana 91, 124
Bowles, Samuel 167
Brazil, 97, 124, 130
Burkina Faso 119
Burma 95

Calvin, John 45
Cambodia 90, 195-6

Canada 78, 196
Cape Verde 130
Carlyle, Thomas 63
caste 115
Chad 203
Chadwick, Edwin 79, 120
child labour 111, 118
China 82-3, 116, 124, 130, 158
Chile 124
choice 104-5
   *See also* civil and political rights
civil and political rights 111,
   113-14, 116, 123-4, 165, 194-5
   *See also* income and civil and
     political rights
code, moral 179, 181-3
communitarianism 201-2
community, moral 179-81
competition 107-9
conditional payments 195-6
consciousness 135-8
consequentialism 30, 182
consumption 85
contentment 8, 41-3, 136-75
   *See also* income and
     contentment, subjective
     well-being
Costa Rica 117
control 153
corporate welfare 193
criteria *vs* symptoms 139
cultural identity 104-5

Czech Republic 114, 116

Declaration of Independence 43, 191
democracy 105, 109
Descartes, R. 135-8, 145
desire 18-19, 144-5
dignity 8, 31, 41-3, 103-31
    *See also* child labour, civil rights, gender, income and dignity, income relative, job quality, unemployment
Dominican Republic 124
Dutch Republic 45-6, 76
duty 25, 32-3

Easterlin, Richard 7, 73, 90, 170
Earned Income Tax Credit 195
education 118, 123, 153, 193
Egypt 86, 130
emotions 140-2
ends *vs* means 14
Engels, Friedrich 126
environment 100, 152
Epicurus 17-19
equality 109
Ethiopia 95, 99, 114, 199
ethnicity 114
eudaimonism 24

famine 91
fear 140-2
felicific calculus 27-30, 34
Ferguson, Niall 116
first-person authority 136-40, 145-8
France 78, 95, 97, 116, 130
Francis of Assisi, St 145
Frank, Robert 192
freedom of the will 23
function, human 15-16

Galbraith, John 155
Gandhi 115

gender 28, 88, 98-9, 111, 113-14, 117, 122
genital mutilation 114
Germany 124, 154
Gilbert, W.S. 108
Gintis, Herbert 167
God 22
goods, rival and non-rival 160-3
government 91, 94, 191-200
grace, divine 21-3, 35
Graham, Carol 159
greatest happiness principle 28-32
Greece 113
Guatemala 90, 114
Guinea Bissau 200

Haiti 124
health 58-9
    and civilization 69-70
    component of happiness 47
    convergence 80-1
    and corruption 92, 199
    and education 88
    and globalization 71-3
    and institutions 88, 90-94
    and sanitation 79-80, 88
    statistics 46-7, 68-76, 81, 85, 168
    and technology 53-4, 67-8, 77-9, 86-90
    *See also* income and health
healthcare 89-90, 193
hedonic treadmill 50, 162
hedonism 17-19, 26
heredity vs environment 40, 166-67
Hesiod, 47
Hobbes, Thomas 60-1
Hume, David 26
Huntington, Samuel 204

immortality 22, 37
income 9
    causes of 171-2 197-8, 190, 200-1
    and child labour 118

and civil and political rights
  115-16
concerns over 161
convergence 80
and contentment 51
and dignity 52, 112
and education 117-8
and health 65-76, 80-8
and immorality 49
inequality 130, 156, 196, 200
as measure of the good life
  190-1, 197
relative 121-31, 155-9, 162
statistics 46
and subjective wellbeing
  153-62
and violence 95, 97, 99
and welfare 51-2
*See also* poverty, hedonic
  treadmill
India 80, 82-3, 87, 91, 95, 97, 115,
  156
Indonesia 85, 130
Industrial Revolution 72-6, 120-1
infrastructure 193
insurance 162-3, 194
intellectual property rights 203
Israel 95, 156
Italy 77-78, 86, 113

Jamaica 124
Japan 83, 97, 130, 155
job quality 121-122
Jong-Il, Kim 201
justice 25

Kant, Immanuel 25, 32-3, 35, 180
Korea 124
Krugman, Paul 117
Kyrgyzstan 159

Landes, David 71
leisure 106, 183-4
literacy 41, 118
Locke, John 61-2

Lokshin, Michael 157, 161
Lucas, Robert 66
luck 14, 59
Lucretius, 50
Lycurgus 49

Malaysia 82, 89
Malawi 157
Malthus, Thomas 73
Malaysia 130
Mandeville, Bernard 125
market 37
marriage 42, 105, 153, 165, 170
Marx, Karl 63-4, 121
McGuire, James 89
McMahon 189
Medicine 77-79
Mexico 124, 130
military expenditures 198-9
Mill, J.S. 7, 30-32, 36, 63-4, 115,
  183, 186, 121
Millennium Development Goals
  65
morality 179-88, 189-90
More, Thomas 52-3, 59, 185
Mozambique 82, 118
Mugabe, Robert 201

Namibia 130
nation state 97
Nepal 199
New Zealand 71
Nicaragua 118, 130
Niger 71

*oikeioisis* 184
Oswald, Andrew 154

peasants 150
Painter, George 53
Papua New Guinea 94, 99
Paraguay 130
Park, Mungo 71
passions of the soul 137-8
personality 166-7

Peru 94, 99, 114, 130
Pettinato, Stefano 159
Petty, William 54
Philippines 95, 128, 130
philosophy 16, 19, 106-7
Pinker, Stephen 166-7
Plato 49, 107-8
pleasure 15-19, 26-8, 30-1, 34, 142-3
Pogge, Thomas 202
Poland 77
Poor Laws (British) 79, 120
Pope, Alexander 62
population control 185-7
Porter, Roy 70, 72, 95
poverty 66, 156-68
    as social condition 48-9, 126-9, 195
    statistics 69
prestige 104, 108-10, 125-6, 155, 160, 173
Priam, King 20, 34
privacy of experience 136-7
property rights 196, 200-2

quantification 27-8

Ravallion, Martin 157, 161
religion 153
respect 108, 155
rights, natural 181-3, 197
    *See also* civil and political rights
Rosenstein-Rodan 129-30
Rousseau, Jean Jacques 50, 62-3
Russia 97, 130, 153, 161
Russell, Bertrand 60
Rwanda 195
Ryle, Gilbert 143

Schama, Simon 45
Schopenhauer, Arthur 144-5
Scotus, John Duns 24-5, 35
self-sufficiency 14
Sen, Amartya 7, 91, 119, 170
Senegal 158

set-point theory 40, 164-6
sex 19
Sidgwick, Henry 36-7, 186
Simon, Julian 54
Skocpol, Theda 149
slavery 42, 72
Smith, Adam, 48-9, 118, 120-1, 125-6, 189
Snow, John 79
social role 105, 160-1
South Africa 97, 117
Soviet Union 117
Sri Lanka 90
Stoics 19-21, 184-5
Stylites, St Simeon 110
suicide 158
sumptuary laws 49, 125
Sweden 162, 196

Tacitus 49
Tahiti 70, 71
Tanzania 128-9
television 85, 104, 158, 160
Teresa of Avila, St 146
terminally ill 104
torture 59
Tuchman, Barbara 168

uneasiness 62, 161
Uganda 92, 199
unemployment 119-121, 130-1, 153
United Kingdom 66-9, 72-6, 78-80, 82, 87, 94-5, 118-19, 121-2, 126, 128, 130, 156, 195-6, 206
United States 71, 78, 82, 84, 87, 90, 95, 97, 114, 120, 124, 128, 130, 153-6, 158, 160-2, 195-6, 203
utilitarianism 26-32
utility 26, 154-6

vaccines 206
Vietnam 66-8, 87
violence 96-9, 114

virtue 15-16, 19-20, 23, 35

wanting 144-5
war 94-6
Weber, Max 191
welfare 8, 41-3, 57-100
    *See also* health, income and
        welfare, violence, war
welfare economics 190
well-being, subjective 9
    correlates 151-60, 166-7
    and health 168-71
    and institutions 163
    and leisure 162, 194
    as measure of the good 172
     polls 150-2
    as source of income growth
        171-2
    and unemployment 153, 169
    *See also* income and subjective
        wellbeing, set point theory
will, goodness of 32-3
wisdom 20-1
Wittgenstein, Ludwig 138-40
Wollenscraft, Mary 115
worthwhileness 105-8

Zimbabwe 91, 124

# St. Andrews Studies in Philosophy and Public Affairs

This series originates in the Centre for Ethics, Philosophy and Public Affairs, University of St Andrews and is under the general editorship of John Haldane. The series includes monographs, collections of essays and occasional anthologies of source material representing study in those areas of philosophy most relevant to topics of public importance.

'Highly interesting, lucid and challenging studies of key issues of public concern, by a wide spectrum of writers, including some of the most interesting and influential thinkers of the day. This series is a must for academic libraries.' **Nicholas Rescher, University of Pittsburgh, founding editor, Public Affairs Quarterly**

'St. Andrews Studies in Philosophy and Public Affairs is an important new series that will advance the academic and public discussions of major social issues and policies.' **Hugh LaFollette, editor, Oxford Handbook of Practical Ethics**

'These works are indispensable resources for scholars, students, and practitioners in all disciplines concerned with the ethical dimensions of public policy.' **Fred Miller Jr, Director, Social Philosophy & Policy Center, Bowling Green, OH.**

## Vol. I: Values, Education and the Human World

### Edited by John Haldane

274 pp., £17.95/$29.90 1-84540-000-3 (pbk.)

The Nature of Values by *John Haldane*; Problems of Values Education by *David Carr*; A Cultural Crisis: The Devaluation of Values; Revaluation of Values by *Anthony Quinton*; Education, Value and the Sense of Awe; The Pursuit of Excellence by *Anthony O'Hear*; The Aim of Education; The Context of Education by *Richard Pring;* Meeting Educational Needs; Good Teaching by *Mary Warnock;* Political Society, Civil Society; Languages of Morals by *Jonathan Sacks;* Values, Religion and Education; Diagnosis? Prognosis? Cure? by *Stewart Sutherland;* Science and Poetry; Atoms, Memes and Individuals by *Mary Midgley;* The Threat of Scientism; The New Marx by *Bryan Appleyard*

'A forthright attack on the "empiricist orthodoxy" that, with its disastrous effects on education, permeates the modern world.' **Paul Standish, University of Sheffield**

'The collection is well organised, reasonably focused and highly engaging. Without exception, the essays are well written and thought-provoking ... [the contributors have] managed very effectively the task of being both scholarly and accessible [and] have admirably fulfilled their brief to appeal to the general educated public.' **Journal of the Philosophy of Education**

'A multidisciplinary offering of a particular camp with passionately argued cases which should appeal to many with general interests in education, values and moral philosophy.' **Robert Bowie, New Blackfriars**

# Vol. II: Philosophy and Its Public Role
## Edited by William Aiken & John Haldane

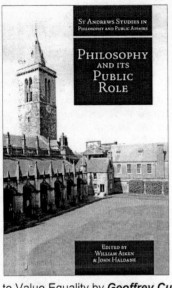

272 pp., £17.95/$29.90 1-84540-003-8 (pbk.)

The book brings together moral, social and political philosophers from Britain, Canada, New Zealand and the US. Topics discussed range from the public responsibility of intellectuals to the justice of military tribunals, and from posthumous reproduction to the death penalty.

American Philosophy and its Public Role by **John Haldane**; Do Intellectuals have a Special Public Responsibility? by **Bob Brecher**; Impartial Public Reason and its Critics by **John Arthur**; Human Nature, Society and Education by **David Carr**; Philosophy, Values and Schooling by **Terence McLaughlin**; Is Cultural Membership a Good? by **Wendy Donner**; Consent and Posthumous Reproduction by **Andrew Moore**; Three Ways to Value Equality by **Geoffrey Cupit**; Mitigating our Consumption by **Bart Gruzalski**; Globalisation and the New Economy by **James Child**; Statistical and Identifiable Deaths by **Richard Brook**; Human Rights: Constitutional and International by **Rex Martin**; Military Tribunals by **Lisa Portmess**; A Deterrence Theory of Punishment by **Anthony Ellis**; Retributivism and Public Norms by **Jonathan Jacobs**; Capital Punishment and Societal Self-Defence by **Dan Farrell**

---

# III: Relativism and the Foundations of Liberalism
## Graham Long

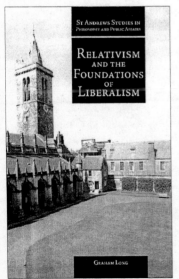

276 pp., £30.00/$59.00 1-84540-004-6 (cloth)

This book aims to refute claims that moral relativism is flawed and incompatible with liberalism. First, it argues that relativism provides a plausible account of moral justification. Drawing on the analyses of thinkers such as Harman, Nagel and Habermas, it develops an alternative account of 'coherence relativism'. Turning to liberalism, the book argues that moral relativism underpins the claims of liberalism. The political liberalism of Rawls and Barry is founded on an unacknowledged commitment to a relativist account of justification. In combining these two elements, the book offers a new understanding of relativism, and demonstrates its relevance for contemporary liberal thought.
This monograph won the 2003 thesis prize from the Political Studies Association.

---

## Vol. IV: Human Life, Action and Ethics: Essays by G.E.M. Anscombe

### ed. Mary Geach and Luke Gormally

320 pp., £17.95/$34.90 1-84540-061-5 (pbk.)

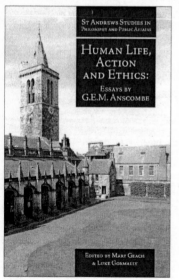

This is the first collection of essays by the celebrated philosopher Elizabeth Anscombe since the publication of three volumes of her papers in 1981. This new collection includes:
a) articles published subsequent to those volumes and not hitherto gathered,
b) previously unpublished papers on human nature and practical philosophy, together with
c) the classic essay 'Modern Moral Philosophy', and a few otherwise difficult to obtain early pieces such as her *Listener* article 'Does Oxford Moral Philosophy Corrupt the Youth?'. The appearance of this volume is a major publishing event.

'The most brilliant of Wittgenstein's students . . . an original and formidable philosopher.' **Simon Blackburn, *Times Literary Supplement***

'The essays reprinted here show the extraordinary originality and great interest of Anscombe's work in action theory and moral philosophy.' **Philippa Foot**

'The editors and the publishers have done philosophy a great service.'
**Alasdair MacIntyre**

'In the latter half of the twentieth century Anscombe could hold her own with any philosopher in the world.' **Anthony Kenny**

'Elizabeth Anscombe thought deeply, wrote beautifully, and was never taken in by pretence.' **Roger Scruton**

'Truly one of the great philosophers of the twentieth century.' **Hilary Putnam**

'The undoubted giant among women philosophers, a writer of immense breadth, authority and penetration ... a truly original philosopher.' **Mary Warnock**

---

# Vol. V: The Institution of Intellectual Values: Realism and Idealism in Higher Education

### Gordon Graham

290 p., £25/$49.90 1-84540-002-X (cloth)

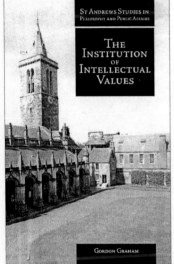

This is a revised and expanded version of the much praised short book *Universities: The Recovery of An Idea*. It contains chapters on the history of universities; the value of university education; the nature of research; the management and funding of universities plus additional essays on such subjects as human nature and the study of the humanities, interdisciplinary versus multidisciplinary study, information systems and the concept of a library, the prospects for e-learning, reforming universities, intellectual integrity and the realities of funding, and spiritual values and the knowledge economy.

'Graham has written an elegant and extraordinarily refreshing book, with no fudging of his own opinions and judgements ... It deserves a very wide readership and will surely stand as a point of reference for years to come.' **Gordon Johnson, *Times Higher Education Supplement***

'A short reflective treatise on British university education that deserves to be widely read . . .its appeal is universal and deserves the attention of a wide audience.'
***Political Studies Review***

'Those who care about universities should thank Gordon Graham for doing what has needed doing so urgently'.
**Anthony O'Hear, *Philosophy***

'Though densely and cogently argued, this book is extremely readable and indeed deserves to be widely read'.
***Philosophical Quarterly***

# Vol. VII: Life, Liberty and the Pursuit of Utility

## Happiness in philosophical and economic thought

### Anthony Kenny, Charles Kenny

275 pp., £17.95/$34.90 1-84540-052-6 (pbk.)

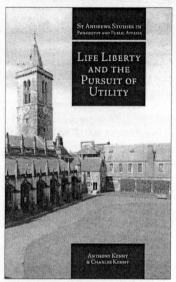

A volume on the nature, ingredients, causes and consequences of human happiness by the father and son team of Anthony and Charles Kenny. The book is an updating of Johnson's famous lines:

*How small of all that human hearts endure
That part which laws or kings can cause or cure!
Still to ourselves in every place consigned
Our own felicity we make or find.*

*Contents:* Introduction; The Supreme Good; Aristotelian Happiness; Utilitarian Happiness; Material Welfare; Subjective Wellbeing; Conclusion: The Good Life; Public Policy, Personal Responsibility and the Good Life.

Charles Kenny is an economist and policy adviser at the World Bank. Sir Anthony Kenny was formerly Master of Balliol College, Oxford, and is currently president of the British Academy. His many books include *Medieval Philosophy*, *A Brief History of Western Philosophy*, *The Oxford Illustrated History of Western Philosophy*, *Ancient Philosophy* and *Wittgenstein*.

---

## Vol. VIII: Distributing Healthcare

### Edited by Niall Maclean

275 pp., £17.95/$34.90 1-84540-051-8 (pbk.)

How ought a society to distribute its publicly funded healthcare resources? Few questions are in more urgent need of an answer. This multidisciplinary investigation brings together the insights of philosophy, clinical science, health economics, operational research and public policy analysis.

Contributors include Howard Glennerster (LSE), Elias Mossialos (LSE), Len Fleck (Michigan State University), John Appleby and Anthony Harrison (King's Fund), and Professor Reinhardt Busse (TU Berlin).

Niall Maclean is a postdoctoral research fellow at the Centre for Ethics, Philosophy and Public Affairs, University of St Andrews.